...tulations on your choice and thank you for
...sing our publication. If you wish you to be kept
...ed about our new publications in your field of
..., we would kindly ask you to tick the boxes for all
...bjects on which you wish to receive our catalogues
...ook forward to serving you and to hearing from you
again.

- ☐ African Studies
- ☐ Ancient Near Eastern Studies
- ☐ Anthropology/Sociology
- ☐ Archaeology
- ☐ Bible Studies
- ☐ Biology
- ☐ Central Asian Studies
- ☐ Classical Antiquity
- ☐ English Language & Literature
- ☐ Sinology, Japanology, Korean Studies
- ☐ French Language & Literature
- ☐ Geology & Palaeontology
- ☐ History
- ☐ History of Science/Medicine
- ☐ Indology
- ☐ Islamic & Middle Eastern Studies
- ☐ Judaic Studies
- ☐ Middle Ages, Renaissance, Reformation
- ☐ Patristics
- ☐ Philosophy
- ☐ Religion
- ☐ South-East Asian & Oceanic Studies

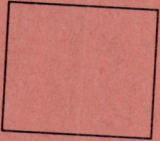

E·J·BRILL
P.O. BOX 9000
2300 PA LEIDEN
HOLLAND

DREAMING, RELIGION AND SOCIETY
IN AFRICA

STUDIES ON RELIGION IN AFRICA

SUPPLEMENTS TO THE JOURNAL OF RELIGION IN AFRICA

VII

DREAMING, RELIGION AND SOCIETY IN AFRICA

EDITED BY

M.C. JĘDREJ AND ROSALIND SHAW

E.J. BRILL
LEIDEN • NEW YORK • KÖLN
1992

The paper in this book meets the guidelines for permanence and durability of the Committee on Production Guidelines for Book Longevity of the Council on Library Resources.

Library of Congress Cataloging-in-Publication Data

Dreaming, religion, and society in Africa / edited by M.C. Jędrej and Rosalind Shaw.
      p.   cm.—(Studies on religion in Africa, ISSN 0169-9814; 7)
Includes bibliographical references and index.
ISBN 9004089365 (hard: alk. paper)
    1. Dreams. 2. Africans—Psychology. 3. Dreams—Religious aspects. 4. Africa, Sub-Saharan—Religious life and customs.
I. Jędrej, M.C. (M. Charles) II. Shaw, Rosalind. III. Series.
BF1078.D727   1992
154.6'3'096—dc20
                                                         92-111
                                                           CIP

ISSN   0169-9814
ISBN   90 04 08936 5

CONTENTS

PREFACE

When the Traditional Cosmology Society of Edinburgh planned to hold a conference in Aberdeen around the general theme of analogy the President of the society, Emily Lyle, kindly agreed to a suggestion from Rosalind Shaw that the last day of the conference be devoted to the particular matter of dreaming, cosmology and society in Africa. Charles Jędrej was then asked to participate as joint convener. The papers from this last day are published here as they were presented in August 1986, though some authors have taken the opportunity to revise and make minor changes. Keith Ray was unfortunately unable to attend and present his contribution personally and Simon Charsley agreed to our suggestion that he write a different essay surveying the field of dreaming in African independent churches. Dr. Charsley's original constribution, a case study of "Dreams in a Ugandan church", has been published in vol. 57 of *Africa* (1987). While preparing the papers for publication our attention was drawn to a publication from the Centre d'Etudes Ethnologiques Bandundu, Zaire, entitled *La Symbolique du Rêve chez les Yansi* by Mubuy Mubay Mpier. This work, published in 1982, is a major contribution to the topic, and we were pleased when the author agreed to the inclusion of extracts translated and edited by M. C. Jędrej in the present volume. We would like to thank CEEBA for permission to publish these extracts.

The publication of this volume would not have been possible without the material support of the Carnegie Trust for the Universities of Scotland and from the University of Aberdeen, the University of Edinburgh and Tufts University (U.S.A.). It is a pleasure to record our gratitude to these institutions for their recognition of a line of scholarship which has always had a Scottish flavour ever since Andrew Lang debated with the English intellectualists about dreams, religion and society.

Aberdeen, 1988   M.C.J.
                                                                                               R.S.

INTRODUCTION

DREAMING, RELIGION AND SOCIETY IN AFRICA

M.C. JĘDREJ AND ROSALIND SHAW

Dreaming and "othering"

When C.G. Jung visited East Africa in 1925, he perceived it as equivalent to a region of the mind. Eventually disturbed by the conjunction of what he saw as two primitive worlds, both in the external surroundings of his waking life and in the inner region of his dreams, he left with the conclusion that his visit "had been not so much an objective scientific project as an intensely personal one, and that any attempt to go deeper into it touched every possible sore spot in my own psychology" (Jung 1967:303).

Jung's association between Africa and inner states was part of a general preoccupation of that time. However, while his attitude to the inner world was one in which assimilation of the Ego into the landscape was sought, Freud's was starkly colonial: dreams were an indication of the savage wilderness within us which had to be subdued and civilized (see, e.g., Roazen 1975: 161-2). The Europe which Freud and Jung inhabited – and shaped – in the early part of this century was one in which imperialist expansion was accompanied by a parallel concern with control over a world *within*. As well as the birth of psychoanalysis, this was the era of psychic experiments, of literature in the H.G. Wells genre about other worlds of the imagination, and of a dramatic multiplication of theories about the origin and development of thought in general and religious ideas in particular.

The important role of dreams in such speculation had already been secured by the nineteenth century sociologists and ethnologists, notably Spencer, Tylor and Lang. Tylor (1871) following Spencer (1882) argued that the key idea of "soul", from which flowed other religious ideas, practices, institutions and even human culture, arose in the minds of primitive humans trying to come to terms with dream experiences but without the disciplines of science and rationality. Such "primitive thought" was characterised, it was claimed, by the inability to distinguish between objective and subjective reality; thus experiences of dreams appeared to be as real as experiences while awake. Western thought, by contrast, was deemed to have overcome these errors. Unlike Freud and Jung, then, Tylor and Spencer saw Western thought as uniformly different from "primitive thought", rather than as containing areas of an archaic landscape. These claims were challenged by Lang (1898), however, who argued that instead of lacking the ability to distinguish between dreaming and waking experiences (such that dreamed ghosts seemed real), early humans might have had the ability to experience psychic phenomena, to "really" perceive ghosts, which "civilized" people have lost (see, e.g. 1898: 49-60)

A different association again between inner states and non-Western "others" was drawn by Lévy-Bruhl (1966, orig. 1922) who was sceptical of the Tylorian claim that the latter confused dreams and waking life. Indeed the existence of a distinction between dreaming and waking experience is fundamental to what Lévy-Bruhl called the "mystical" nature of the "primitive mentality". Because people may take both dreams and waking experiences into account, he observed, it does not follow that they confuse these. On the contrary, on the basis that dream experiences are sometimes judged to be "more valuable than the perceptions of the preceding day" (1966:99), he argued that the dream is the medium through which mystical representations, which pervade everyday life, manifest themselves (1966:113). Accordingly, Lévy-Bruhl maintained, when there is an apparent contradiction between dream perceptions and waking perceptions, those of the dream are considered to be more trustworthy, and reality has to be adjusted accordingly.

In these early theoretical positions, then, dreams were used in the construction of contrasts between Western and non-Western conceptual predicaments. If, for psychoanalysts, "the savage world" was both "out there" and "in here", for the nineteenth century ethnologists as well as for Lévy-Bruhl both its outer and inner dimensions were located at a safe remove, in the world of "the other":

Freud/Jung: Our dreams are like their waking reality *(analogy)*,
Tylor/Spencer: Their dreaming and waking realities are confused; ours are not *(opposition)*,
Lang: They have abilities in waking life which we can only imagine in dreams *(encompassment)*.
Lévy-Bruhl: Their dreams are more important than their waking reality; we reverse this *(reversal)*.

Enough has been written about such processes of "othering" through comparisons of homogenised "Western" and "non-Western" modes of thought to make a lengthy critique in relation to dreaming unnecessary. But to what extent have studies of dreaming in African contexts been shaped by these positions, and to what extent have they gone beyond them?

Studies of dreaming in Africa

Of these positions, those of Lang, Freud and Jung have had the least currency in studies of dreaming in African societies. In the 1920s Seligman, whose anthropological research in the Sudan and New Guinea was greatly influenced by psychoanalytic ideas, drew attention to the implications for a universal psychology of the widespread occurrence of (apparently) identical dream symbolism among historically and culturally unrelated peoples (e.g. 1924). More recently, Jung's ideas are manifest in the interfusing of inner psychic archetypes revealed in dreams with accounts of "Bushman" cosmologies in the writings of Laurens van der Post (Barnard 1989). But Freud's massive impact upon Western folk-models pushed dreaming to the margins of social anthropology, sociology and history, since dreams came to be defined as being of more relevance to individual (and universal) psychology than to the analysis of social and cultural phenomena.

A tradition of psychological anthropology has, however, endured in the U.S.A., with the consequence that there have arisen marked regional contrasts in the use of psychoanalytic concepts as authorised forms of knowledge in anthropological studies of dreams. American psychological anthropology has undergone a long period of development in relation to a wealth of studies of dreaming in North and South American Indian societies, the ethnographic regions which have been most prominent in the work of American anthropologists. Here the assumption that dreams are principally of individual and/or universal significance formed the basis for studies which either treated cultures as akin to individuals, or which searched for universal psychological motivations in cross-cultural studies. Some of those interested in a relationship between culture and personality, for instance, used dreams as psychological data (eg. Eggan 1949; Devereux 1951), and among psychoanalytically-inclined anthropologists the view that dreams are a privileged route in every culture to unconscious mental processes has been entrenched for some time (e.g., Roheim 1932).

The boundary-conscious British social anthropology of the 1940s and '50s, on the other hand, had a strong avoidance-relationship with psychoanalysis. Since it was primarily through ethnographic research in Africa at that time that British social anthropology was developing its concepts and theories, we find few explicitly psychoanalytic studies in Africanist anthropology. In his early work on Tallensi kinship, Meyer Fortes' Freudian perspective was only revealed with any clarity in footnotes (e.g., 1949: 37, n.1), and was camouflaged by substituting the Oedipus of Greek mythology for the Oedipus of Freudian theory as one of the two paradigms in his study of personhood, *Oedipus and Job in West African Religion* (1959; see Horton 1983: 74-79). Since

Seligman, it has been American anthropologists who have conducted psychological anthropological studies of dreams in African contexts (e.g., Johnson 1978; R. LeVine 1966; S. LeVine 1981).

Anthropological applications of Freud's ideas have not, in the main, been concerned with contrasts between "ourselves" and "others", but rather with the delineation of common patterns of thought and affect, albeit modified by cultural differences (see, e.g., Seligman 1932:219). This has not been true of recent developments of the Tylorian position, however. Tylor's ideas about the confusion of subjectivity and objectivity in "primitive thought" have enjoyed something of a revival in recent debates between anthropologists and philosophers about rationality in non-Western conceptual systems. Although dreams do not have the prominence in this debate that they had in the works of Tylor and Spencer, they are part of Hallpike's neo-Tylorean examination of the cognitive capacities of non-literate peoples (1979). In many non-Western cultures, he observes, dreams are ascribed an objective reality and an external origin. On this basis he claims that in such cultures, instead of having a conception of the mind as generating its own images, people are not "capable of recognizing the subjective basis of dreams" (1979:419), and he uses this claim to support his argument that in "primitive thought", child-like conceptual realism and pre-operational thinking prevail.

On the basis of a study of the development of dream concepts among Hausa children (Shweder and LeVine 1975), however, Shweder (1982) challenges Hallpike's position. According to this study, Hausa ten-year-olds, like Western adults, adopt a rationalist/subjectivist view of dreaming, claiming that dreams are unreal and internal in origin. Hausa adults, however, find this inadequate, and say instead that dreams are a kind of vision which gives them access to an external, objective realm of the wandering soul. Shweder concludes that "Hausa are not only capable of a 'subjectivist' view of dreams. They entertain that viewpoint as ten-year-olds, and later reject it!" (1982:362). Although we cannot properly speak of Lang's influence here, his position might nevertheless be viewed as a precursor of such contemporary challenges to Tylorian explanations as that of Schweder: both kinds of argument are in terms of an awareness of an alternate reality instead of a confusion between subjective and objective perceptions. But whereas for Lang the issue was that of the objective reality of psychic experiences, for contemporary interpretive anthropology it is that of the culturally defined character of reality, in which the the opposition between "subjective" and "objective" reality in Western thought is itself a cultural construction (see, e.g., Tedlock 1987).

Lévy-Bruhl's view is, as we have seen, that non-Western cognitive systems give dreams the status of superior realities. Some of the African examplés he cites, such as the report that a Zulu will treat a friend as an enemy because of a dream in which the latter intended to harm him (1966:104-5), are uncritically reproduced by later writers such as Caillois (1966). Perhaps one of the most celebrated cases is that from Asante, of whom Rattray has reported that if a husband learns that another has dreamed of sexual intercourse with his wife, he will sue the dreamer for adultery (1927:193). Lincoln has referred to this report as evidence that for some peoples "the dream experience is regarded as having a greater reality than an actual experience" (1935:28-9).[1]

However, this use of such reports makes it difficult to maintain against Tylor respect for a qualitative distinction between dream and waking experiences. In any case, if the sources are examined carefully, the reports deal with phenomena rather more complex than Lévy-Bruhl's theory of a kind of inverted Cartesianism would admit. As regards the Asante case, Rattray writes: "if you dream that you have had sexual intercourse with another man's wife and anyone hears of it and tells her husband then you will be fined the usual adultery fees, for your soul and hers have had sexual intercourse" (1927:193). If the last clause is ignored and tacitly replaced with the assumption that sexual intercourse and adultery for Asante are much the same sorts of things as they are in Western contexts, then one arrives easily at the conclusion that it is the evaluation of the reality of dreams which must differ. Yet the statement can be seen as saying more about the nature of sex and adultery according to Asante than about their notions of dreams. Crucially, conception and reproduction involve *ntoro*, "spirit substance" or "soul stuff", which is inherited patrilineally. Adultery involves the meeting of the *ntoro* of the two men in the woman's body, which in the case of a pregnant woman will cause the death of the child, such that the adulterer was at one time dealt with as a murderer (*awudifo*). Adultery payments were not simply compensation, but were also necessary for the propitiation of "the ancestral ghosts and the nonhuman spiritual powers" (Rattray 1927:55). It is not, then, that Asante are confused about the real status of dreamed sexual intercourse, but rather that the conceptual status of real sexual intercourse involves literally a "confusion", a blending, of material and non-material components.

Since, like the Freudians and the Tylorians, Lévy-Bruhl is in the end addressing himself to the fundamental properties of what he saw as the "primitive mind", he is rendered peculiarly insensitive to the consequences of qualitatively different social and cultural situations. Progress beyond these perspectives has, however, been hampered by the fragmentary nature of studies of dreaming in African societies. Although it could be argued that this peicemeal treatment reflects the empirical situation, since the significance of dreaming in Africa is far from homogeneous, this uneven distribution of significance within and between African societies is itself a topic which should deserve our attention.

Of greater relevance to an explanation of this patchy treatment, we believe, is the marginalisation of dreaming in British social anthropology, as well as in African religious studies. Material on dreams seems to have been present in the field notes of many Africanist anthropologists working on religion, symbols and modes of thought, but very few have made more than cursory remarks about dreaming in published articles and monographs. Nadel writes that he "used to record all the dreams of the Nupe men with whom I was in daily contact" (1954:67), but includes only three pages on dream interpretation in *Nupe Religion* as part of his chapter on divination. Rehfisch – rare in his specific focus upon dreaming – gives a description of a dramatic dream-event among the Mambila, in which the dreamer, apparently dead or dying, perceived herself as awakening not just from sleep but from death (1969). Evans-Pritchard, writing before the positivist rejection of phenomena deemed to be "individual" and "internal" became anthropological orthodoxy, explored the role of dreams in Zande ideas of causality and accountability (1937; see below). But until very recently, social anthropologists have typically categorised dreams as individual rather than social phenomena and relegated them, along with private thoughts and emotions, to psychology (apparently unaware that psychologists, in the heyday of *their* positivist phase, have been behaviourists for most of this century). It is therefore ironic that a valuable early article on *social* influences on dreaming among the Zulu was written by Gilmore Lee, a psychologist (1958). Later, dreams continued to be bypassed in structuralist explorations of African myths, symbols and rituals. Conversely, when Kuper (1979; 1983) applied structural analysis to dream accounts, it was not his African research which he drew upon for material.

In African religious studies, scattered references are often made to the role of dreams in mediating contact between deities, ancestors and human beings. But most of those in African religious studies have tended to concentrate upon selected aspects of African religions which closely parallel dominant forms within Western Christianity, such as ideas of a supreme being, prayer and sacrifice, with the consequence that again little attention has been paid to dreaming. Those few who have done so have focused upon Christian and Islamic examples. Fisher discusses the role of dreaming and dream-interpretation in conversion to Islam (1979), while Sanneh describes the practices of Muslim dream-incubation through spiritual retreat (*khalwa*) and dream-divination (*istikhara*) among Jakhanke clerics (1979). In his study of religious dreams and militant African political movements, Mbiti adopts a normative stance, suggesting that political leaders and others should "exercise restraint in putting God at the centre of their dreams which are intended for public consumption" (1976:47). Studies of dreaming in independent African churches, however, have been exceptions to the general neglect of dreaming in

Africanist anthropology and religious studies, since here the use of dreams is sometimes a prominent institutional form (see Charsley, this volume).

Recently, with the re-centering upon the subject in anthropology, dreams have been rediscovered in the course of innovative approaches to religious and social experience in African contexts. Wendy James explores the form of knowledge to which dreams give access in her study of moral knowledge among the Uduk (1988:78-83). Beryl Bellman uses Kpelle ideas about dreaming to criticise the writings of the social phenomenologist Shutz on multiple realities (1975:165-178). Michael Jackson's ethnographic novel *Barawa* uses Kuranko interpretations of his dreams and his interpretations of Kuranko dreams to articulate his developing understanding of Kuranko perspectives (1986). Once again, however, in none of these accounts is dreaming a major focus. Fernandez' monumental work *Bwiti* (1982) comes closest to providing this. In it, he traces the development of Fang ideas about dreams and revelatory knowledge into the "world-reconstructing" visions and sermons of Bwiti, a new religious movement which heals the dislocations of a colonised Fang world through integrative cosmology and ritual. It has been from outwith anthropology, on the other hand, that African scholars have researched dreams and dreaming and it is hoped that further African scholarship will augment multidisciplinary engagement with the topic, adding to the contributions of Sanneh *(op. cit.)* and Mbiti *(op. cit.)* from religious studies, Chimombo (1989) from African literature, and Mpier (1982 and this volume) from social psychology.

In other regions of the world, the study of dreaming is currently enjoying renewed attention from fresh perspectives. O'Flaherty (1984), for example, explores the place of dreaming in the history of Indian religious thought, while the contributors to a recent collection of mostly Amerindian studies of dreaming edited by Barbara Tedlock (1987) approach the topic from semiotic, sociolinguistic, psychological and interpretive anthropological perspectives. Studies which approach dreaming as a crucial sphere of cultural meaning, then, have replaced early theoretical concerns with dreams as providing a basis for the construction of dichotomies between "Western" and "non-Western" modes of thought.

Yet further dichotomies remain entrenched. In social anthropology, at least, the categorisation of dreaming as outside the "proper" subject-matter of the discipline appears to have resulted in a more enduring and sharply-drawn separation of "meaning" from "power" and of "the subjective" from "the social" in relation to dreaming than in other spheres, such as ritual or myth. The consequence has been a polarisation in both anthropology and other disciplines in African studies in which dreaming has (with the exception of the works of Fernandez and James cited above) either been marginalised and discounted or treated as a privileged semantic sphere more or less divorced from power and social praxis. In the present volume, a reconciliation is attempted. A dominant theme in many of the contributions is the intermeshing of meaning and experience with power and social action. This is explored in the following two sections on accountability and authorisation, and identity, agency and specialists. Other dominant focii are the embeddedness of dreaming in ritual and everyday life, and the contextual construction of meaning, which are explored in the section on symbols, ritual and dream interpretation. These emphases are combined in the concluding section on dreaming and African Christianity.

Accountability and authorisation

Recollections and accounts of dreams are often associated with a complex linkage between the extraordinary and the mundane in everyday life. Usually distinct from the "practical consciousness" of daily life, they involve a different kind of knowledge and intentionality. Rarely is a woman cooking the evening meal because of a dream, or fetching water because of a dream, or a man broadcasting seed or herding cattle or milking a cow because of a dream he had, or any of the hundreds of other daily tasks undertaken by men and women. The exception, and it is an exception which proves the rule, occurs in myths which tell of the time when these now mundane tasks were first performed by human beings as a consequence of a dream. All of this points to the relevance of what C. Wright Mills has called "vocabularies of motive" (Mills 1940; see also Scott and Lyman 1968): accepted and shared sets of terms which constitute the explanations people use to account for their actions. Since questions are raised and explanations offered when conduct departs from the routine, the intelligibility of these departures will depend upon the socially available and adequate answers to likely queries. Dreams, then, are often among the terms which people use to construct acceptable accounts, to explain to themselves and to others otherwise extraordinary and unintelligible actions.

This is well brought out, despite the lingering influence of Lévy-Bruhl and Seligman, in Evans-Pritchard's classic Azande study.[2] According to Azande, dreams in general are likened to oracles, and are evaluated as being just as truthful as the pronouncements of the rubbing board oracle (1937:378). Bad dreams are perceived not merely as signs of witchcraft but as direct experiences of it (1937:134-47), and their dreamers are compared to the witchdoctor who, after eating medicines, is able to see witchcraft while awake (1937:178).[3] Although Evans-Pritchard does not develop his suggestion that "the memory of dream images may influence subsequent behaviours and subsequent happenings may intrude upon the memory of dream images so that they conform to one another" (1937:384), he cites intriguing examples of this recursive relationship between dream memories and action from the accounts of his informants:

> A man dreams that he is having sexual intercourse with a woman. This predicts a successful love affair, and if the dreamer recognizes the girl with whom he is having intercourse he does his best to make his dream come true ...

> A man dreams a dream about a woman, with whom he has not previously had relations, that he has intercourse with her. He awakes from this dream, awakes from sleep, and turns round on his bed so that his head rests where his feet had rested at the bottom of the bed and he lies down to sleep an uneventful sleep. As he is about to rise at daybreak he considers the dream he has dreamt. When he turned on his bed and slept with his feet at the head of the bed, then the woman about whom he had dreamt began to dream a dream on her part that she lay with him.

> While the man is walking about he sees this woman, and since she liked him before he begins to solicit her and she consents to his suggestions and he has congress with her. They sit together and flirt and he says to her, "Oh my sister, the dream has indeed spoken truly for I dreamt that I sat with you and now I remember what happened in the dream". She says to him, "A dream is a cunning person. I dreamt my dream also ..." (1937:381).

Since in Zande thought dreams are broadly "true", they are available to provide acceptable accounts for action. This availability, however, is dependent upon indigenous theories of dreaming; where such theories assert that dreams may, as among the Tikopia, be sent by spirits to mislead the dreamer, they have very different potential in providing vocabularies of motive (Firth 1934: 68; c.f. Firth 1985).

Access to such vocabularies, moreover, may be restricted to certain categories of people. Evans-Pritchard noted that Zande oracles play an important part in the subordination of women to men (1937:284, 371), since women are excluded from the rubbing board oracle and above all from the poison oracle. The unavailability of accounts based on these oracles constitutes a severe restriction upon intelligible courses of action – behaviour which is not unaccountable – which women would consider available to them at times of crisis. Although Evans-Pritchard does not provide this information, we can speculate that the existence of a vocabulary of dreams as a sub-set of the general oracular set might provide Zande women with an alternative means of originating and mediating departures from routines. In the present volume, Reynolds describes the restrictions which are sometimes placed upon Zezuru children's access to dreams sent from the dead ("such dreams are not dreamt by children"). Such dreams may initially account for other unusual aspects of behaviour as a "call" from the shades, and may eventually become accepted as part of an internal initiation into the role of healer.

The use of dreams in providing accountability thus shades into their use in authorisation. Considered in such ways, it is clear that we are concerned with an ensemble of dreaming rather than "the dream" in the abstract. The dream is, as Hudson (1985) puts it, feral and elusive. When it appears as something shared between people, it has crossed a boundary and is transformed (or perhaps translated) into a domesticated dream, a recollection. Charsley in this volume points out that it is this process which so richly permeates the account with potential meanings, meanings which are projected back onto the dream itself. And, of course, the pursuit of more "accurate" versions of the dream elaborates and enriches while approaching no nearer to the "reality" of the feral dream. This distinction between feral and domesticated dreams is analogous to that drawn by Malinowski between individual and offical dreams (1927:93), or by Lincoln between individual and "culture-pattern" dreams (1935:22). These are not two *types* of dream, however, but varying degrees of domestication of the feral dream.

Where a concept of what Lincoln has called "culture-pattern" dreams exists, this presupposes a system of authorisation in which the former are accorded "official" status. Frequently, such a system involves specialists who have a more privileged access than most people to the knowledge perceived as inherent in dreams, and who thereby exercise control over dream-interpretation (Mpier, Reynolds and Shaw, this volume), as well as other spheres of life to which dreams may be relevant – witchcraft accusation, the timing and content of rituals (Jędrej and Mpier, this volume), and membership or leadership within a church (Charsley and Curley, this volume), for example. In the right context, then, dream narratives can acquire a strongly performative force: when authorised, they themselves become means of authorisation. One consequence of this use of dreams as "authorising discourses" is the often highly negotiated character of dream-narratives and dream-interpretation. This is particularly prominent in competitive situations in which power is constituted through knowledge, as when ritual and occupational specialists compete for acceptance and renown (see Reynolds, Shaw and Dilley, this volume), candidates compete for ritual office (Ray, this volume), and members of a church compete for influence (Curley and Charsley, this volume).

Also relevant here is the extent to which ideas concerning dreams and dream-interpretation are systematised in different societies. Among some peoples, dreams are rarely recounted to others and dream-interpretation is a fairly brief and informal procedure, yet such knowledge is uniformly distributed throughout society (Holy, this volume). Elsewhere, the intersection of institutional forms with dreaming and dream-narration appears to be accompanied by a greater degree of formalisation, discursiveness and control over definitions and interpretations of dreams by elites and dominant groups. Thus among Yansi clan elders and medicine-owners, who are defined as wise dream interpreters and accurate oracular dreamers, the elaborate distinctions made between different kinds and qualities of dreams (such as "true dreams" versus "dreams of the head") can be seen as part of a discourse of conceptual authority (Mpier, this volume). An especially elaborate body of knowledge is manifest in African Islam, in which specialists define certain dreams as true revelations and others as Satanic in accordance with Muslim dream theory, and literate knowledge as embodied in Islamic dream-interpretation manuals is accorded particular power and prestige (see Fisher 1979; Dilley and Shaw, this volume).

The processes discussed in this section – the construction of acceptable accounts, the definition of "official" dreams and the systematising of dream interpretations – can all be too easily be viewed in partial (and implicitly functionalist) terms such as the legitimation of change and the negotiation of status. It is necessary to recast such one-dimensional understandings of the politics of dreaming through a view of power as inseperable from ontology. Such a recasting is attempted in the next section.

Identity, agency and specialists

The studies by Reynolds, Shaw, Ray and Dilley in this volume examine aspects of the institutionalisation of dreaming with respect to religious and craft specialists. As among non-specialists, dreaming may become part of a set of procedures concerned with elaborating, promoting and defending personal identities, by simultaneously singling someone out and assigning them to a category. In negotiating a special identity through dreaming there is an important potential for ambivalence wherein dreams are perceived as both intensely personal and as deriving from outside, as both "me" and "not me". This ambivalence constitutes what we might call the duality of agency in dreaming: if dreams come from someone or something outside, the actions I perform in my dream may be subsumed within the agency of another. Sometimes this duality is turned back upon itself to induce a kind of intellectual vertigo in narratives. There are familiar examples of this in Western and Eastern literature and philosophy: Orestes dreams of the Furies and they are dreaming him; Chuang-Tzu poses the question of whether the butterfly was in his dream or he was in the butterfly's; Alice dreams of being dreamed by the Red King and is told not to wake him up lest she go out like a candle; this is also the theme of Borges' story of the dreamer dreamt in "The Circular Ruins."

Such processes are explored in Reynolds' study of Zezuru children and healers, for whom dreaming and dream-telling are a means of both individuation and socialisation, part of the Zezuru repertoire of what Foucault has called "techniques of the self." Central to these techniques of the self is the experience of being acted upon even as one acts; in the process of being chosen by the spirits as potential healers, children themselves exercise choices. For the child, the spirits are active agents who send experiences which are received passively in dreams; at the same time, these dreams may be used by the child to actively "bargain" for – or to resist – the identity of a spiritual mediator with parents and experienced healers. Yet there is no simple dichotomy of "passive" dream experiences and "active" negotiation in waking life; both strands are interwoven, and feed back into each other. Knowing what interpretation is given to certain dreams, for example, the child

> ... can repress some or all of his dreams; he can recall more dreams; he can match his behaviour to the interpretations; or he can reject the interpretation and take care not to participate in the metaphor that links family and the supernatural.

This negotiation of identity has itself a double quality, since the construction of individuality and conformity to socially-recognised patterns of behaviour are both part of the same process of becoming (or avoiding becoming) a healer.

Unlike the norm of passive receptivity among Zezuru healers, the power of Temne diviners, as described in Shaw's study, depends upon active accomplishment in dreaming. Temne diviners derive their abilities from an initiatory dream in which they establish a contractual relationship with a patron spirit, and from subsequent encounters with this and other spirits in the "dream town" of *ro-mere,* striking bargains with them and piercing the "darkness" which conceals the knowledge they own. Diviners claim to dream with perfect control and with oracular truth, but represent most ordinary people as passively acted upon in their dreams by spirits, ancestors or witches, either as their victims or as recipients of revelations. This asymmetry in agency is repeated in processes of dream-telling during divination, in which diviners do not merely pronounce on the meaning of a client's dream, but may also ascribe a specific dream to a client who had until then been unaware of having dreamed it. Since control of inner knowledge and personal secrets is central to Temne selfhood, the diviner's assertion of his "divinerhood" in the process of establishing and maintaining his position as a ritual specialist involves the extension of ontological hegemony over his clients. The contrast between his retention of his own agency and his client's renouncement of it in dream recollections and dream narratives is thus used as the basis for the diviner's claims to superior knowledge.

Shaw states, however, that we should not assume that Temne diviners do not themselves participate in the ideas about dreams and dreaming which they deploy. This point is also emphasised in Ray's conclusion to his study of Igbo succession dreams. Ray is concerned with a form of ritual kingship among the Igbo as it persisted into the early decades of the twentieth century, and with certain contemporary processes of succession to ritual office. After the death of the sacred king, the *eze Nri,* and an interregnum of seven years which followed, it was not unusual for there to have been a number of rival candidates for the office. Succession here, and in a number of contemporary ritual offices which Ray describes, is "ascribed" insofar as the incumbent is required to be chosen by the spirit of his predecessor, or by the deity whose power the ritual office mediates. In the case of the *eze Nri* a group of assessors would deliberate on the choice of one of the rivals, but their decisions were based at least as much upon a reading of extra-human signs of divine nomination as upon an awareness of both the personal qualities and lineage interests of the protagonists. One of the ways by which such extra-human signs were communicated was via dreams, in which the previous incumbent appeared to the candidate and handed over some of the key insignia to him; such dreams, however, had to be accompanied by other kinds of signs such as omens and prophecies. One might say that the candidate's dream-telling, his interpretation of events in his household as omens, and his attempts to make prophetic statements were all deployed as cumulative means of "achieving" an ascribed religious status.

However, in Igbo thought each person's life-course is predestined through the agency of the *chi,* a spiritual entity belonging to each individual, although usually this destiny can be modified by the *ikenga,* the personnification of the individual's right hand and power to achieve. Telling a "succession" dream, therefore, is at the same time an active strategy for self-advancement and a manifestation both of the agency of the spiritual entity behind the office and of the candidate's *chi.* There is no contradiction between the tactical use of dreams and omens and the conviction that one *is,* in fact, the chosen one of the spirits. In Igbo succession to religious office, then, not only remembered dreams but even the tactical use of dream-narratives may be ultimately subsumed under the agency of a semi-autonomous entity, the candidate's *chi,* which is both "him" and "not him".

Dilley's study concerns the importance of dreams in the activities of Tukulor weavers. Weaving is said to have its origins in the spirit world, whence the craft was acquired by an ancestor and handed down to man in the time of myth. Through the mediation of dreaming, the spirit world remains a source of inspiration to weavers, who attribute their skill and their designs to knowledge acquired from *jinn* of the forest. As creative individuals believed to hold magical powers of transformation, and whose sources of creativity are external to themselves and to society, weavers regard their inspirational dreams as part of their personal stock of knowledge, and hardly ever divulge them. At his most innovative and skillful, therefore, the dream-inspired weaver is in a way passive: the source of his skill and speed are external to him, and he weaves a dreamt design. Such dreams are also, Dilley observes, a means of resolving the paradox of an ideal equality between weavers in Tukulor social ideology and the reality of individual differences in levels of ability. At the same time, inspirational dreams form part of the basis of a hierarchical distinction between craftsman and musician groups whose "black lore" derives from the *jinn*, and marabout clerics (who are variously the custodians of Islamic knowledge, orthodoxy and reformation) whose "white lore" derives from Allah and his angels.

As Reynolds observes, and as these four studies exemplify, techniques of self-construction are inseparable from those through which we seek to direct others. Or to put it another way, the political, strategic aspects of dream-telling are inseparable from lived experience. In focusing upon the former, however, a denial of the latter is often implied in the language used. Kiernan, for example, writes that "the sociological emphasis isolates as its primary datum the dream-told-to-others, an essentially social act, which leads to an analysis of dreams as social assets, which can be manipulated to advantage or disadvantage" (1985:304). But such a one-dimensional view of intentionality in terms of social manipulation alone would ignore the inseperability of agency and ontology in the essays discussed in this section. Zezuru children who petition both parents *and* spirits for the identity of a healer, Temne diviners' clients who partially renounce their interpretation of reality in the face of divinatory authority, Igbo candidates for ritual office whose very competitiveness is subsumed by their understanding and experience of a personal *chi* and Tukulor weavers who do not normally divulge the dreams which inspire them are not just manipulating dreams as social assets, but also negotiating their experience of self and reality. Curley's essay in this volume on membership dreams in an independent church in Cameroun (discussed below) also represents an important corrective to the "dreams as social/political bargaining chips" position. Here, while new members' dreams are clearly strategic, they do not just authorise a new status but form the basis for the experiential reconstruction of a new self in line with the church's definition of itself as consisting of "saved" souls. We are not, of course, suggesting that we can (as Temne diviners claim) have direct access to other people's dream experiences, but we can nevertheless explore dimensions of identity and ontology associated with remembered and narrated dreams. It should not be assumed that we are invariably dealing with individuals who do not experience their dream-recollections as phenomenological realities, however tactically they may deploy them.

Symbols, ritual and interpretation

As the titles of the next three papers imply, there is a shift from a concern with dreams and a particular institutional complex (healing, divination, kingship, craftsmanship) to a perspective which begins by considering dreaming as a generalized feature of each society. Although the authors of the studies of dreaming among Yansi, Berti and Ingessana each have different theoretical interests, it is nevertheless clear that the diversity among these reports is also a reflection of the different ways in which these African cultures have appropriated dreaming. Berti "only rarely tell others in the morning what they dreamt about or discuss their dreams with others" and "a dreamless night" is normal, while by contrast Yansi begin each day with a discussion of the dreams of the night. Berti hold that people dream when they are anxious, but for Ingessana dreams are commonly cited as cause for concern, while both are obviously true for the Yansi. There are among Ingessana and Yansi different kinds of dreams insofar as certain persons claim to be able to dream dreams which no one else is capable of and these dreams are attributed with a peculiar importance which has material consequences extending widely through the society. The Berti population, on the other hand, appears to be homogeneous with regard to the status and significance of dreams. There are no dream specialists, either as interpreters or as dreamers.

Mubuy Mubay Mpier, whose own interests are in the field of social psychology, concentrates on the semantics of Yansi dream discussion and the role such discussion is given in structuring and punctuating the minor and major contingencies which comprise quotidian life. Though dreaming can be described as integral to the Yansi witchcraft-sorcery-medicine complex (and in this respect is comparable to dreaming in Zande oracles and witchcraft), Mpier is primarily concerned with Yansi attitudes and discriminations as regards dreams and dreaming. Yansi make a series of discriminations between recollected dreams which engage with reality, and those which are discounted as mere fantasy. Such judgements are made in the context not just of Yansi notions about dreams but also of what are for Yansi significant levels of reality. Distinctions between medium and content are not relentlessly sustained, and there is instead an active concern with boundaries and relations between humans and animals, between the living and the dead, elders, medicine custodians and ordinary people.

Ladislav Holy's study represents a shift of focus to the semiotics of dream interpretation. Berti make a radical distinction between dream-recollections which are literally accounts of privileged glimpses by the soul into the future beyond the here and now in which the physical body is located, and those dream-recollections which are distinguished by the presence of one or more of a certain number of images recognised as figures. All Berti are able to grasp the meaning of such dream accounts, though some are more or less skilled "readers" than others, and Holy analyses the "grammar" which endows these accounts with significance. This system of rules is not absolutely systematic, and recourse has to be made to extra-dream contexts, such as the current status of the dreamer (e.g., if a woman, and whether pregnant or not) to deal with certain equivocal signifiers, notably "gun" and "snake".

A theme which recurs in all three studies is symbolic reversal in dream images. This theme is taken up in the study of Ingessana dreaming, partly because of the structuralist preoccupations of the author, and partly because of its striking manifestation in this particular culture. What emerges, and is of considerable general interest, is the intimate relationship between major dream images and particular ritual institutions, concepts and practices. Indeed among Ingessana this intimacy is recognised in the use of the same word to refer both to dreams in general and to a particular life-promoting cult group. It is argued that it is the place of dream accounts in such configurations which endows them with an acceptability as accounts not just of dreams but of otherwise contingent lines of conduct, patterns of behaviour, etc. It may be suggested that such specific relationships between dreaming and indigenous ritual institutions may render dreaming less available for capture as a kind of bridgehead by other systems of religious ideas, rituals and ethics in their penetration of local and particular traditions.

Moreover, it is in a variety of local circumstances that the historical diffusion of Christianity and Islam takes place. In this respect it is worth remarking that Berti are now an Arabic-speaking Islamic people while Ingessana, though surounded by Sudanese Islamic people and penetrated by Muslim merchants, have remained relatively unconverted, certainly in the early 'seventies when the field research upon which the present study is based was carried out. In other words, when considering the role of dreams in these historical processes, it is not sound to make deductions from general statements about the (presumed) ubiquity of dreams in black African life, the Old Testament and the tradition of dream interpretation in Arabian Islam.

Dreaming and African Christianity

McKenzie's study is based upon archival research amongst the letters and journals of Yoruba catechists of the Church Missionary Society written during the great transitional period in the middle of the nineteenth century. As McKenzie points out, what the catechists recorded was for an audience not in sympathy with Yoruba religion. Yet it was not only the dreams of converts to Christianity which were recorded, but also of those still adhering to Yoruba deities. McKenzie is thus able to compare accounts of dreams involving conventional Yoruba religious themes with those in which Christian and Yoruba imagery are interwoven, and which thereby articulate transformations of personal religious identity during this period of profound religious change. There is a continuity, he suggests, between these transformations among nineteenth century converts and those of the independent churches of the twentieth century.

Curley's study, based upon field research, is of an independent church in Cameroun. Most people who join the church recount a dream that they experienced shortly before joining. The conversion dream is regarded as an indication of religious fervour, and thus shows that the person is qualified to become a member of the sect. As time goes on, the dream becomes an emblem which summarises the life of the individual, calling attention to the personal identity of the church member and testifying to the transformation which occured when that person joined the church. The conversion dreams also comprise an important part of the collective knowledge of the church community. They are not only the private dreams of individual church members, but they also offer public evidence of the church's ability to change people's lives.

Curley theorises that the lack of exegesis of dream narratives and the importance of the manifest content is related to the recent origins of the church, and that as it develops and matures this may change. He observes that at this stage in its development the church is concerned with its distinctive identity and with the membership as set apart from the rest of the population. Since the church defines itself in terms of the ontological condition of its individual members as new "saved" persons, the identity and experience of the individual are of prime concern, and it is through conversion dreams that these are negotiated.

Charsley, in a major review of the literature on dreaming in independent African churches, challenges a number of taken-for-granted positions. These include the validity of the distinction between individual dreams and stereotyped dreams, the ubiquity of dreaming as a feature of independent African churches, and a necessary connection between pre-Christian and Christian concern with dreaming. Five circumstances are distinguished in which dreaming may be relevant: in the foundation of a church; in the emergence of a church's distinctive features; in the process of becoming a member; as a contribution to the content of church activity; and as an element in the development of special powers, such as those of prophecy and healing. In his conclusion, Charsley critically assesses functionalist and historical explanations of dreaming in independent churches. He finds the former especially weak, not only because of the questionable stability of such churches, a stability which is presupposed in one way or another by the notion of function, but also because Charsley's own fieldwork leads him "to doubt whether dream telling solves more problems than it creates". As for historical connections, these cannot be presumed in advance on the basis of some dream life abstracted from other levels of reality, and which may be more or less successfully tapped by traditional and Christian religious institutions. Above all there is the crucial difficulty of conceptualising and specifying the connections between entities such as a novel institution – the church – and a prior indigenous culture. Is it, for example, the cultural background of the membership (who may be immigrants from diverse localities) or is it the society in which the church is geographically located which is relevant? Or perhaps some other society in which the church itself originated?

If, following Charsley, we do not simply presume connections between pre-Christian and Christian uses of dreaming, we are in a better position to investigate these. As McKenzie's material on nineteenth century Yoruba religion demonstrates, accounts of dreams from historical sources may be more plentiful than we imagine, and may provide insights into the re-negotiation of religious ideas and images during periods of religious and political transition which take us beyond the question of historical and cultural survivals.

Conclusion

We began this Inroduction by examining the failure of Africanist anthropology and religious studies to problematise dreams and dreaming. In this volume, the contributors develop directions for such problematising. Unlike the evolutionist world of the late 19th. and early 20th. century Europe with which we began, however, there is no unified metadiscourse today in terms of which dreaming can be situated. This is a polyphonic collection. As we have seen, some contributors to this volume have begun to remedy the neglect of dreaming in Africanist symbolic and semiotic analysis, some explore the politics of experience in the construction of identity via dreams and some trace the relationship between dream-narratives and historical transformations, while Roy Willis' "Afterword" frames these contributions in terms of psychological processes of meaning-construction. It seems more useful, in the present exploratory stage of this topic, not to suppress such diversity by the imposition of a single encompassing theme. It is hoped that, by raising the above issues and by making lacunae more visable (such as the dearth of material on dreaming in African Islam), this collection will stimulate further studies in Africa and will contribute to a wider rethinking of the anthropology of dreaming.

NOTES

1. Hallowell has cited the same case as indicative of a continuity of the moral responsibility of the self through dreams and waking life (1955:107).
2. Mary Douglas has also characterised Evans-Pritchard's theoretical concern in this work as "tracing accountability" (1980: 11-13)
3. The importance of the body in dreaming suggested by such ingestion of "dream-medicine" has probably been obscured by the Tylorian emphasis on the soul. Note that the Greeks used to take their bodies to certain temples where they would lie on special beds *(kline,* hence "clinic") and incubate diagnostic dreams (Dodds 1951).

REFERENCES

BARNARD, A., 1989, The lost world of Laurens van der Post? *Current Anthropology* 30, 104-114.

BELLMAN, B., 1975, *Village of Curers and Assassins: on the production of Fala Kpelle cosmological categories.* The Hague: Mouton.

CAILLOIS, R., 1966, Logical and philosophical problems of the dream. In G. von Grunebaum and R. Caillois (eds.), *The Dream and Human Society.* Berkeley: University of California Press.

CHIMOMBO, S., 1989, Dreams and Ntara's *Man of Africa. Journal of Religion in Africa* XIX: 48-70.

DEVEREUX, G., 1951, *Dream and Reality.* New York: International Universities Press.

DODDS, E.R., 1951, *The Greeks and the Irrational.* Berkeley: University of California Press.

DOUGLAS, M., 1980, *Evans-Pritchard.* London: Fontana.

DURKHEIM, E., 1915, *The Elementary Forms of the Religious Life.* London: George Allen & Unwin.

EGGAN, D., 1949, The significance of dreams for anthropological research. *American Anthropologist*, 51: 171-198.

EVANS-PRITCHARD, E.E., 1937, *Witchcraft, Oracles and Magic among the Azande.* Oxford: Clarendon Press.

FERNANDEZ, J.W., 1982, *Bwiti: an ethnography of the religious imagination in Africa.* Princeton: Princeton University Press.

FIRTH, R., 1934, The meaning of dreams in Tikopia. In E.E. Evans-Pritchard, R. Firth *et al* (eds.), *Essays Presented to C. G. Seligman.* London: Kegan Paul, Trench and Trubner.
1985, Degrees of intelligibility. In J. Overing (ed.), *Reason and Morality.* London: Tavistock.

FISHER, H.J., 1979, Dreams and conversion in Black Africa. In N. Levtzion (ed.), *Conversion to Islam.* New York: Holmes and Meier

FORTES, M., 1949, *The Web of Kinship among the Tallensi.* London: Oxford University Press.
1959, *Oedipus and Job in West African Religion.* Cambridge: Cambridge University Press.

HALLOWELL, A.L., 1955, *Culture and Experience.* Philadelphia: University of Pennsylvania Press.

HALLPIKE, C.R., 1979, *The Foundations of Primitive Thought.* Oxford: Oxford University Press.

HORTON, R., 1983, Social psychologies, African and Western. In M. Fortes, *Oedipus and Job in West African Religion.* Cambridge: Cambridge University Press (reissue).

HUDSON, L., 1985, *Nightlife: the interpretation of dreams.* London: Weidenfeld and Nicholson.

JACKSON, M., 1986, *Barawa and the Ways Birds Fly in the Sky.* Washington: Smithsonian Institution Press.

JAMES, W., 1988, *The Listening Ebony. Moral knowledge, religion and power among the Uduk of Sudan.* Oxford: Clarendon Press.

JOHNSON, K.E., 1978, Modernity and dream content. A Ugandan example. *Ethos* 6, 212-20.

JUNG, C.G., 1967, *Memories, Dreams, Reflections.* London: Fontana.

KIERNAN, J. P., 1985, The social stuff of revelation: pattern and purpose in Zionist dreams and visions. *Africa* 55: 304-318.

KUPER, A., 1979, The structure of dreams. *Man* 14: 645-622.
    1983, The structure of dream sequences. *Culture, Medicine and Psychiatry* 7: 153-175.
LANG, A., 1898, *The Making of Religion*. London: Longmans, Green & Co.
LEE, S.G., 1958, Social influences in Zulu dreaming. *Journal of Social Psychology* 47:265-83.
LE VINE, R., 1966, *Dreams and Deeds. Achievement motivation in Nigeria*. Chicago: Chicago University Press.
LE VINE, S., 1981, Dreams of the informant about the researcher: some difficulties inherent in the research relationship. *Ethos* 9: 276-93.
LEVY-BRUHL, L., 1966 (orig. 1922), *Primitive Mentality*. Boston: Beacon Press.
LINCOLN, J.S., 1935, *The Dream in Primitive Cultures*. London: Crosset Press.
MALINOWSKI, B., 1927, *Sex and Repression in Savage Society*, London: Kegan Paul, Trench and Trubner.
MBITI, J.S., 1976, God, dreams and African militancy. In J. Pobee (ed.), *Religion in a Pluralistic Society*. Leiden: E. J. Brill.
MILLS, C.W., 1940, Situated actions and vocabularies of motive. *American Review of Sociology* 5: 904-913.
MPIER, M.M., 1982, *La Symbolique du Rêve chez les Yansi et les Populations Voisines*. Bandundu, Zaire: CEEBA Publications.
NADEL, S.F., 1954, *Nupe Religion*, London: Routledge and Kegan Paul.
O'FLAHERTY, W.D., 1984, *Dreams, Illusions and Other Realities*. Chicago: University of Chicago Press.
RATTRAY, R.S., 1927, *Religion and Art in Ashanti*. Oxford: Oxford University Press.
REHFISCH, F., 1969, Death, dreams and the ancestors in Mambila culture. In M. Douglas and P. Kaberry (eds.) *Man in Africa*. London: Tavistock.
ROAZEN, P., 1975, *Freud and his Followers*. New York: Alfred A. Knopf.
ROHEIM, G., 1932, Psycho-analysis of primitive cultural types. *The International Journal of Pschyo-Analysis* 13: 1-224.
SANNEH, L., 1979, *The Jakhanke: the history of an Islamic clerical people of the Senegambia*. London: International African Institute.
SCOTT, M.G. and LYMAN, S.M., 1968, Accounts. *American Sociological Review*, 33: 46-62.
SELIGMAN, C.G., 1924, Anthropology and psychology. *Journal of the Royal Anthropological Institute* 54: 13-46.
    1932, Anthropological perspective and psychological theory. *Journal of the Royal Anthropological Institute* lxiii: 193-228.
SHWEDER, R., 1982, On savages and other children: a review of *The Foundations of Primitive Thought* by C.R. Hallpike. *American Anthropologist*, 84: 354-366.
SHWEDER, R. and LE VINE, R., 1975, Dream concepts of Hausa children. *Ethos*, 3: 209-230.
SPENCER, H., 1882, *The Priciples of Sociology*, Vol. I. London: Williams and Norgate.
TEDLOCK, B. (ed.) 1987, *Dreaming. Anthropological and psychological interpretations*. Cambridge: Cambridge University Press.
TYLOR, E., 1889 (orig. 1871), *Primitive Culture*. London: H. Holt & Co.
VON GRUNEBAUM, G., 1966, Introduction: the cultural function of the dream as illustrated by classical Islam. In G. von Grunebaum and R. Caillois (eds.), *The Dream and Human Society*. Berkeley: University of California Press.

DREAMS AND THE CONSTITUTION OF SELF AMONG THE ZEZURU

PAMELA REYNOLDS
University of Zimbabwe

Dreams as techniques of the self

For two years, 1982 and 1983, I worked with sixty traditional healers in three areas of Mashonaland in Zimbabwe. One area is rural (Musami), another peri-urban (Mabvuku) and the third urban (Mbare). I was studying the transmission of knowledge across generations and, in the process, learnt something about the role of dreams in what Foucault (1984) has called the techniques of self. During the course of the study I was struck by the quality of the relationships between healers and children (often grandparents and grandchildren) which seemed to allow for an unusual degree of individual expression and examination both of self and other. The relationships seemed to offer more than the help and companionship that is often observed between the old and young among the Zezuru: it offered a forum for the transmission of knowledge and an arena for the exploration of self. This exploration was conducted in part through the use of dreams.

Foucault (1984: 369) said that just as it is necessary to study and compare the different techniques of the production of objects and the direction of men by men through government, one must also question techniques of the self. These, he believed, can be found in all cultures in different forms. The analysis of techniques of the self is difficult because they are often invisible and because they are frequently linked to the techniques for the direction of others. This paper examines dreams as part of the repertoire available for the constitution of self and for the direction of others.

In exploring ideas on the genealogy of ethics, Foucault concentrates on the relationship between the individual and a symbolic system. He wrote:

> So it is not enough to say that the subject is constituted in a symbolic system. It is not just in the play of symbols that the subject is constituted. It is constituted in real practices – histori-cally analyzable practices. There is a technology of the constitution of the self which cuts across symbolic systems while using them. (1984: 369)

Rorty (1986) reminds us of the quarrel between poetry and philosophy, the tension between an effort to achieve self-creation by the recognition of contingency and an effort to achieve universality by the transcendence of contingency. Nietzche, he says, first saw self-knowledge as self-creation and Freud showed us how every human can generate a self-description. He tracked home "conscience to its origin in the contingencies of our upbringing" (Rorty 1986).

In this paper I trace Zezuru healers' use of dreams as part of their strategy for coping with the contingencies of their upbringing. Dreams are seen as part of the description of self.

Dreams and the symbolic system

For anthropologists symbols are taken as being characteristic of sets or groups of people, of institutions or of types of situation. Anthropologists are occupied with "the symbolism of collectivity – of myth, of ritual, of social structure" (Firth 1973: 207). In contrast, psychologists study, not exclusively but basically, symbolic forms presented by individuals. Firth illustrates the intricacy of the relationship between private and public symbolism and identifies the central problem facing anthropologists interested in the psychological domain as "the translation from individual to social dimension" (1973: 150). My intention here is to trace the ways in which Zezuru healers translate the social dimension in constituting themselves as individuals in the process of becoming socially recognised mediators.

I shall place the symbolic system as an axis first in the links between the supernatural, traditional healers (n'anga) and individuals, and then as an axis around which the child can constitute his or her self (see Figures One and Two). A detailed description of the symbolic system will not be given here. There are many kinds of spirit that are said to influence the living. There are spirits of ancient popluations whose descendants are unknown; spirits of the chiefs of the past (mhondoro); spirits of ordinary people who possess their own descendants (vadzimu); spirits of witches (varoyi); spirits of lost souls (ngozi); alien spirits (mashave) including river spirits (njuzu). I use "shades" to refer to all or any spirit and "ancestors" to refer to spirits of dead kin.[1]

There are symbols that appear in dreams which many of the n'anga with whom I worked claim have universal meaning. Some of these are:

the symbol	the meaning
field	life
green maize	life
mountain	life span
grain	mudzimu (i.e. life)
digging a trench	death (in the family)
death of a stranger	death of kin
car full of people	death
ploughing	death
flying	shades moving (communicating)
flying (in a child's dream)	growth
being on a hill	shade's visit
bird flying	shade
black clouds	shades addressing one
white python	one's own shade
lion chasing	shades touching (testing one)

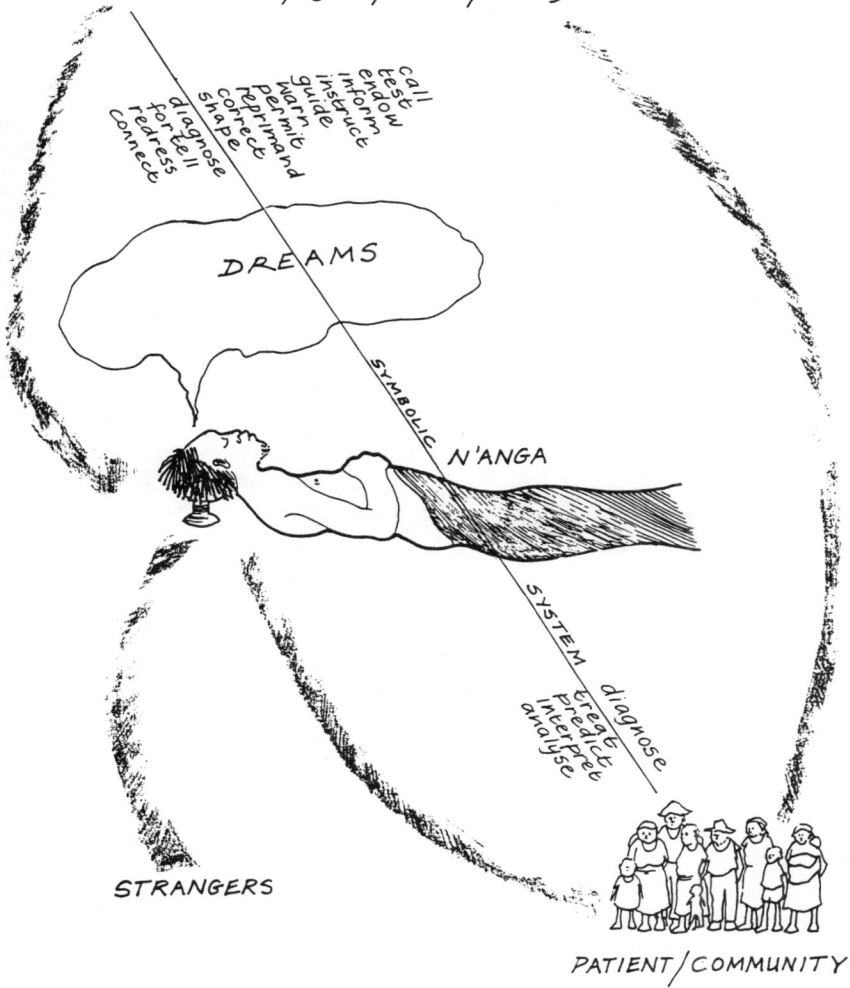

SHADES: mhondoro/ngozi/shave/varoyi

call
test
endow
inform
instruct
guide
warn
reprimand
correct
shape
diagnose
foretell
redress
connect

DREAMS

SYMBOLIC

N'ANGA

SYSTEM

diagnose
treat
predict
interpret
analyse

STRANGERS

PATIENT/COMMUNITY

Figure 1: Dreams as Mediators

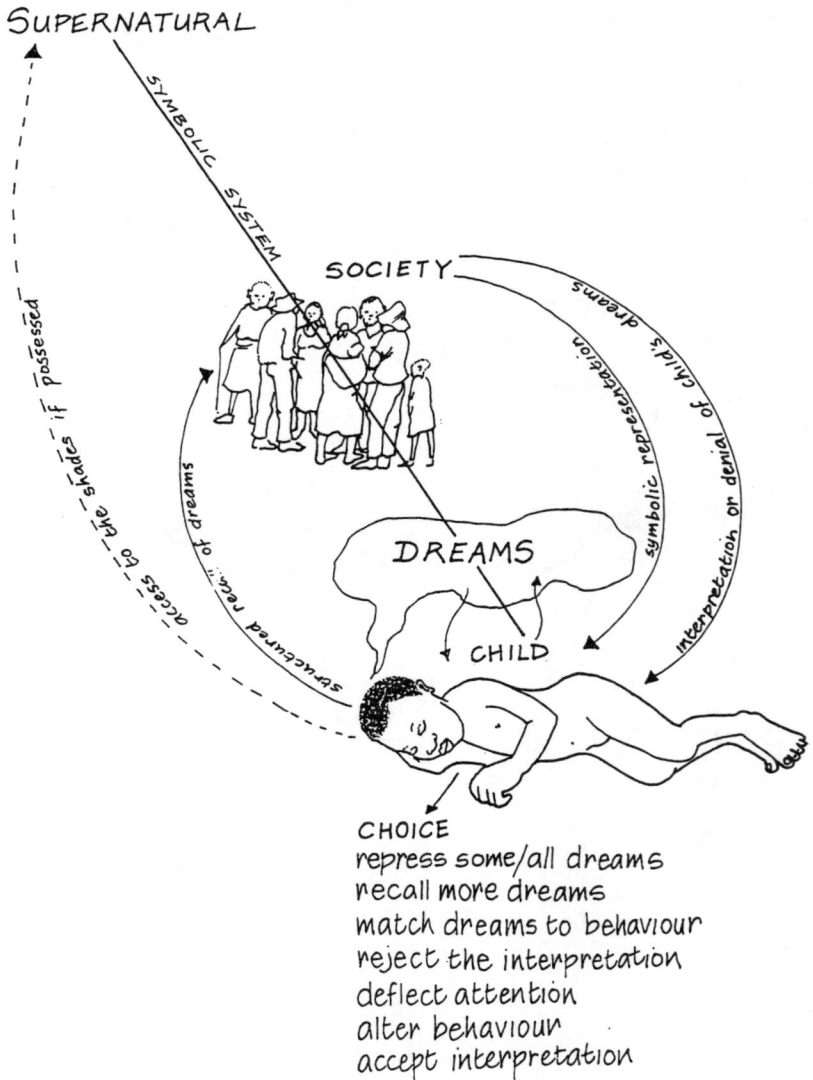

Figure 2: Dreams and the Child

I did not systematically inquire about symbols, nor have I attempted to analyze them. It seems probable that there is sufficient concurrence among healers as to symbolic significance to render the sort of analysis that Turner made among the Ndembu fruitful. It is clear that the composition of the symbolic system alters over time (for example, it is a new notion that a car load of people represents death – and quite accurate in Zimbabwe). The system is not static, immutable, but reflects the changing contributions made at each level.

Dreams as conduits

In Figure One the shades, dreams, *n'anga,* and individuals (or individuals within communities) are placed along the axis. The figure represents the play that is made of the symbolic system with dreams as one point of mediation. Perhaps we can draw an analogy between the symbolic system and an electrical current that is tapped at different points.

The shades (whether *mhondoro, vadzimu, mashave, varoyi,* or *ngozi)* are said to use the dreams of *n'anga* to achieve many purposes. Before I examine these, two points must be made. One is that the shades infiltrate anyone's dreams, not only the dreams of *n'anga.* Anyone can draw insight from the shades via dreams, and even the power to cure some ailments and foretell some events. Access from the shades to individuals and from individuals to the shades is not wholly dependent on the mediation of diviners and/or healers. The second point is that neither the shades nor individuals are dependant on dreams as a medium for communication: dreams are but one piece of technology – "our TV screens", as one *n'anga* explained it.

An analysis of the dreams told to me by *n'anga* suggests that the shades use dreams to call, test, endow, inform, instruct, guide, warn, permit, reprimand, correct and shape healers; and they use healers' dreams to reach the community in order to diagnose patients, to foretell the future, to call for the redress of neglect, to caution against immoral behaviour, and to make connections between the past and the present. The shades of witches *(varoyi)* or lost souls *(ngozi)* use dreams for nefarious ends to cause harm, or demand retribution, or scare the dreamer into compliance. The shades, using dreams and other means, bestow power but also revoke it. They are hard task-masters and take their pound of flesh (usually in the form of beer). People do not become *n'anga* lightly; there is a sense of unease, of responsibility, even of slight illness that is seen to accompany their calling. The shades endow some people with power yet they offer no security of tenure. Moral transgressions, neglect, mistakes, disobedience, laziness, greed, even the process of ageing, may result in abandonment by the shades and loss of power which may lead to madness.

Dreams are seen to offer protection to *n'anga* as they foretell major incidents, thus allowing them to prepare to meet them. When one *n'anga* was taken into the mountains by the comrades during the war and beaten during interrogation to see if he was a "sell-out", he felt aggrieved at his spirits for not having warned him. In fact, while being interrogated he became possessed and, as the ancestors supported the liberation struggle, the comrades accepted his protestations of innocence.

We have seen some of the ways in which the shades may be said to use dreams. The norm holds that the healer is passive in that he is a conduit in the process of communication between the ancestors and their descendants. He is said to be the pocket to the shade(s).[2] The process of identification and authentication of someone as a healer is said to be controlled by his kin and community. In studying the histories of healers' coming-out and in watching phases of the process it seemed to me that they were actively engaged in petitioning kin for acknowledgement and support of their claims and, hence, for ritual and material investment. The aspirant healer canvases for support from among senior healers, knowing that their recognition of the possessing shade's genealogy and good intentions are vital in authenticating the healer's claims.

Dreams are used to bolster the aspirant healer's case; he garners them and presents them like signatures on petitions. In doing so he appropriates symbols. The symbols appear in his dreams. He selects which dreams to offer for interpretation. He decides whether or not to accept the interpretation, seeking other explanations in some cases. He decides whether or not to act in accord with the interpretation. It is up to the individual to continue to present dreams or symptoms or patterns of behaviour that draw his kins' attention to his singularity and his needs. He acts out his call. His behaviour must accord with his call across time: he must follow the path through a series of variable, flexible yet determining stages.

Once recognised as possessed, the healer must persuade the community that he has been endowed with spiritual power by living in accord with the moral precepts said to be imposed by the shades. He is obliged to treat and should take care not to seem mercenary in his handling of patients. In order to remind the community of the special relationship he has with the supernatural world, the healer holds numerous rituals to which kin and neighbours are invited.

The healer's moral conduct, service to the community, attendance at ritual functions, performance of rituals, are all seen to be avenues of communication with the shade. The healer takes care to make public gestures of respect towards the shade, like taking snuff or removing his shoes before entering his *banya* (spirit's house). The shades are addressed before patients are treated, major decisions are taken or herbs collected.

In summary: the shades inform the healer through dreams (though not only through dreams) and, in return, the healer gives thanks and pays respect to the shades, receives fees on behalf of the shades and lives in accord with the shades' precepts. Using power and information derived from the shades, a healer diagnoses, treats, predicts, interprets and analyses. In return for his public services the healer receives respect (though he is often regarded with ambivalence); reward (though he says that fees belong to the shades and he may use them only as directed by the shades); and recognition (though it is conditional). No healer is secure in his command of power from the shades nor respect from the community. He is constantly involved in a process of negotiation with both spheres and, in part, the currency of negotiations is dreams. Through the dreams of patients and the dreams about patients a healer has privileged access to others' minds.

Dreams and the child

We have seen how dreams can be used by healers to direct others. Let us now look more closely at the use of dreams to constitute self. Let us shake the kaleidoscope and re-arrange the pieces to yield another diagram, the one depicted in Figure Two. Here dreams mediate between the child and society and the supernatural.

The child dreams, drawing from society the symbols which clothe dreams or, at least, into which dreams are moulded in order to be communicated. He offers up some of his dreams for comment. Adults swing between dismissing children's dreams as meaningless and interpreting them as direct messages from the shades. It is often said that children's dreams are simply to do with growing. Sometimes a child reports his dreams and finds that they provoke anxiety in adults and may even result in punishment. For some this is an early collision with people's ambivalence towards those who have direct truck with the supernatural.

Sometimes families seek interpretation of children's dreams from *n'anga*. These dreams have already been twice selected: once by the child and once by his kin. A child's dream brought to a *n'anga* is likely to be given an interpretation involving the influence of the shades. I have examples of children's dreams which have been interpreted to show that an ancestor is appealing through the child for a debt to be paid (often the mother's cow); or a *ngozi* calling for compensation to be made to his family for his death which was caused by a *mujibha* (a messenger) during the Liberation War; or a *shave* impressing upon the family that the child has been selected as a "pocket" to be possessed later.

Whether or not the family acts on the interpretation depends on the occurrence of the dream in relation to a sequence of other events or signs, including incidents of illness or misfortune. Seldom would much significance be given to a child's dream in isolation. Adults may be sceptical of the power of dreams, especially in children, but many reserve their opinion in case subsequent events prove them wrong. While ancestors are seen to be benevolent and to act on behalf of the interests of the family, they can be punitive and can display unworthy emotions like envy, jealousy and wrath. In order to persuade the family of their immediate needs they often strike through a child, causing illness or even death to the child. A child's dreams may presage such feared interference from the ancestors.

A child knows what interpretation is given to his dreams. To some extent, he chooses what to do with it: he can repress some or all of his dreams; he can recall more dreams; he can match his behaviour to the interpretation; or he can reject the interpretation and take care not to participate in the metaphor that links family and the supernatural.

Remembrances of dreams in childhood

In recalling incidents and dreams from their childhood that presaged future possession, many *n'anga* emphasize the resistance with which the signs were initially met. The resistance partly reflects the sense of vocation as coming from outside. Parents are often said to ignore signs of possession in their children, hoping that nothing will come of them. They do so partly because possession is seen as a mixed blessing as has been suggested above, partly because the costs involved can be substantial, and partly because if a spirit is incautiously accepted and it turns out to be a witch or *ngozi* it is difficult to chase.[3] A family may test a spirit even after it has been authenticated at a *bira* (ritual of bringing out the spirit, when senior *n'anga* question the spirit on its genealogy and intention), withholding the cloth and axe due the spirit. Calling is often seen to confict with a family's Christian beliefs.

One healer recalls that as a young child he dreamt of dancing on hides and of lions chasing him – sometimes he would climb a tree and fall, sometimes run into a river, sometimes fly. These dreams would commonly be interpreted as a spirit testing the will and courage of the dreamer: each feature has symbolic resonance, for example, the river is the home of the *njuzu*, spirits who confer potent healing powers. When the child used to tell his mother these dreams she would beat him, saying "Such dreams are not dreamt by children". Later he dreamt of falling stars that would crash and break into pieces. He would pick up the largest piece and jump into a river. An Apostolic priest was consulted and said the dreams predicted the child's death. The boy's mother burnt *mbanda* (an aromatic herb used like incense) to chase the dreams. They worsened as the spirit was angered. Later, as a young man, he had hallucinations in which the skyscrapers of Salisbury (now Harare) grew tiny, and in which he could see through cars and make out the engine parts, and in which he could see the medicine in people's pockets. These occurred shortly before his family finally accepted that he had been called.

Other *n'anga* remember dreams in their childhood of flying, of grabbing a lion's mouth, of being covered in a black and white cloth, of being thrashed with an ox's tail, of being the centre of a *bira* dance, of being under water, of caves full of healers' paraphenalia, of black pythons around the neck, and of herbs. Sometimes a family member clearly leads a child in the process of emerging as a healer. Here is one female healer's story. As a young adolescent she began to dream of herbs and her family accepted that she had been called. Her father was informed in a dream that his daughter's spirit was male and that he must collect and handle the herbs revealed in her dreams as, if she touched them, she would not bear children. Earlier signs had warned of her future possession: in Grade One at school she would become blind when told to write; at the age of eight she would fall into the river *en route* to school. It was interpreted by her parents that her spirit was forbidding her to attend school. (This is a theme that quite often emerges in healers' recall of their childhood experiences.) He respected her, as "she had taken his father's name", that is, she was posesssed by the spirit of his father who, before his death, had foretold that he would possess his son's first born.[4] And so it had come to pass. On the healer's birth, a ritual had been held to appease the baby's grandfather's spirit in the hope that he would wait and allow the child to mature before possessing her. When the healer married she bore twins, both of whom died because, she said, a ritual of appeasement had not been held partly because she was living far from home. She commented: "Having children is not as easy as buying bread".

I have collected many other dreams as recalled by *n'anga* from their childhood. Even if the dreams are invested with significance using hindsight they are informative in revealing the process through which *n'anga* claim to have passed, that is, they confirm the norm offered by society. Or, as Bachelard phrased it, "mediated childhood is more than the sum of our memories" (1971: 126).

Power and meaning in children's dreams

Some *n'anga* feel that children dream of useless things that mean nothing to the child until the age of understanding. This they place at about age seven. Most *n'anga* hold that the dreams of children are meaningful, that they have power, and that attention ought to be paid to them. Some say that children's dreams are more meaningful than adults' because "their hearts are pure". Jung said that children sometimes have archetypal dreams, which he explains "by the fact that when consciousness begins to dawn, when the child begins to feel that *he* is, he is still close to the original psychological world from which he has just emerged: a condition of deep consciousness" (1968: 106). Jung believed that a "veil of forgetfulness is drawn upon these experiences, usually at the age of four to six" (1968: 107). He continued:

> I have seen cases of ethereal children, so to speak, who had an extraordinary awareness of these psychic facts and were living their life in archetypal dreams and could not adapt. Recently I saw a case of a little girl of ten who had some most amazing mythological dreams. Her father consulted me about these dreams. I could not tell him what I thought because they contained an uncanny prognosis. The little girl died a year later of an infectious disease. She had never been born entirely. (*ibid.*)

I offer Jung's story not to suggest strong parallels between psychoanalysis and Zezuru healing patterns, but to suggest that it is not uncommon for children to be seen as emanating from and returning to the world of spirits. As Bachelard (1971: 127) says, "childhood, in its archetypal quality, is *communicable*" and "childhood … causes a great abundance of fundamental archetypes" (1971: 124).

Some *n'anga* say the interpretation of dreams "is natural", that the meaning is clear, that interpretative ability does not improve over time or with experience. These views accord with Jung's when he says, "the dream is its own interpretation" (1968: 92). Other healers say that making connections between dreams and incidents that follow teach one how to interpret dreams. Many know medicine that improves the recall of dreams, and some say it helps to make dreams prophetic.[5] The ingredients usually include a vulture's brain and ear (the area around it), which are mixed with herbs placed in incisions in the skin which should be pricked with a vulture's nail. The vulture's heart is cooked with herbs and eaten. The medicine is given to trusted children, those with a good heart and an interest in the healing business. There are medicines to chase nightmares, and they can also be used as protection against the police!

Dreams are seen to possess an active power. For example, one healer often dreams of flying and warns her husband not to waken her as if he does she will die while dreaming thus. Berglund claims that, "The reality of dreams in Zulu thinking does not limit itself merely to the seen and the heard. It includes the experienced also. Pain in the shoulders after a night of dreams is most definitely spoken of as the shades' activities" (1976: 98). Evans-Pritchard has recorded of the Zande that their bad dreams were commonly interpreted in terms of witchcraft – not as symbols of witchcraft but as actual experiences of it (cited in Firth 1973: 218).

N'anga say that the shades of dead children can enter adults' dreams. Few grant them power or influence, although a senior healer said that the shades of abandoned children, especially those dumped in toilets (there has been, since Independence, a rash of "baby dumping" that has brought draconian sentences on the young mothers), can cause more havoc than other aggrieved spirits. They may even kill bachelors, which is a terrible fate as "they still have their children in their stomachs". In some sense these *ngozi* (the spirits of abandoned children) draw on the power of the shades, who are angered at the waste of their gifts, that is, the birth of children.[6]

Some healers interpret their own children's dreams when they are possessed. Many healers tell children the uses of herbs that the children say are revealed to them in their dreams. For example, a sixteen-year-old girl told her mother's mother (an old and widely respected healer) that the night before she had dreamt of a herb and had collected it from the bush on waking. She asked her grandmother how to use it and was told to crush the leaves into tea or porridge and administer it as protection against witches or sexually transmitted diseases. It could also, the old woman said, be rubbed into incisions around the navel to relieve stomach pain. The incident illustrates my thesis: that the technical knowledge that is a necessary but not sufficient skill in healing is often learnt as a child, that a child can be an active partner in the learning process, and that a child can use dreams as part of the conversation between himself and a healer (most often a grandparent). In claiming to have had the plant revealed to her by the shades in a dream, the girl acted in accord with the norm that says healing is not a learnt skill but one endowed by the shades. No contradiction of the norm is seen in the fact that her grandmother told her how to use and prepare the plant as medicine. Her dream legitimised her inquiry. She used the dream to gain knowledge. Unless the girl is prepared to adopt the language (whether consciously or unconsciously) of the symbolic system, she cannot participate in the healing process.

Dreams and technical knowledge

All healers who claim to be possessed or guided by the shades say that their technical knowledge (their knowledge of *materia medica*) is revealed to them in dreams. They deny that they are taught to identify plants, classify species, prepare medicines or diagnose illnesses. Apart from minor ailments, every treatment must be revealed in dreams for each patient, even if the illness is one often treated by them. Dreams may appear in short spells of sleep during treatment sessions. Spiritual power must be tapped anew for each consultation. *N'anga* quickly feel the displeasure of the shades if the latter refuse to reveal the ingredients of medicines. *N'anga* constantly tap the power of the shades, and the timbre of the relationship between shades and *n'anga* is frequently gauged.

Technical knowledge is acquired over time. The shades introduce healers to progressively more complicated illnesses and gradually extend their range of competence. Recent "graduates" refer difficult cases to their seniors, saying the spirit has not yet revealed the treatment to them. The ingredients are pictured in dreams. In the case of herbs, the whole plant is illustrated and the part to be used picked out. Most medicines are made of a number of ingredients: some *n'anga* say that these are revealed in a series of dreams, sometimes across several nights, and others in the same dream. The dream always shows where the plant may be found, but not necessarily the exact spot. Many *n'anga* experiment with new ingredients on themselves before prescribing them. Names are seldom given in dreams: healers ask others to identify those not known to them. A healer, who held high office in a national traditional healers' organization, claimed that his *mudzimu* had revealed to him an extraordinary set of myths to do with healing that had been drawn from Greek, Biblical and Zezuru mythology. He said that his spirits gave the Latin names of herbs revealed in his dreams.

As technical knowledge is not taught but revealed, it is no use teaching a child how to identify plants, classify species, prepare "medicines", etc., unless the child is guided at least by a *shave*. Without spiritual guidance the child will simply forget. Therefore, a child with a quick, agile, interested mind that holds information and acquires more will be seen to be spiritually guided. In attaching himself to a healer within the family and in offering his company, doing as bid, assisting with the collection of herbs and preparation of medicines, the child is declaring himself to be in communication with the supernatural. The process through which knowledge is acquired is said to be tough – like "climbing an anthill" *(kukwira churu)* because it represents contact with the shades and is seen as a time of testing by the shades. Herbal training courses are thus dismissed as worthless. No healer can guarantee the transmission of his knowledge to future generations, as the acquisition of knowledge depends upon spiritual endowment. Herbs acquired from another source, even another healer, are often cast away by one's own spirit.

Conclusion: dreams and connections

Dreams are invisible to all but the dreamer. Most dreams are discarded. A problem is *what* is remembered, recounted, as distinct from what is experienced in dreams – the latter is forever closed to outsiders. Structures emerge in the telling. Crises lend meaning to dreams, and the process of self-description shapes their recall. Kuper (1983: 174) hypothesises that dreams, like myths, are based on systematic transformations, and he suggests that the structure of dreams "is so reminiscent of the structure of myths discovered by Lévi-Strauss, that (in analysing their structure) we may even be learning something about the psychology of cognition in general".

Zulu believe that without dreams, true and uninterrupted living is not possible. They say "Dreams are our eyes in the work" (Berglund 1976: 98). Zezuru believe the same: dreamless nights are said to be unhealthy. Dreams mediate between the shades and the living. It seems, too, that it was not only for Freud that dreams represented "the most important road to the subterranean forces which determine the parapraxes in everyday life" (A. Freud 1981: 216).

I shall offer a dream of a *n'anga* to make a final point: that dreams make connections between personal problems and the burden of an epoch, and between the present and the past. Kazembe is a fairly young healer, but his reputation is growing rapidly. He showed signs of future possession as a small child. His mother would take him to the fields and he would become violently ill, falling unconscious, and would have to be carried home. Those were the only signs in his childhood that he remembers, but as a young man working as a domestic servant in Salisbury he used to see antelope asleep in his room. He became ill, and a long process of consultation with *n'anga* followed, including an encounter with *njuzu* spirits. Kazembe has three spirits, one of which is from the early ancestors and is the son of a spirit who has possessed ten members of Kazembe's family down the generations. The spirit was instructed by his father to possess a member of the line during the Liberation War in order to protect the family. The spirit possessed an elder during the wars between the Shona and Ndebele in the last century.

Kazembe is shown in dreams the miracles that the elder performed against Ndebele warriors. He told me one of these dreams:

> I dreamt of a homestead on top of a mountain. On the steep slope of the hill was a stone structure like Zimbabwe. Zulu came to attack the village. I saw them beside a river – I saw dust and trees shaking. I took a spear and struck it into the ground and the water in the river turned to blood to prevent their crossing. The whole village began to run away out of the stone structure through small gaps in the walls to the village of Nyamapanga.

Kazembe says that it was a very frightening dream. He thinks the incident happened. He struck the spear in the dream, but it was really the elder whom his spirit then possessed. What concerns us here is that the story of the river turning to blood is known in the area, and it is not disputed that Kazembe's spirit was involved. Besides, the area delineated in the dream was a troublesome place to go during the Liberation War. Soldiers in Smith's army were badly stung by bees; a snake without a head or tail (because it was so long) was often seen there; a red cloth was found there; motorists would travel and travel at night and in the morning find themselves in the same spot. The dreams fit local myths about the original claim to ownership of the land. The dreams knit together the people's experiences of war. Kazembe told me his dreams just after the War of Liberation had ended and at a time when he was treating children traumatised by their experiences during the war. His treatment depended in part on their dreams.

NOTES

1. The spirits of dead kin are those that have, through ritual, been secured a place among the host of shades said to influence the living: these exclude the spirits of the dead that were not recognized as having achieved full adult status while alive, for example, the spirits of children or infertile women or impotent men or murderers.
2. The majority of *n'anga* in Zimbabwe are female, yet I shall keep to traditional grammatical form in using masculine pronouns.
3. Compare Favret-Saada who, writing of "unwitchers" in France, says that, "Everyone in the Bocage is sufficiently aware of the dangers and servitude attached to magic power to know that it is a poisoned gift which one must not touch unless one's desire to do so is sufficiently strong" (1980: 19 n.11).
4. Berglund (1976: 100) says that Zulu believe the shades can determine that a child in the womb will be a diviner.
5. Berglund (1976: 114) mentions a plant used by Zulu to make dreams clear.
6. Zulu believe that children can appear as shades in dreams but they deny that they have power. Berglund writes:

> To Zulu all human beings are potential shades ... All are emphatic that children, including infants, are and become shades, disregarding the fact that they may not have been "brought back" to the homestead in the customary *ukubuyisa* rituals. Asked what happens to children when they die, an informant said: "They become *amadlozi* (shades), but they remain children. No child has power in the homestead. So the shade of a child has no power". People are explicit that even children appear in dreams, particularly to their mothers. "Sometimes even to the fathers, especially small boys. When the father is wondering what has happened with the child, then he sees the child in a dream. The father simply sees the boy. Then he (the father) wakes up." All are convinced that no shade of a child can either give advice or exercise influence of any kind: "That is impossible. It is merely a child. What can a child say?" (1976: 119).

Acknowledgements

I thank Colleen Cousins for drawing the diagrams and Michael Bourdillon and Charles Jędrej for commenting on an earlier draft of the paper.

REFERENCES

BACHELARD, G., 1971, *The Poetics of Reverie. Childhood, language and the cosmos*, tr. D. Russell, Boston: Beacon Press.
BERGLUND, A.I., 1976, *Zulu Thought-Patterns and Symbolism*. London: Hurst and Co.
FAVRET-SAADA, J., 1980, *Deadly Words. Witchcraft in the Bocage*. Tr. C. Cullen, Cambridge: Cambridge University Press.
FIRTH, R., 1973, *Symbols, Public and Private*. London: George Allen and Unwin.
FOUCAULT, M., 1984, *The Foucault Reader*. Ed. P. Rabinow, New York: Pantheon Books.
FREUD, A., 1981, *Psychoanalytic Psychology of Normal Development 1970-1980*. London: The Hogarth Press.
JUNG, C., 1968, *Analytical Psychology: its theory and practice. The Tavistock Lectures*. London: Routledge and Kegan Paul.

KUPER, A., 1983, The structure of dream sequences, *Culture, Medicine and Psychiatry* 7: 153-175.
RORTY, R., 1986, The contingency of selfhood. Northcliffe Lecture, University College London.
SINGER, J., 1981, *Daydreaming and Fantasy*. Oxford: Oxford University Press.
TURNER, V., 1981, *The Drums of Affliction. A study of religious processes among the Ndembu of Zambia*. London: Hutchinson.

DREAMING AS ACCOMPLISHMENT:
POWER, THE INDIVIDUAL AND TEMNE DIVINATION

ROSALIND SHAW

Tufts University (U.S.A.)

> For their beleefe, I can heare of none that they have, but in such as
> they themselves imagine to see in their dreames, and so worship the
> pictures, whereof wee sawe some like unto Divels. (John Sparke,
> 1564, in Markham [ed.] 1878)

This sixteenth century account characterises the religious ideas of the inhabitants of the Isle de Los (Hair 1987), many of whom belonged to groups closely related linguistically to the Temne. If we read Sparke to be claiming that their concepts of spirits are illusory phantasmagoria derived from dreams, he anticipates by three hundred years aspects of Edward Tylor's "dream theory" of the origin of religion (1871). Today, of course, ethnographic concern for an appropriate translation of culture is manifest in an emphasis upon culturally specific metaphysical frameworks in terms of which dreams may be ascribed not only reality but also authority as crucial sources of knowledge (e.g. Lienhardt 1961:149; Overing 1985:13). This point has been emphasised in relation to the Temne of north-western Sierra Leone by Littlejohn in his analysis of conceptual patterns articulated in the Temne house:

> I wish to stress that it is not the case that the Temne do not distinguish between dreams and
> wakeful perception; they do. The point is that dreams count for as much as wakeful perception
> ... While experience neither in dreams nor wakeful perception can be said to be categorized
> with the Temne, both are subject to the same characterizations; both, for example, can have
> the character of "present reality", both can have the character of "forewarning" ... (1960:71).

Given that it is within specific conceptual contexts that dreams acquire reality and authority, how are such reality-conferring contexts spread within a society? Or to put it another way, if dreams are a source of knowledge, how is this knowledge socially distributed? For like other phenomena which are deemed to be universal and naturally based (such as human fertility, for example: MacCormack 1982), dreaming is subject to cultural definitions, and these definitions may themselves be shaped by very heterogeneous group and individual interests. We only have access, moreover, to dream-narratives produced by individuals acting in specific social situations, in which the concepts which frame and define dreams may be strategically deployed. This introduces further potential for variation, since different categories of people may have differential access to those contexts in which the reality and status of not only the dream but also, by extension, the *dreamer* are affirmed, denied, or negotiated.

This intermeshing of concepts, agency, authority and ontology is particularly clear in the case of ritual specialists whose claims to special abilities involve dreams. Among the Temne, the vision and knowledge of diviners are largely attributed to accomplishment in dreaming, through which they become experts on the dreams of their clients. Not only, then, do their dreams have power; they have power over other people's dreams.

Temne cosmology and divination

Within what cosmological understandings do dreams and the findings of divination acquire reality and authority among the Temne? As with many other peoples on the Guinea Coast of West Africa, "the Temne" has been a rather fluid category historically, characterised by a high degree of cultural borrowing and considerable absorption of invading, migrant or neighbouring peoples (see Rodney 1970; Wylie 1977). The consequences of this historical process can be seen in the heterogeneity of different areas of Temneland and in the cultural overlap between those who define themselves as "Temne" and those who are aligned with other ethnic identities. Nevertheless, in my research in two locations in south-eastern Temneland (Matotoka, Tane Chiefdom, and Petbana Masimbo, Bombali Sebora Chiefdom) and among migrants from many other parts of Temneland in the national capital of Freetown and the diamond mining centre of Koidu, two features of knowledge and ritual have been ubiquitous, and do not appear to be shared by neighbouring peoples. These are, firstly, the highly elaborate nature of Temne cosmological ideas, and secondly the large repertoire of techniques used by Temne diviners.

The Temne are, as far as I know, unique in the Guinea Coast region in having ideas of multiple worlds. Usually, four worlds are distinguished:

no-ru or *da-ru,* the visible world inhabited by human beings;
ro-soki, inhabited by the spirits;
ro-kerfi, inhabited by the ancestors or "old ones";
ro-seron, inhabited by witches.

Ro-soki, ro-kerfi and *ro-seron* are described as "towns" *(ta-pet)* which are invisible to ordinary people, but are "all around us": "there is only darkness *(an-sum)* between us", I was often told. Although we cannot see them, their inhabitants, being more powerful than we are, can see us: superior power, for the Temne, entails superior vision and knowledge. Yet certain people known as *an-soki* are nonetheless able to penetrate this "darkness" with special vision inhering in their possession of "four eyes" *(e-for y-anle),* consisting of two ordinary and two invisible eyes. Among such people are diviners, powerful hunters, warriors and blacksmiths, cult association officials, twins and witches.

The inclusion of this latter category of witches, however, renders all *an-soki* implicitly suspect as potential witches.

Accounts of either *ro-kerfi* or *ro-soki* are difficult to elicit at all, beyond descriptions of individual spirits in *ro-soki*, but I have often heard *ro-seron*, the world of witches, describes in graphically detailed terms. Like a surreal version of Freetown, it is said to be a large town whose inhabitants drive Mercedes cars and own palatial houses made of gold and precious stones. On its streets, one can buy a snack of roast "beefsticks" of human meat, as well as special clothes with transformative powers. In order to become temporarily transformed into a wild animal in the human world, *no-ru*, one can put on a "witch-gown" *(an-thoro)* in *ro-seron* in order to change into, for example, an elephant, a crocodile, or a chimpanzee. Cult associations parallel to those in *no-ru* operate, but in *ro-seron* membership is dependent upon one's ability to supply human victims (especially children) or rice crops for communal feasts.

No-ru, the world of ordinary human beings, is not described in terms of urban imagery, but is implicitly likened to a refined human head. A Temne creation myth collected in the nineteenth century, but no longer remembered today, describes this world as having been placed by God *(K-uru)* on the head of a giant, whose hair is the earth's vegetation, which is infested by human beings and animals, the earth's equivalent of head-lice (Schlenker 1861:12-15). Significantly, as Littlejohn has observed, the word *no-ru* is cognate with the verb "to plait" *(-ru)*, implying "that the giant's hair has been combed and wrought" (Littlejohn 1963:2). It seems likely that the name for God *(K-uru)* may be similarly derived, meaning literally "one who braids", indicating a deity who creates by ordering, patterning and refining the earth. Further connections between plaiting the head, creating civilized human beings and cultivating the earth have been noted by Lamp (1983; 1985) in the initiation rituals of the male *ra-Bay* and female *an-Bondo* cult associations.

Passage between *no-ru* and their own regions is unproblematic for the inhabitants of *ro-soki, ro-kerfi* and *ro-seron,* all of whom have their own habitats in this world as well. The ancestors, for example, cohabit on such close terms with their living descendants in the latters' villages that it is considered unwise to sweep the house after nightfall in case their benevolent presence is swept out. These "old ones" share the responsibility for the protection and fertility of their community with non-ancestral "town" or "lineage spirits" who also, as these names suggest, inhabit the village. "Bush spirits" are very different: they are described as looking so terrifying that anyone who sees their true appearance will go mad, and they are randomly destructive to rice crops and to female fertility. A further association between types of spirit and the character of the space they inhabit can be seen in river spirits. Just as the river is between town and bush, since villages are built near a water source, river spirits are "in between" town and bush spirits:

> The river joins bush with town. The river demon occupies a place midway between the other two, as powerful as the one but like the other bestowing riches. (Littlejohn 1963:5)

It is not, however, upon the village community that river spirits bestow prosperity, but individuals. A man seeking wealth or, more usually, a woman seeking children will establish a one-to-one contractual relationship with a spirit inhabiting a strikingly beautiful pebble found on the river bank, taking the stone home and promising to make a sacrifice in return for a child or for success. Appropriately, then, it is with the private, individual sphere between the social and the purely asocial that river spirits are associated. Witches, finally, live in the village and appear to belong to the community, but secretly behave like destructive forces of the outside in a whole range of malevolent activities such as invisibly eating children, stealing the "substance" of a rice crop, shooting enemies with a "witch-gun" and attacking people in the form of wild animals of the bush.

Some of these ideas have been restructured in a more dualistic manner by Muslims. Islam was brought into Temneland in the eighteenth and nineteenth centuries by Susu, Mandinka and Fula migrants (see Skinner 1978; Turay 1971: 61-155; Wylie 1977: 32-40). In contrast to north-western Temneland, where chiefdoms are explicitly defined as "Islamic", the south-eastern part of Temneland in which I carried out most of my fieldwork is semi-Islamised. The definition of who is or is not a Muslim is highly flexible, and those who do so define themselves have used Islamic ideas and forms to reconstruct Temne concepts rather than to replace them. For instance, the world of the ancestors is viewed by some Muslim Temne not as a permanent ancestral destination but as a transitional region where the dead await their relegation to one of two additional worlds: Paradise *(ro-riyana)* or Hell *(ro-yanama:* see Turay 1971: 102-4). This elaboration and moral dualism extends to concepts of the spirits, to whom a category of "Muslim spirits" *(e-yina)* has been added, these Muslim spirits being often characterised as "good", while non-Islamic Temne spirits, *an-kerfi,* are sometimes described as being "bad" by contrast. Far from reducing the complexity of Temne concepts, then, Islamisation (in south-eastern Temneland at least) has generated further cosmological elaboration.

A plural and elaborated cosmos requires elaborated forms of mediation. Diviners *(an-thupes;* sing. *o-thupes),* by far the most ubiquitous professional mediators, are present in nearly every village, using one or more divinatory techniques. Over thirty methods are used by Temne diviners, and the terminology of most of these – including one which Temne claim to be the "traditional" Temne method (see Shaw 1978) – indicates an origin from Mande peoples such as the Susu, the Mandinka and the Kuranko. Moreover, techniques defined as "Islamic" are now in the majority. Temne diviners who categorise themselves and their methods in this way range from those who use Islamic elements such as prayer beads, Arabic slates and Qur'anic prayers and can read little or no Arabic, to those who have facility with the Islamic divination and dream-interpretation manuals which are in circulation throughout North and West Africa.

This proliferation of methods, their originally Mande provenance, and the high proportion of Muslim techniques indicate the extent to which diviners, in competition with each other for renown and a large clientele, have been active in incorporating elements of the practices and ideas of powerful and prestigious outsiders. Historically, diviners have played a pivotal role in the process of Islamisation over the past two centuries. In the first place, Muslim Susu, Mandinka and Fula diviners were employed by Temne chiefs, achieving considerable influence and often marrying into chiefly families (Skinner *ibid.:* Turay *ibid.*). In the second place Temne diviners, in response to these powerful competitors, adopted these strangers' divination techniques, as well as incorporating Islamic forms into methods they were already using. As part of this process, Islamic cosmological ideas – for example an overwhelming emphasis upon the supreme deity Ala (Allah), a key mediatory role for the archangel Jibril (Gabriel), and a new category of Muslim spirits (*e-yina;* sing. *an-yina*) – were added to and interwoven with existing religious concepts.

On the basis of (1) the constant interaction between Temne and Mande groups which has characterised Temne history over the past four centuries (see Rodney 1970; Wylie 1977), (2) the Mande origin of Temne divination methods, and (3) the innovatory and "world-reconstructing"[1] strategies on the part of diviners competing with each other during the period of Islamisation, it is tempting to ascribe the elaborate *non*-Islamic cosmological patterns among the Temne to the incorporative and "cosmogonic" work of diviners as well.[2]

Dreaming and mediation

An alternative means of mediation between the regions and inhabitants of the cosmos is through dreams *(me-re)* and dreaming *(worep)*. Witches are described (and, when confessing, describe themselves) as coming and going between *no-ru* and *ro-seron* in their dreams, consuming the "life" *(an-nesem)* of people and of their farms. It is also said (mostly by male diviners) that in dreams, women are vulnerable to sexual intercourse with bush spirits, who assume in the dream the form of a brother, and who thereby cause barrenness, miscarriages and the birth of deformed children. But not all extra-human contacts in dreaming are as undesirable as those in dreams of witches and bush spirits: in common with many other African cultures, dreams are also an important vehicle for communication from the ancestors, who are described as "the old ones who have gone to the place of truths" *(an-baki po kone ro-ten)*, and whose messages are valued accordingly.

Not only the world of the ancestors, but the other regions outside *no-ru* are also described as sources of "truths" *(ta-ten)*, items of effective knowledge to which access can sometimes be gained through dreaming. An association between sleep, dreaming and "truths" finds symbolic expression in the significance of the left hand. Littlejohn (1973) has characterised the right/left opposition among the Temne as articulating the contrast between inclusion in and exclusion from society, such that whereas the right hand is treated as dominant and endowed with positive qualities during ordinary waking life and its patterns of social interaction, the left hand is often described as taking over when the individual is removed from the community during sleep and after death. After death, it is only the left hand which is said to be able to give God a "true" account of the individual's life. In sleep the left hand's power manifests itself, through a kind of literal physical translation, in a commonly-reported experience in which it becomes immensely heavy. If it falls on one's chest, one wakes up feeling crushed by an enormous weight, and is unable to either move or call out. Littlejohn argues that in these, and other, contexts, what is signified is that "truth" is associated with the extra-social. He observes, in connection with the experience of the heavy left hand during sleep, that "Weight is for ... [the Temne] a virtue of truth or of the power which becomes equivalent to truth" *(op.cit.:* 297), and he concludes that "not-being-in-proper-relation-with-others is for them a condition of perception of truth" *(op.cit.:* 298). Truth, then, has an extra-social source.

Dreaming is thus a valuable but dangerous means of mediation potentially available to non-specialists. Although close visual contact with spirits in waking experience commonly results in madness or death for ordinary human beings, such contact in dreams is possible – though still dangerous – even for those who do not have the penetrative vision of "four eyes" because sleep is said to be a "darkness" *(an-sum)*. "Darkness", as we have seen, is a visual impenetrability normally separating the worlds of *ro-soki, ro-kerfi* and *ro-seron* and their inhabitants from *no-ru*. Yet, just as the distinctness of separate shapes disappears at night, if one can enter this darkness the distance between humans, ancestors and spirits can be reduced.[3] Through dreams, we enter yet another region, called "the place of dreams", *ro-mere,* which is said to be close to *ro-soki.* Some people appear to use the term as a metaphor for the dreaming state itself, but more often, like the other invisible worlds, *ro-mere* is spoken of as a definite spatial location – as a town again, in fact. Unlike them, however, it is not cited in reply to questions about other worlds, but is mentioned in conversations about dreaming specifically.

Reaching *ro-mere* is in itself often described as something of an attainment, since dreaming is not held to be a universal phenomenon: as Littlejohn, again, has observed, people ask "can you dream?", not "do you dream?" (1978: 13). This view of dreaming as an accomplishment requiring personal power is one often expressed by diviners.

One diviner's view of ro-mere

Continued access to the powerful "truths" located outside *no-ru* via a patron spirit or ancestor is considered to be a prerequisite for the mediatory role of the diviner *(o-thupes)*, and it is therefore not surprising that we find particularly detailed accounts of dreams, dreaming and the world of *ro-mere* among diviners. The following description is from Pa Yamba, a Freetown diviner and official of the male cult association, *an-Poro*, in response to my questions.

R.S.:   What is *ro-mere?*

P.Y.:   *Ro-mere* is a big town dreamers go to. If you go to bed and go to *ro-mere*, things happen there just the same as they happen here. There are small differences. Your mind *[an-mera]* will not know you have been in *no-ru*. *Do-mere:* it's just as if you've always been there. It's the *an-yina* ["soul", "shadow" or "Muslim spirit"] that goes there. It's different from *ro-soki*, but close to it. Only in *ro-mere* are you able to talk to them [the spirits]; *ro-mere* is their own place, and you can talk to them there. They're just neighbouring towns *[ro-soki* and *ro-mere]*. There are times you see strange things which are dangerous. You'll look at them but something else helps you go away because it's a dangerous place. At times an *a-yina* helps you, or a spirit *[u-kerfi]*, or an "old one". Not all people dream; only those who have "strong heads" *[baki ra-bonp]* and those who the ancestors are after.

R.S.:   Do those people have four eyes?

P.Y.:   Anyone who dreams is a person God *[K-uru]* gives eyes to see. So they're the same. Diviners dream more than most people – they have prophesies that come true. In diviners' dreams, they're in perfect control. But there are ordinary people who sweat after dreaming. There are people who dream and see spirits *[e-kerfi]*. If they wake up they have to be helped or they'll die. When someone dreams, what happens to him is just like *no-ru*. If he comes across "bad people" [witches] and they put medicine in his eyes, he'll get four eyes. It's something like when we're near death. I don't have four eyes now, but I do when I sleep. There are other four eyes that people are born with. These people, if God says they'll have a long life, nobody can challenge them. Before people die they dream a lot, and some even dream their death.

R.S.:   Can an "old one" reborn as a child dream his past life?

P.Y.:   He can dream *ro-soki*[4] but not his past life in *no-ru*. (22nd November 1978, Freetown)

According to Pa Yamba, then, *ro-mere* is closely parallel to *no-ru*, but is experientially autonomous and self-contained: "it's just as if you've always been there", you cannot remember *no-ru*. In this, however, he differs from certain other diviners whose methods – notably that of *an-listikar*, which is described below – involve seeking in dreams for the solutions to problems brought by their clients, which presupposes some continuity of awareness between *no-ru* and *ro-mere*. That part of the person which goes to *ro-mere* is called *an-yina,* which is usually translated as the individual's "soul". This term may have originated with Islamisation, since it is the same as that used to denote a non-human Muslim spirit. It is unclear to which of these meanings Pa Yamba was referring.

In discussing the kinds of people who dream, Pa Yamba distinguishes between those who have a "strong head" and are given "four-eyed" vision in dreams by God ("Anyone who dreams is a person God gives eyes to see") and those more powerful individuals who are born with four eyes in the first place. The connection between dreams and God, and the assertion that one needs a "strong head" in order to participate in the world of *ro-mere* is perhaps an echo of the connection between the head and the world manifest in the nineteenth century Temne creation myth outlined earlier, in which the world was placed by God on the giant's head. Despite their having "strong heads", however, the vulnerability of ordinary people, "who sweat after dreaming", is contrasted by Pa Yamba with the perfect control and prophetic truth of diviners' dreams. Finally, the link between dreaming and death is stressed.

Pa Yamba's extremely rich account integrates certain normative conceptions about dreaming with his own ideas about the inability to remember *no-ru* while in *ro-mere.* Moreover, given the fact that Pa Yamba is a diviner, and that a diviner's power depends upon his or her ability to mediate between clients' problems in *no-ru* and the "truths" of the other worlds, his emphasis upon the greater frequency, mastery and "truth" of diviners' dreams is clearly a strategically appropriate conceptualisation. Since a great many people besides diviners evidently do dream, this could be a potential threat to the diviner's position, dreams being to a certain extent an alternative form of "do-it-yourself" divination available to ordinary individuals. This is not, I think, unconnected with the fact that diviners make claims of superiority for both the quality and the quantity of their dreams, and seek to appropriate other people's dreaming. For not only do diviners claim authority over the interpretation of the dreams of others (with the implication that ordinary people understand their dreams less clearly), but during diagnosis diviners can also *ascribe* a dream to a client or accused party, of which the latter may have had no prior knowledge.

Secrecy and identity

The implications of such hegemonic claims over the personal experience of others may be clarified here by briefly describing the importance of secret knowledge in Temne society. In common with many other African representations of selfhood, inner knowledge and experience constitute a crucial source of personal identity for Temne. As Godfrey Lienhardt has recently stressed, much of what has been written about African ideas of personhood rightly puts to the fore a person's place within their social group, but this collectivist definition has tended to deflect attention from the importance of what is *hidden* and *private* within the individual (1985: 143-6). Among the Temne, as well as many other Sierra Leonean and Liberian peoples (see, e.g., Bellman 1984; Bledsoe and Robey 1986; Jackson 1977, esp. pp. 219-220), secrecy pervades social life and social relationships, particularly power relationships. For members of the male and female cult associations, for chiefs and subchiefs, for certain occupational specialists, and for men and women simply as men and women, secret knowledge is used as a basic organizing principle by which people define themselves as members of particular groups and as sharing in the power controlled by these groups. As many Temne express it, secrecy creates a "darkness" which keeps different groups separate.

But, as among the Kpelle, who say that "to know oneself" is to know one's own hidden power (Bellman 1975: 50-51), hidden knowledge is also used to promote *individual* identities and personal power. Because hierarchies of power are articulated by means of hierarchies of secrecy and revelation, subordinates are expected not to keep secrets from superiors, but superiors can retain their own personal knowledge, and thereby their own personal power. In practice, of course, social relationships involve a considerable degree of negotiation, in which one's own secrets, however apparently trivial, are defended.

Because most divination is conducted in private, the personal secrets of individual clients are usually safeguarded. This, along with the diviner's status as a specialist in hidden knowledge, and the client's desire for help, means that when diviners appropriate the inner knowledge of their clients by interpreting or ascribing dreams, they are usually not challenged. Diviners' claims to be able to not only interpret but also to "see" through the darkness hiding their clients' dreams can thus be viewed in terms of the hegemonic dominance of these ritual specialists, whose livelihood depends upon their clients' assent to their conceptual and ontological authority (see, e.g., Gramsi 1971: 12-13). This is by no means to suggest, however, that this dominance is consciously deployed in a state of cynical detachment from the conceptions which both inform and derive from their activities as diviners. On the contrary, I would argue that we have no reason to doubt that the ideas and reported experiences of most diviners, most of the time, are a phenomenological reality. Despite clients' provisional assent to divinatory authority during the session itself, however, diviners' pronouncements are not always accepted or acted upon. The extent of the diviner's hegemony over dreaming can be seen in an outline of the contexts in which dreams are recounted.

Contexts of dream narratives

1. The most straightforward of these contexts is that in which a person relates a dream they judge to be important to someone around them – a relative or a friend. The significance of the dream may be in the form of a fairly straightforward message. Ancestral dreams are quite common, in which, for instance, a dead relative tells the dreamer that he or she is suffering hardship in *ro-kerfi* and needs a sacrifice. Or if a person has initiated a relationship with a personal river spirit in order to acquire wealth or children, and if this spirit has taken a liking to them, it may appear in a dream, often in the form of a snake, and reveal its name.

Alternatively, the significance of a dream may be contained more cryptically, if its images are judged to require interpretation. Some interpretations recur frequently. It means good fortune, for instance, to dream of flying, or of crossing a river, or of something white, such as a white person. This colour symbolism, in which "white" is auspicious and "black" inauspicious, is not the same for all contexts, and is not applied to black *people:* a black person in a dream is, of course, an ordinary human being. However, if you dream of a person dressed in black, it means they are going to die, or at least to get ill. Sometimes meanings are reversed: dreaming that you are laughing means misfortune; dreaming that you are crying means that something is going to make you happy. Most people know these, and construct their own dream interpretations around them, and may also select a form of sacrifice themselves which they feel to be appropriate in order to secure a favourable or avert an unfavourable future outcome.

Some are explicit about the fact that they thereby avoid expensive sacrifices. When I was studying migrant Temne diviners in Kono, the diamond district, a Temne diamond digger, Abdul, helped me by introducing me to the area and to people. He told me: "I don't go to diviners myself, because if they tell me to make a cow or a chicken sacrifice I may not be able to afford to. Instead I just make a sacrifice when a dream tells me I should." He went on to tell me that he was helping me with my work because he had "dreamed" me before I arrived, although the white woman he had dreamed of had had a different face. She had been the wife of a diamond dealer, and he had walked in and asked where her husband was. She told him he was out, and gave him fifty cents. Dreaming of a white person is an omen of impending good fortune, so in the morning he made a sacrifice of two kola nuts, giving a white one to a yellow-complexioned person and a red one to a black-complexioned person.

2. In the second context of dream-narration, the dream is reported to and interpreted by a diviner. When a dream is felt to be disturbing or particularly puzzling, it may be taken to a private diviner for interpretation and for the

correct sacrifice to be prescribed. Diviners' interpretations of dreams do not seem significantly different from those of non-specialists, but if they are literate Muslim diviners they may also consult Islamic dream-interpretation manuals, which are highly prestigious sources of knowledge unavailable to most people.

In this context, whether or not to consult a diviner is the individual's decision. Another Temne diamond digger in Kono, Saidu, told me of a dream, which he had taken to a Temne Muslim diviner. He said:

> At one time, I dreamed a river with plenty of water. A boat was brought. I boarded the boat. I went across the river. When day broke, I went and told one man who knows about dreams [a Muslim diviner, *u-more*]. This man told me that the year will not end before I get money. So he showed me the sacrifice to make, and *K-uru* [God] answered. I got money. I got a diamond. (17th. November 1978, Koidu)

This interpretation was straightforward, because everyone knows that dreaming of crossing a river means good fortune, but unlike Abdul, he went to a diviner because, he said, he wanted to be sure that the sacrifice he gave was the right one. He was told to offer seven white kola nuts, white moulded rice flour, and water. There is, then, considerable individual latitude at this level over what people do with their own dreams: whether or not they choose to ignore them, *or* to act upon their own interpretations of them without the aid of a diviner, *or* to select which diviner to see if they do decide to consult one, and to either accept and act upon the diviner's interpretation and prescribed sacrifice, *or* to get a second opinion by consulting another diviner afterwards.

3. In the third context, however, there are normative limits to this interpretive independence. One ought, for example, to report to the chief any dream in which the town is on fire, because this means that a plot is being hatched against him (Littlejohn 1978: 13). One should also report any dream whose imagery constitutes a commonly-agreed omen of witchcraft in the town, such as seeing someone turn into a wild animal, or seeing people cooking and eating meat. A public divination session should then be called in which the dream may have to be recounted and used as evidence against specific people recognised in the dream who were said to have turned into animals or to have eaten meat. These suspected witches are then interrogated, accused, and sometimes given ordeals. When they eventually confess, they may also narrate dreams of their own witchcraft activities. Clearly, there is considerable scope for "strategic dreaming" here in the context of disputes and rivalry.

4. In the fourth context, a fairly stereotyped dream is assigned to a sick client in a diviner's diagnosis. These "pre-packaged" dreams take several different forms, the following three being common themes:

(a) Firstly, a man who is sick, mad or suffering financial misfortune may be told that this is due to a sexual relationship he has cultivated in his dreams with a female water spirit called *an-yaron,* or "Mami Wata" in Krio, who is depicted as a mermaid. In this relationship, *an-yaron* makes her lover fabulously wealthy as long as he remains sexually faithful to her in the waking world of *no-ru* or, in some accounts, as long as he takes her comb and does not return it. If he is unfaithful to her, or if she manages to get her comb back, *an-yaron* will kill him or, if she particularly likes him, she will merely make him ill, insane, or impoverished.

(b) Secondly, a common diviners' diagnosis for a woman who is barren, who has menstrual irregularities, a miscarriage, or simply persistent stomach pains is the type of dream described above in which a bush spirit makes love to her, often in the form of a brother.[5]

(c) Thirdly, a sick child suffering from stomach problems may be diagnosed as having been fed human meat in a dream by a witch intending to recruit the child as a fellow-witch. Although a witch grows a second stomach called *an-kuntha* specifically for the purpose of digesting human meat, an ordinary person's digestive system cannot cope with this, and until they develop such an organ themselves, their stomach will swell up painfully. A child who receives this diagnosis is considered blameless, however.

In cases like these, the diviner asks the client if they remember having had a dream in which these fairly standard scenarios occurred. The client, who is usually ignorant of having had such a dream until he or she is so informed by the diviner, will most often agree, since unless they do a cure will not be given. This is not, of course, to deny that anyone has dreams like these, but to bring out the point that such dream narratives usually originate in the context of diagnosis, and from the diviner rather than the client. A diviner who assigns a "pre-packaged" dream in this way is asserting ontological hegemony. The source of the client's problem is in a dream which they do not remember, but which the diviner knows all about, thereby making claims over the client's private experience and sense of self. Clients in this situation are not entirely powerless, however, because even after agreeing that they remember the dream they have been assigned, they can still nevertheless consult another diviner afterwards, although the pressure caused by the illness itself makes it harder for them to pick and choose.

5. In contrast to the relative passivity of clients in relation to their dreams within divination sessions, diviners' uses of their own dreams are active and purposive. One divination method which relies exclusively upon dreams, for example is *an-listikar,* the Temne version of the Islamic dream-divination technique, *istikhara* ("asking favour of heaven"; see Trimingham 1959: 123). Here, the diviner constructs an Islamic amulet or simply writes a passage from the *Qur'an* together with the client's name on a piece of paper, and prays to Allah for the solution to the client's problem before going to sleep with his head resting on the written sheet. The answer is revealed in the diviner's dreams.

Dreams can also be used in conjunction with any of the wide variety of Temne diviners' techniques, including those which are not classified as "Islamic". In this case, they are used as a means by which the spirits or ancestors either confirm the diagnosis arrived at in a divination session, or reveal what cure should be carried out in a particular case. Not only, then, are diviners' dreams considered to be effective sources of "truth", but diviners also have the power to apply their dreams, to translate them into practice, far more than most people. This power accorded to the diviner's position is itself derived from an initiatory dream, which constitutes the sixth context to be examined here.

6. Diviners insist that no-one can be a diviner unless they have had an initiatory dream in which a contractual relationship is established with either a spirit or an ancestor, or both. This patron ancestor is usually a deceased diviner of the same sex who was a close relative, while a diviner's patron spirit is usually of the opposite sex. In return for a sacrifice (usually of a sheep if the future diviner can afford it), the spirit or ancestor bestows the ability to divine, and thereafter facilitates the diviner's access to the "truths" of the other worlds. One diviner, Pa Ahmadu, described how he had come to use river-pebble divination *(an-bere):*

> I had no training: I got the knowledge from God. While I slept, I dreamt that a spirit tied me up and said we should do this work together. When I woke up the next morning, I could do it, and gave an egg to the spirit. (Pa Ahmadu Conteh, 17th. May 1978, Mabure, Bombali Sebora Chiefdom.)

A woman diviner in the diamond district, Ya Mabinti, related how her dead aunt had taught her to use cowrie shell divination in her dream:

> In the first dream my aunt showed me how to use the cowries. I woke up and started doing it. Then I was in *ro-mere,* and I saw these cowries first in a heap, then a circle. When I woke up, I was afraid. (Ya Mabinti, 24th. October 1978, Koidu.)

In these examples, the dream functions as a spontaneous "call", and contains all the training required. Equally often, however, the dream is the culmination of a period of training and apprenticeship to a parent or relative or to an Arabic teacher who practices divination. But whatever training an apprentice diviner has, it is the initiatory encounter with the patron spirit or ancestor which is crucial. In the dream narrative of a successful Muslim diviner, Pa Abdul, the same patron spirit is described as having maintained a relationship with several generations of a family through dreams:

> The gift I have is a lineage gift. My great-grandfather was a great warrior. When he died, my grandfather, Pa Kaper Bongo, took over the warriorship. When he died, he left his gift with his son, who was a famous hunter. When my father died, he called me to him in a sacred forest near Makump. My eyes were tied with a white cloth, and I slept. I saw a fine white lady, who said that my father had asked her to transfer the gift to me, and asked me what kind of gift I

would like: to be a famous warrior, hunter, chief or Muslim? I replied that I wanted to learn Arabic and to learn what is hidden. I said, "Whenever something is hidden, I was to know how to find it." After this, she stretched out her hand and we greeted each other. Then she gave me a red cloth with perfume in it. Anyone who has this perfume and puts it in their eyes can see hidden things ... I disappeared when I went to sleep and spoke to the lady. I was gone for two days; the lady had taken me to *ro-soki*. When she left me and I came back, I was not myself. I was dizzy for seven days. When I got back, sacrifices were made ... So I do not need to prepare any medicines: the gift is inside me. (Abdul Conteh, 23rd November 1977, Magburaka.)

This gift bestowed by the patron spirit and passed down through the patri-lineage is, then, not specific to divination, but could also be used to achieve extraordinary success in other specialisations such as hunting, war and being a chief. The assertion in this narrative about having been taken to *ro-soki* is unusual, since diviners normally encounter their spirit patrons in *ro-mere,* the place of dreams, and it may be that this assertion to have gone further than most diviners, into the abode of the spirits themselves, constitutes a claim to divinatory superiority. Pa Abdul is very successful, and often claims that his power and vision are more "wonderful" than those of other diviners.

Another unusual and thereby rather revealing example is a dream related by Pa Biyare, a diviner who had been apprenticed for about ten years to his father, a famous diviner who used the river pebble method of divination, *an-bere.* He said: "My father told me in a dream: this work is yours. Take it. But you have to have some patience yet" (Pa Biyare, 13th. October 1978, Makeni). What is significant about this is the fact that his father was still alive at that time, this being the only account I heard in which a living rather than a dead relative figured in such a dream. Accordingly, the apprentice diviner was told in it that he would have to wait patiently before he could be given his full power as a diviner, and he therefore offered no sacrifice afterwards. What this reveals is firstly, how crucial an initiatory dream is regarded to be in authorising the role of the diviner. Secondly, the atypical nature of Pa Biyare's dream can perhaps be seen as derived from the fact that he was extremely eager to take over his father's position as a powerful and high-status diviner. This, together with the previous example, exemplifies not only the variability possible in this type of dream-account, within certain similarities of pattern, but also demonstrates the strategic, negotiative basis of such variation.

7. The final context to be described here is that of my own interaction with diviners and their clients, which was of course the context in which my knowledge of Temne dreaming was produced. It seems highly probable that this situation would have involved some restructuring of dream-accounts. Personal interests obviously loomed fairly large in this interaction on my part. On the one hand, this was the fieldwork for my doctorate, but on the other hand my research into divination and diviners was also an end in itself. On the

part of the diviners who worked with me, I was sometimes seen as an "important client", a source of status. In addition, some would emphasise to me that they were telling me things because I resembled a spirit: the "otherness" of diviners' patron spirits usually consists in their being white and female.

My work on divination was incorporated into my own dreams, and *vice versa*. Sometimes I took diviners my dreams to interpret, and when I was learning the river pebble method of divination *(an-bere)*, I wondered if I would produce an initiatory dream to accompany it. Instead, a little while afterwards I had a dream about fieldwork. I dreamed that a close friend who was conducting research in Sierra Leone at the same time as myself was killed by a creature which drained the life out of her. During this process, my friend retained her objectivity, not attempting to escape, but observing her own annihilation as I screamed at her to run away. In a later sequence I was involved in a struggle with the same creature, but managed to break free.

I brought the dream to Pa Yamba for divination, partly because I found it deeply disturbing and felt the need to put it into someone's hands, and partly because I was interested in contrasting his interpretation with mine. To me, the dream had been about my concern over what I considered to be my excessive objectivity in fieldwork. When I related the dream to Pa Yamba, who used mirror-gazing divination *(an-memne)* to perceive the diagnosis, he told me that my mind *(an-mera)* was waking up, and that certain dreams that I had came true. But if I had not escaped in the dream, I would have been in serious danger, because the creature was a bad spirit who inhabited the area in which I was staying. He prescribed a protective sacrifice of a black umbrella and a length of black material, and offered to perform the ritual for me, which would have involved opening the umbrella over me and covering me with the material.

Like Abdul, the diamond digger mentioned above who interpreted his own dreams and avoided potentially expensive sacrifices which diviners might prescribe, I was satisfied with my interpretation of the dream. I was unwilling to deplete my diminishing fieldwork grant by having further sacrifices in addition to those I had already undergone: only the previous week, Pa Yamba had performed a relatively expensive sacrifice for me. And like other diviners' clients, I ungenerously took into consideration Pa Yamba's economic interests in evaluating his choice of offering. It was the rainy season, umbrellas were expensive, and he would retain my "sacrificial" umbrella and black material as well as his fee afterwards. But most importantly, the context in which I consulted Pa Yamba involved a different relationship between power and knowledge than that which usually obtains between diviners and clients. My own hegemonic claims as an "interpeter of culture" were rather similar to his claims to be an interpreter of dreams. My perspective sometimes shifted towards Pa Yamba's interpretation of my dream when I was startled by an unfamiliar noise at night. But the consequence of my sceptical considerations – considerations which, in fact, contradicted my own interpretation of my dream as a warning against detachment – was that I did not have the sacrifice.

Conclusions

In comparing these contexts, a scale from individual passivity to individual power in relation to dreaming is apparent. At one extreme is the person accused of witchcraft through being an object in another person's dream narrative, at the other extreme are firstly the diviner who has successfully appropriated the truth and power of dreaming and exercises hegemony over other people's dreams, and secondly the anthropologist whose appropriation of "the translation of culture" encompasses the diviner's own interpretative claims, while in between diviners' clients negotiate control over their own experience. In relation to this scale of ontological autonomy, many conceptions about dreaming have spheres of relevance; they are specific to certain positions on the scale. Dream symbols which have explicitly interpetable meanings, for instance, are reproduced in contexts in which non-specialist individuals have the power of choice, and either interpret their own dreams, or select a diviner specifically for dream interpretation. Symbols and their meanings are not employed, however, in contexts in which diviners ascribe to their usually sick and therefore relatively passive clients the standardised dream narratives involving being fed witch-meat, sexual intercourse with a bush spirit, or a spoiled relationship with Mami Wata. The "pre-packaged" dream is itself the diagnosis here, and it would be unthinkable, for example, for a diviner diagnosing a child's stomach pain to add to his description of the child's dream that the witch responsible had been wearing white, and that this was an omen of impending good fortune.

Again, symbols and their interpretation are not a feature of diviners' dreams. Diviners' dreams do not have "significance" in this way; they are not used in relationships in which meaning as such is conferred, negotiated, authorised by others. This is not to say that the initiatory dreams of apprentice diviners are not confirmed by their teachers, or that diviners' clients cannot either accept or reject diagnoses based upon divinatory dreams: diviners' dreams are confirmed or discounted as bases for divinatory *praxis*. But neither initiatory dreams nor divinatory dreams are translated into significata beyond themselves; instead, they are "translated" into action.[6]

That dreams originating from ordinary people require interpretation, whereas dreams originating from diviners are a basis for praxis may be seen as deriving from the fact that diviners, whose powers are defined in terms of extra-social knowledge, are in competition not only with each other, but also with the potential dream-knowledge of their clients. I have argued above that the proliferation of divination methods and the elaboration of cosmological ideas in Temne history may have been means of generating and renewing assent to diviners' conceptual authority. Of particular relevance here are diviners' elaborate ideas about *ro-mere* as a distinct region, both wonderful and terrifying, fraught with dangers to ordinary people. Vivid descriptions of close encounters with denizens of other worlds in the "dream town" of *ro-mere,* while certainly not restricted to diviners, are nevertheless more prominent in their accounts than in those of non-specialists. An especially elaborate and formalised body of ideas concerning dreams, moreover, is controlled by literate Muslim diviners whose powerful and prestigious knowledge is embodied in Islamic dream-interpretation manuals. To these conceptions about dreaming, non- specialists have no direct access. The above elaborations of "dream- knowledge", together with control over dream-interpretation, the power to ascribe dreams to others, and claims to special qualities required for "accomplished" dreaming are, I suggest, among the means by which diviners' conceptual hegemony is sustained. It is central to my argument, however, that diviners participate in the conceptions they perpetuate. What obtains, then, is a form of the control of experience (Lienhardt 1961) whereby hegemonic dominance operates not only upon others but also upon *oneself,* constructing lived experiences of divinatory dreaming as "accomplishment".

NOTES

Fieldwork in Sierra Leone was carried out in 1977 and 1978, with the financial support of the (then) Social Science Research Council, the Emslie Horniman Anthropological Research Fund, and the Central Research Fund of the University of London. I would like to thank Keith Ray for encouraging me to tackle the topic of dreams and dreaming.

1. Cf. Fernandez' (1982) analysis of cosmological reconstruction as a response to European colonialism in the Bwiti cult of the Fang.
2. Bloch (1967) similarly argues that the complexity and obscurity of Merina astrological cosmology are attributable to the elaborations of astrologers competing for prestige.
3. In the Islamic divination technique known as *an-yina Musa,* a medium enters a trance also described as a "darkness" in which he or she is neither in this world nor in *ro-soki,* but can see and communicate with the latter's inhabitants.
4. The fact that Pa Yamba spoke of *ro-soki* instead of *ro-kerfi,* the world of the ancestors, suggests that he was using *ro-soki* in its alternative sense as a generic term including all invisible regions, rather than the world of the spirits specifically.
5. Littlejohn (1960) has observed a connection between this dream scenario and men's perceptions of the wife's brother *(o-nasin)* as an incursive affine who "plunders" the household. This dream narrative is primarily a product of the divination sessions of diviners, most of whom are male, rather than of the women who are thus diagnosed.

6. See Dilley, this volume, on the "translation" of Tukolor weavers' dreams into cloth designs and weaving techniques rather than into "meanings".

REFERENCES

BELLMAN, B.L., 1975, *Village of Curers and Assassins. On the production of Fala Kpelle cosmological categories.* The Hague: Mouton.
1984, *The Language of Secrecy: symbols and metaphors in Poro ritual.* New Brunswick: Rutgers University Press.
BLEDSOE, C. & ROBEY, K., 1986, Arabic literacy and secrecy among the Mende of Sierra Leone. *Man* 21: 202-226.
BLOCH, M., 1967, Astrology and writing in Madagascar. In J. Goody (ed.), *Literacy in Traditional Societies.* Cambridge: Cambridge University Press.
FERNANDEZ, J., 1982, Edification by puzzlement. In I. Karp and C. Bird (eds.) *Explorations in African Systems of Thought.* Bloomington: Indiana University Press.
GRAMSCI, A., 1971, The Intellectuals. In *Selections from Prison Notebooks* (ed. and trans. Q. Hoare and G. Nowell-Smith). London: Lawrence and Wishart.
HAIR, P. Personal communication of 28/10/1987.
JACKSON, M., 1977, *The Kuranko: dimensions of social reality in a West African society.* London: C. Hurst and Co.
LAMP, F., 1978, Frogs into princes: the Temne Rabai initiation, *African Arts* XI: 38-49.
1983, Balancing the Lopsided Load: dimension and sequence in the arts of the Temne. Unpublished Ms.
1985, Cosmos, cosmetics and the spirit of Bondo, *African Arts* XVIII: 28-43 and 98-99.
LIENHARDT, R G. 1961, *Divinity and Experience: the religion of the Dinka.* Oxford: Clarendon Press.
1985, Self: public, private. Some African representations. In M. Carrithers, S. Collins and S. Lukes (eds.), *The Category of the Person.* Cambridge: Cambridge University Press.
LITTLEJOHN, J., 1960, The Temne house. *Sierra Leone Studies* (n.s.) XIV: 63-79.
1963, Temne Space. *Anthropological Quarterly* XXXVI: 1-17.
1973, Temne right and left: an essay on the choreography of everyday life. In R. Needham (ed.), *Right and Left.* Chicago: University of Chicago Press.
1978, Aspects of medicine among the Temne of Sierra Leone. London: Social Science Research Council Report no. HR 4873.
MacCORMACK, C., (ed.), 1982, *The Ethnography of Fertility and Birth.* London: Academic Press.
MARKHAM, C.R., (ed), 1878, *The Hawkins Voyages.* London: Hakluyt Society.
OVERING, J., 1985, Introduction to J. Overing (ed.), *Reason and Morality.* London: Tavistock.
RODNEY, W., 1970, *A History of the Upper Guinea Coast: 1545-1800.* Oxford: Clarendon Press.
SCHLENKER, C.F., 1861, *A Collection of Temne Traditions, Fables and Proverbs.* London: Church Missionary Society.
SHAW, R., 1978, *An-bere:* a traditional form of Temne divination. *Africana Research Bulletin* (Fourah Bay College, Sierra Leone) IX: 3-24.
SKINNER, D.E., 1978, Mande settlement and the development of Islamic institutions in Sierra Leone. *International Journal of African Historical Studies* 11: 32-62.

TRIMINGHAM, J.S., 1959, *Islam in West Africa*. Oxford: Clarendon Press.
TURAY, A.K., 1971, Loanwords in Temne: a study of the sources and processes of lexical borrowing in a Sierra Leonean language. Unpublished PhD thesis, University of London (SOAS).
TYLOR, E, 1889 (orig. 1871), *Primitive Culture*. London: H. Holt and Co.
WYLIE, K.C., 1977, *The Political Kingdoms of the Temne: Temne government in Sierra Leone 1825-1910*. New York: Africana Publishing Company.

DREAMS OF GRANDEUR: THE CALL TO OFFICE IN NORTHCENTRAL IGBO RELIGIOUS LEADERSHIP

KEITH RAY

St David's University College (University of Wales)

> A strange thought seized Edogo now. Could it be that their father had deliberately sent Oduche to the religion of the white man so as to disqualify him for the priesthood of Ulu? ... No, that was not the reason. The priest wanted to have a hand in the choice of his successor. It was what anyone who knew Ezeulu would expect him to do. But was he not presuming too much? The choice of a priest lay with the deity. Was it likely that he would let the old priest force his hand? Although Edogo and Obika did not seem attracted to the office that would not prevent the deity choosing either of them or even Oduche, out of spite. Edogo's thinking now became confused. If Ulu should choose him to be Chief Priest, what would he do? (Achebe 1974: 92)

Passages such as this reveal Achebe the novelist's insight into complex cultural processes. What he is here distilling is the kind of calculation that so typifies Igbo approaches to difficult questions of succession to office. Rarely in such contexts are human agency and motivation weighed in isolation from ideas concerning strategems of the gods. Wealth, farming prowess, trading and business acumen, wisdom and a reputation for fair-dealing are among the most important qualities of aspiring office-holders in Igbo society, but evidence of extraordinary powers and the support of divine will are equally prerequisites. While the demonstration of worldly worthiness is continuous, if often chequered, the demonstration of extra-human powers is necessarily more restricted, and it is a feature of "crisis management" in situations of succession to office that such powers are called into play by those who seek advantage.

In the present paper I set out to examine the use of dreams, omens and prophecy as the principal demonstrations of extra-human powers in the candidacy for religious office. In so doing, I am seeking in part to take the study of dreaming in Igbo society beyond the stereotype that Igbo dreaming is simply a consequence of "achievement motivation" (Le Vine 1966).

Dreaming, omens and prophecy feature in the claims of rival candidates for offices ranging from that of the periodic bearer of the "medicine" bundle *(Onumonu)* which constitutes a manifestation of a local deity, through the chief earth-priest of certain Igbo towns, to the sacred king of the Umueri Igbo. The role of divination in the succession process is a means of both interpreting and further validating the message of a dream, the meaning of an omen, or the significance of a prophecy. As such, the situation is quite different from many other systems of succession, where divination is used as a way of deciding upon one claim or candidate rather than another, or even of effecting the selection of a successor from unknown candidacy (Goody 1966: 21-3).

The particular view of dreams presented here, then, is one which emphasises the strategic, but which also acknowledges the perception of dreams as media for divine messages. Omens make manifest the experience of dreams, and successful prophecy is evidence of the power of the dreamer and omen-reader. Only rarely does this sequence occur, but the context of such occurrence is significant. Just how this is so will, I hope, become clear.

Igbo deities and religious office

In common with many parts of Africa, an organised cult of the earth has existed as a fundamental feature of religious organisation in Igboland. This cult emphasises the link between the earth and the fertility of crops and people. It is this association which may account for the widespread (but not pan-Igbo) description of the spirit *(alusi)* of the land or earth as a female deity, referred to variously as *Ala, Ani, Ana, Ale,* or *Ane* (c.f. Meek 1937: 25-31; Horton 1954). *Ana* (as I shall refer to the deity here) is typically regarded as the fount of morality, the cult of *Ana* providing prescriptions and guidelines concerning social and ritual action.

The relationship of *Ana* to other deities is, for the most part, unproblematic, except that her or his position vis-a-vis *Chukwu* or *Chineke,* the high god, is somewhat ambiguous. Debates concerning the relative seniority of *Chukwu* or *Ana* have been recorded at village level (see, for instance, Arazu's interview in Isichei 1977: 175-6) and feature prominently in academic discourse. *Ana,* like *Chukwu,* is associated with the creation and sustenance of life, and it has been suggested by some researchers that *Ana* may, prior to the missionary era, have occupied the central role in Igbo religious thought now claimed for *Chukwu* (Echeruo 1979; Nwoga 1984a: 29-31).

Apart from the notion of *chi,* a personal deity bound up with the individual's own destiny, there are a number of other deities (generically, *alusi, agbara,* etc.) common to most if not all parts of Igboland, as well as the yam deity *Ifejioku* (and variants), and the market-day or village quarter-gods, *Eke, Orie, Afo,* and *Nkwo.* Of more restricted provenance are gods such as *Amadioha,* associated with thunder in southern Igboland, or *Anyanwu,* associated with the sun in northern Igboland. It is local deities, however, which comprise the bulk of the beings actively and abundantly venerated in shrines across Igboland. These tend to be spirits attributed to the waters of rivers, or inhabiting hills, rocks or trees, and they are generally considered, as *genii loci,* to be autochthonous. In addition, there are medicine-cult deities usually asserted to have been introduced from powerful religious foci such as the Nri ritual centres described below.

During the course of daily religious activities, prayers and offerings are made at the various shrines *(onu,* lit. "mouths") belonging to whichever deity is being addressed. In the case of the autochthonous deities, worship at the shrine of one may serve for relay to another, if it is made clear to which of the deities the offering is destined, in the act of beseeching. In some instances, one deity may actually be envisaged as "standing proxy" for another, a common link being the use of a local river, rock, hill or tree deity as an intermediary for *Ana.*

There are also human intermediaries. Most commonly these are household heads, minimal lineage *(umunna)* heads, maximal lineage elders and other leaders *(ishi nze)* such as the oldest man of a village, the *onyishi.* They offer up prayers and sacrifices daily (but more intensively on special occasions) at shrines dedicated on behalf of the members of the groups whose interests they protect. Within the household, shrines must be set up to the ancestors, to the personal deity *(chi)* of household members, to the *ikenga* (a carving embodying individual power and achievement) of the household head, and to certain locally essential beings in various parts of Igboland, such as *Anyanwu* in the Nsukka area (see map).

Beyond this level, communal shrines are attended to by ritual specialists whose income is derived largely from fees or gifts from supplicants who come to seek help from the deity at whose shrine they preside. The most common title for such priests is *Eze,* prefixed to the name of the shrine deity. At each level of integration of landholding unit (such as household, village, and village-group), there is an *Ezeana* or senior priest of the earth deity (Horton 1954). The role of the shrine priest is to regulate prayers and offerings to the deity at the shrine, to maintain the various shrine facilities (ante-rooms, deity-figures, central paraphenalia and associated sacred places), act as mouthpiece for the deity, modulate relations with other deities through their visible representatives, and observe in the correct manner those festivals held in celebration of the deity's presence or actions.

Any incumbent of a priestly office is automatically a member of the *Ndi Oha* or titled group in northcentral Igbo communities. As such, their role as mouthpiece of the deity extends into the daily affairs of the town in which their shrine is located, and in some instances beyond it. This latter is certainly true when the shrine gains an oracular attribute either as a by-product of kinds of advice given by the priest to supplicants, or by dint of deliberate power-seeking. The power of such oracular shrines to affect events and destinies well beyond the geographical limits of their immediate community is associated with their becoming centres of "pilgrimage". This inevitably brings in greater revenue, and leads both to the recruitment of more priests and to a growth in the complexity of sacrifices and related ritual (Ottenberg 1956).

Closely linked with, but not actually holding, priestly office are diviners (*dibia* or *onye n'agba afa*). Not only are diviners interpreters of events via decipherment of divinatory outcomes, they are also arbiters of propitiatory ritual, since they will direct their clients to make offerings at one rather than another deity's shrine. As such, they wield considerable power and are able to influence the prestige of individual shrines and the fortunes of their attendant priests.

The title system has in the past also provided a connecting thread to the religious life of a broad network of Igbo communities. Progression via initiations through the various grades of the title system is seen not only in terms of status acquisition, but also as a process of personal purification and enhancement of religious and moral authority (Ottenberg 1971; Webb 1981). In many communities the origin and reference-point of the title system was a location known from without as Nri or Nshi, and members of the *Umueri* communities (lineage descended from the mythical apical ancestor, Eri) of the Nri-Awka area were seen as agents of a ritual system which claimed primordial status in Igbo religion on account of its management of the earth-cult (Onwuejeogwu 1981). The nature of this system and the role of dreams in the succession of its sacred kings are key points for consideration hereunder.

Succession to Umueri kingship

There are two forms of kingship which have existed into recent decades in Igboland. The first, in western Igboland, is a considerably centralised and in some respects secularised form which appears to share a number of characteristics and various aspects of terminology and practice with Benin kingship (see Ejiofor 1982). The second is a sacred kingship unique to Igboland and closely associated with the cult of the earth. Kingship in at least one centre, Onitsha, shares attributes of both systems (Henderson 1972).

Sacred kings of the second kind, known as *Eze Nri*, are known to have ruled in two localities in the Awka area into the present century, and there are claims from at least one other place, Enugwu Ukwu, that just such a kingship formerly existed there also. The two localities for which the evidence is unequivocal are Agukwu (known widely simply as Nri) and Oreri. Their immediate sphere of authority was over the *Umueri* lineages scattered among many village-groups from the Anambra river south almost to the Imo river, with isolated groups beyond this area, especially northwards and westwards. The two centres acted as pivots of a ritual system which regulated the cult of the earth which, as noted above, underpinned the traditional value system of most Igbo communities.

The moral codes enacted and formulated in this core area of the system used to be promulgated throughout Igboland by Nri agents, a further tier of ritual officiants recruited from communities having direct ties of common origin with the two focal settlements (Onwuejeogwu 1981: 165-8).

At Agukwu-Nri and Oreri there were several tiers of office-holders among the king-donating lineages and within a priestly lineage known as the *Adama* or *Umu Diana*. These latter, in close coordination with the Eze Nri, were charged with the maintenance of a complex ritual calendar which controlled the timing of key activities in the agricultural cycle, with the foretelling of drought and pestilence, and with the conduct of magical practices sustaining fertility. Central among the latter was the elaboration and performance of rituals for the cleansing of abominations against the earth, which included such varied offences as yam-theft, the bearing of twins and murder.

The *Umueri* sacred kingship gave rise to some of the most complex cosmologies in northcentral Igbo religion, and fortunately enough of the body of belief and ritual practice survived into the middle years of the present century to have enabled a record to be compiled. Thus, when considering dreams and other portents of succession, there is more material concerning the entire process of selection and elevation of sacred kings than of any other among the ritual specialists and religious leaders discussed in the present paper.

Following the speculations of Frazer (1922), Hocart (1927) and, for Nigeria, Meek (1931), concerning the role of regicide in the definition of kings as spirit-beings or otherwise sacred personages, M.D.W. Jeffreys, a colonial government anthropologist, seemed to have been intent on uncovering vestiges of this practice in the rituals surrounding the death of an Eze Nri. During his investigations into the Nri ritual system in the early 1930s, he was able to discover little other than the vaguest hints in contemporary symbols and rituals to either confirm or refute these notions (Jeffreys 1934). What he was able to do for the first time, however, was to discover details about the complex process of selection and investiture noted only in outline in prior anthropological researches by Northcote Thomas.

The time demanded for an interregnum between the death and burial of one king and the creation of a successor was a minimum of seven years. The interregnum represented both a ritual and a political hiatus. During this period the priestly lineage or *Adama* officiated in all central and critical rituals, and the king's council or *Nzemabua* (Onwuejeogwu 1981: 136—8 and 158-60) presided over all matters of policy. It was also the duty of these two groups to interpret and evaluate the testimonies of any individuals who, during the years of the interregnum, began to receive indications of a supernatural nature that they might have been chosen by the spirits of previous kings, or by other divine ordinance, to become the succeeding Eze Nri. Such candidates would call meetings of the *Adama* and council and would recount omens, visions, or prophecies to them. If there were rival claims, diviners might be nominated to seek to distinguish the more valid candidacy.

After the choice of the successful candidate became known, gifts expressing allegiance or support would begin arriving from local Nri communities, and from centres of prestige elsewhere in Igboland, such as the famous trading town of Onitsha or the oracular centre of Arochukwu. The available accounts of what used to happen next vary, but the most complete version, for Agukwu-Nri, derives from Jeffreys (1934; 1935).

Firstly, the chosen candidate visited and made offerings at all the lineage-shrines which belonged to deceased Eze Nri. He was then given the most important staff of office, the *ofo nri,* by the senior lineage elder of the town, after which he went through a ritual symbolically enacting his death as a human being and his rebirth as a spirit. Following this, he was washed ritually in white clay and dressed in the clothes and regalia of a sacred king. He then embarked upon a ritual journey, visiting a special anthill near Ukpo, raising a sacred lump of white clay called the *odudu* from the bed of the river Anambra, and visiting shrines associated with the legendary founder of the Nri lineages at Aguleri. Finally, he visited and ritually greeted *Osi Mili* (the river Niger) before returning to Agukwu.

Having returned from this journey the new king completed his inauguration by spending a year in seclusion, followed by further symbolic acts of power, such as a complex rite recreating the week in the form of four earthen mounds representing the market-days. He also buried the *odudu* and other ritual paraphenalia before the king's shrine, and (allegedly at Agukwu) obtained the skull of the immediately predeceased king and encased it within his throne in a newly-constructed kingly compound.

The dreamers of Agukwu-Nri kingship

The accounts of dreaming in succession to office discussed in this section were reported by the colonial anthropologists Northcote Thomas and M.D.W. Jeffreys in the early part of this century. In recording these accounts, attention was given to dreams as cultural phenomena associated with offices which could be regarded as underpinning the traditional political system.

Nri Obalike of Uruoji quarter was ruling when the British invaded northcentral Igboland (1902-5). Referred to as "Alike" by Thomas and "Abalike" by Jeffreys, he appears to have been interviewed both by Thomas and by a District Officer in the years either side of 1917 when, in a situation of mounting tension between the kingship and the colonial administration, he was forced to abrogate a number of taboos which (as in the case of twin-killing) the authorities declared illegal. In both interviews, Obalike mentioned a dream as central to his candidacy. He told Thomas that he had experienced difficulties (probably some form of post-operative trauma) while undergoing the elaborate facial scarifications for the *ichi* title. He consulted a diviner as to what to do next, and was told to continue with the initiation.

> ... he replied that he had no money [to do so], but the doctor encouraged him by saying that an alose [spirit] named Ebaba was looking for him... the old people were consulted and they said that he must bring [summon?] Ebaba; and one prophesied that Alike was to be the Ezenri.

> One night Enwelana [Eweleana], the last Ezenri, appeared to him and said that he was the chosen man; thereupon he proceeded to offer sacrifices.

> (Thomas 1913: 49; bracketed comments added)

The account given to the District Officer was quoted apparently verbatim by Jeffreys but neither the Intelligence Report nor its author were identified by him, perhaps because they remained confidential at the time:

> I became *eze Nri* about twenty years ago. God appointed me. The signs were as follows: In the night something came down from the sky, like a vulture, and put something into my hands. I found *ofo* and *alo* in my hands.[1] I heard a voice saying: "You will be *eze Nri*". I do not know why this was. There were many bigger and richer men in Nri at the time. I called the people of all the neighbouring towns and told them.

> (Jeffreys 1934 VII:13)

Nri Obalike then went on to describe how he went to make sacrifice at a number of shrines, and how people far and wide brought tribute to him in recognition of his election. Although it might also result from the superficiality of inquiries, it is just possible that what is left out of consideration in these accounts is as significant as what is included. For instance, there is no mention of the role of the Agukwu *Nzemabua* in deliberating on the dream as evidence; nor is there any account of other associated visions, omens and prophecies which substantiated his claims. It might be assumed that, since so long had elapsed since his election, Nri Obalike had forgotten these details. Yet in the context of what is stated (including a listing of the sixteen towns from which he called representatives to hear of his dream) this is difficult to believe. Rather, it seems likely that he wished to conceal the "miraculous" aspects and any details concerning the structure of power relations *within* Agukwu-Nri, while at the same time emphasising two other aspects: the divine remit for his appointment, and the geographical extent of his powers. In other words, perhaps here was an account which was selective, maybe for the purposes of a particular political strategy in relation to the newly-installed apparatus of colonialism. This strategy would then have amounted to an attempt by the sacred king to outflank the overt pattern of colonial domination.

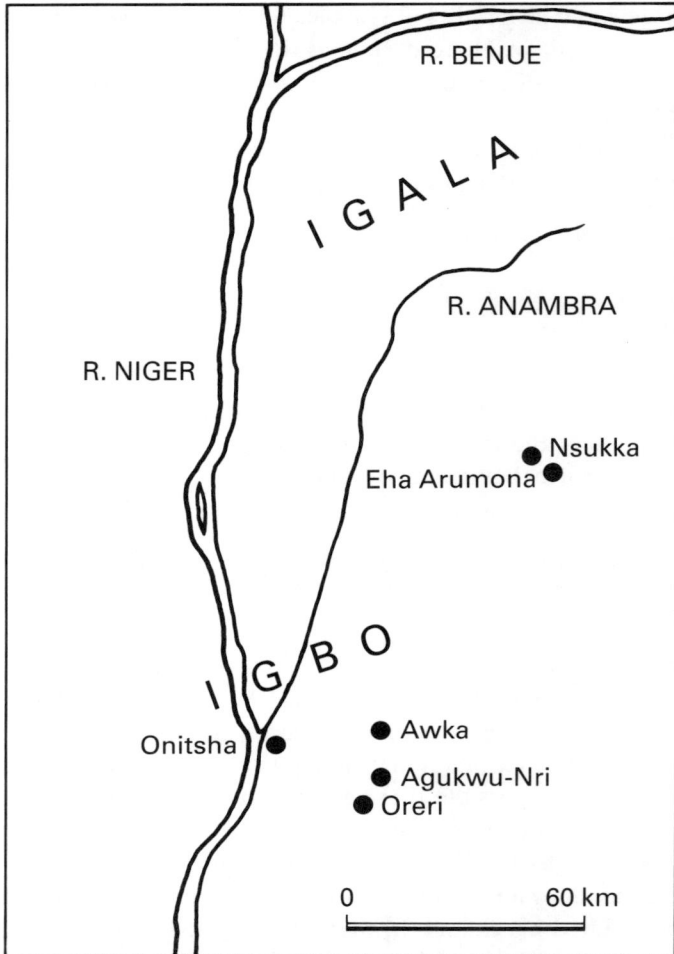

Fig 1. Locations mentioned in the text

Twenty-five years later, Jeffreys was sent to the Nri-Awka area to discover more about the Umunri sacred kingship system, presumably since it still exercised some measure of influence throughout Igboland, and the colonial authorities wished to discover how and why. At the time of his visit to Agukwu-Nri only about half of the required interregnum period of seven years after the death of the previous king had elapsed, but already candidates for the post had begun to emerge. One of the these candidates, Okpoko, appears to have seen in Jeffreys a potential source of accreditation, since he appears to have asked the latter to come to him specifically to record the signs which had already occurred, and which he had begun to use as a justification for potential appointment.

Okpoko stated that the first indication he had that he was being marked out for the kingship was when suddenly one night he was awoken by the main wooden gate at the front entrance to his compound, which began banging as if it had been burst open. He got up and went to check it, only to find that it was in fact securely bolted as he had earlier left it. On several subsequent nights his sleep was disturbed in the same way by the sudden banging of this door. Not long afterwards he had a dream in which Obalike (the now-deceased king) came to him and said "Here are the *ofo* and the *alo*. I hand them to you, for you are to be the next king." Okpoko continued:

> I told my dream to the elders of Agukwu the next day. In the following dry season, the walls of my *ngulu* (compound) started to fall down without any cause, and again, in a dream, I was told by an unknown *mmo* (spirit) that I was to be the next *eze*.

> (Jeffreys 1934, VII 16-17)

The collapse of the compound walls in the dry season (when there is no rainfall, the usual cause of walls collapsing) appears to have been regarded both in Agukwu and in Oreri as a key omen in the call to high religious office because upon taking up the post, the new king rebuilds his main lodge *(obu)* and takes down his compound walls to emphasise his beyond-worldly condition. Jeffreys elsewhere notes (1934 VII: 10) that a part of the rites of candidacy is a formal declaration to the *Nzemabua* that he has been chosen by the *mmo* (spirits) of all past kings.

Okpoko was at pains to emphasise to Jeffreys, however, that there were other reasons why the message to him from the spirit world was clear:

> A little later a number of people from another town came to see me, hearing of the signs that were occurring to me. I told them to go away and not to enter my yard for if any one of them did so, then within a week, a man of their town would fall from a tree and die. They would not listen to me and came in. On their way home they heard that one of their townsmen had fallen off a palm tree and had been killed. I had warned them.

> (Jeffreys 1934, VII: 17)

It may be that such a visit was prompted by concerns with the fertility of crops and the overall wellbeing of the community concerned, since it was believed that these might be in jeopardy if the interregnum were to be too long. The case of someone being killed falling from a tree would not necessarily be regarded as remarkable in this part of Igboland, where fatalities from men slipping while cutting palm-nuts or tapping wine were (and still are) by no means uncommon. Hence Okpoko was quick to back it up with further evidence:

> Then, on another occasion, I was sacrificing at my *obu chi* [shrine to personal destiny as linked to lineage fortunes], when I felt something on my left shoulder. I put my hand there and found three locusts. There were no locusts about, and there had not been any for years. This was

indeed a wonderful sign. I called a meeting of the elder of Agukwu, and, holding the three locusts in one hand, asked what they were. They replied "locusts". I pointed out that there were none about and that I had suddenly felt them upon my arm while sacrificing at my *obu chi*. I then said, within five months there will be many locusts here, and see how my prophecy was fulfilled. The locusts came. If I am to be the new *eze* Nri, the other aspirants will perish, and leave me the undisputed right.

(Jeffreys 1934, VII: 17-18; bracketed comments added)

Jeffreys appended a note to this testimony to the effect that locusts visited the area between November 1930 and January 1931 after an absence of many years. However, he did not elaborate on the significance of the omen itself. The locust is an interesting dual image of the power of the sacred king to summon up either the forces of destruction (if the locusts swarm to devastate crops) or of plenty (if they are less destructively-disposed and can be captured easily: they have been widely considered a food delicacy by the Igbo). Furthermore, they are also associated with the power of the sacred king to effect transformation and perform miracles, as when he visits two white-ant hills at different places in the course of his coronation itinerary and climbs them in an act of symbolic dominion. It is said that the hills can be broken open afterwards to release swarms of locusts. Thus the omen heralding the arrival of the locusts and Okpoko's subsequent prophesy provide an economical but striking image of his imminent association with the kingship.

Much of the interest in Okpoko's account of these signs rests in the fact that he was so actively in pursuit of the kingship despite continual reiteration that he was too poor to bear the burden of the title-taking costs. However, the most significant aspect of his testimony is the fact that he was interviewed while yet a candidate for the kingship rather than already an incumbent. Moreover, there appears to have been some rival activity, and this is perhaps the factor which accounts for the need for omens and prophecy to supplement the "evidence" of dreams. This is a question that I shall return to in the concluding section of the paper.

Omens without dreams at Oreri

One thing which was clear from Jeffrey's account of kingship in Oreri was that it had lost the ritual centrality which it still appeared to enjoy up to 1930 in Agukwu-Nri. Most seriously, there was little precision in the keeping of the ritual calendar, and this had therefore become out of step with the agricultural cycle (Jeffreys 1934 XIII: 31-2). This dislocation was associated with a considerable loss of power, prestige and economic strength as measured in tribute of agricultural products brought to the king from communities near and far in former times in recognition of his role of ensuring agricultural success and prosperity. It is perhaps for this reason that despite the fact that it was only at Oreri that Jeffreys was able to interview a reigning king, the resulting testimony is so slight.

In line with his agenda of questions from Agukwu, Jeffreys asked Nri Okonkwo of Oreri how it was that he became king. Before his accession, Okonkwo had been ill for thirteen years, and had been unable to move about. In an effort to understand what could be done about it, he consulted diviners who said each time they were consulted that it was a sign from the spirits calling upon him to become king. He had had no dreams, and was reluctant to agree with the diagnoses of the diviners. However, one day in the dry season his compound walls appeared spontaneously to collapse, and it was this omen which convinced him that the call was genuine.

The office of *Okpala* is a title in a few Awka-area communities, but does not exist at Agukwu-Nri. At Oreri, the *Okpala* is the chief priest of the *Adama*, with specific responsibility for attendance upon and counselling of the Eze Nri at Oreri. *Okpala* Okaka had taken up his post at exactly the same time as Nri Okonkwo had, some two or three years before Jeffreys interviewed him.

Okaka also makes no mention of dreams about the spirits coming to him. Rather he presented the evidence in terms of omens. Firstly, although not aspiring to the kingship, the link to the kingship was made plain in the fact that his compound walls fell down. Then four snakes, all knotted together, appeared mysteriously one day in his compound and, a little later, a matchet broke in his hand and cut it. After making propitiatory sacrifices:

> I asked as a sign of approval [from the spirits] that my first wife should become pregnant, and that a goat of mine should die suddenly.
>
> (Jeffreys 1934; XII: 4; bracketed comment added)

The goat died, but so too did his first wife. To find out the meaning of all these strange events he consulted a diviner, who said that they were signs that the spirits were calling him to take up the vacant post of Okpala.

Dreaming the Ana: Ezeana Agulu Awka

The remaining accounts of dreaming in succession to office concern the "calling" of ritual specialists. In a passage devoted primarily to a description of the taboos followed by Nri sacred kings, Northcote Thomas noted that similar prohibitions apply to senior officials of the earth-cult, such as the earth priest *Ezeana*, the selection of whom could be as surrounded with extra-human reference as that of sacred kings. The *Ezeana* of Agulu quarter of Awka provided an example:

> He dreamt that the Ana came to his house and called him, saying, "I am hungry: I have come

to you to provide for me. If you fail I will punish you." He [the Ana] was like a man but shone like brass, and was a big as a house. In the morning he went to a doctor and told him his vision; there-upon the quarter brought a cow and other victims to be sacrificed to Ana.

(Thomas 1913: 56; bracketed comment added)

The Ezeana went on to describe how "Nri men" were called in to preside over the sacrifices specified by the diviner, and to tie the ankle cords symbolising office, thus emphasising the link to the kingship enacted in the succession.

Claiming autochthony, Agulu Awka was the Awka quarter which most stressed its links with Nri and with the earth cult. The Awka blacksmiths who travelled throughout Igboland and worked in association with ritual specialists from Nri in this itinerant manner came primarily from Agulu, so the similarity of this call to succession to those from Nri itself should perhaps not be regarded as surprising. The final instance of dreaming and succession described in the next section is a contemporary one.

Dreaming the Onumonu: John Nwamba of Eha Arumona

A number of northcentral Igbo communities acknowledge, albeit indirectly, an influence from Nri upon certain forms of their religious institutions. One such community is that of Eha Arumona (usually written, incorrectly, as Eha Alumona), in the Nsukka area in the north of Igboland. Major deities in Eha Arumona, in common with those of many village-groups on the Nsukka plateau, have an embodiment carried by a human bearer as well as a number of shrines. This embodiment is a bundle of ritual materials known as *Onumonu* or *Awam*. Although each major deity has a shrine-priest, the *Onumonu* is borne by a separate identified office-holder on ritual occasions.[2] While carrying it, the bearer himself "becomes" the *Onumonu* as well as the deity which it embodies. There is no title to this office but, like other religious offices, it is a life-task. The selection of a successor can therefore be as complex a procedure as that for the shrine-priest himself, although the material rewards are inferior.

The *Onumonu* is described as the "son" *(nwa)* of the deity. Most of the time it is stationed within the *Ulo Onumonu* ("house of the *Onumonu*"), an open structure which forms part of the shrine complex for the deity. It becomes activated during festivals of the deity, when petitioned to settle land disputes (where it is thought to have the power to see the true boundaries), and when requested (due to the same powers of perception) to discover the location of harmful medicines which have been deliberately buried for some particular malevolent purpose.

As with the shrine priests of these local major deities, the bearer of the *Onumonu* may be selected by divinatory means. However, the bearer of the *Onumonu* of the deity *Ezeugwuorie* of Amundi village in Eha Arumona claimed to have been called to office by the *Onumonu* itself.

John Nwamba is the current bearer of the *Onumonu*. When asked how it was that he came to occupy this position, he stated that before the previous bearer died, the latter came to him in a dream. A diviner subsequently interpreted this as a sign that Nwamba should try to carry it, in order to see if the deity accepted him. He therefore started to carry the *Onumonu before* the previous bearer had died, and his experience of carrying it introduced him gradually to the transformative aspect of this prospective role. Still he hesitated to take up the office, however.

Subsequently, in further dreams it was not the former bearer but himself who took the form of the *Onumonu*. After this, he accepted that he had been chosen, and while carrying the bundle he began seeing things "through spirit's eyes". The previous office-holder died, and Nwamba has carried *Ezeugwuorie* on its departures from its shrine-home ever since.

There are several points about this testimony which are of significance in relation to succession to other religious offices described above. These points are, firstly, the appearance of the previous incumbent in the sequence of dreams; secondly, the interpretation of the dream by a diviner; thirdly, the initial display of reluctance by the dreamer to believe in the call to office; fourthly, the appearance of the spirit itself to provide the definitive call; and finally, the "proof" of the correctness of the selection in the transfer of other-worldly powers to the chosen candidate.

Conclusion: Igbo dreams, succession, and personal destiny

The degree of consistency among the various accounts of dreaming and portents of succession to religious office described above is, given the variety of interviewers, the range of contexts and the temporal disparities, quite remarkable. Not least notable is the number of cases where dreams are mentioned as the medium whereby the call to office is first communicated. The consistencies even of details of the rendered testimonies about dreams of succession is impressive: the parallels are almost formulaic. Thus the messenger appearing in the dream is either the previous incumbent of the office or a manifestation of the spirit to the service of whom the office is devoted. In some cases the one type of messenger appears in an initial dream, and in a subsequent dream the message is reinforced by the appearance of the other type. In practically every case the principal mode of communication is via the physical placement of the symbols of office in the hands of the dreamer by the messenger. In many instances this act is reinforced by a voice telling the dreamer that he has been chosen for office. Where it is a spirit that is the messenger, its appearance is awesome: descending from the sky or "shining like brass". The use of these images might be dismissed simply as convention, but the subtle differences (such as they can be glimpsed from these accounts) in descriptive terminology do, I think, suggest at root a similarity of experience rather than a lack of imagination.

If nothing else, this highlights the relative neglect of dreaming as a feature of Igbo cultural experience and cosmology (Nwoga 1984b), and points the way to the study of Igbo dream-accounts from a social rather than a cultural-psychological perspective. Le Vine's (1966) study examined private dreams of personal success as a means of identifying underlying cultural values of achievement-motivation. In the present study the identification, in paradoxical contrast, of a form of success-dreaming made public opens out a fuller perspective in which apparently contradictory values can be contextualised

Throughout this essay I have emphasised the strategic nature of the references made to dreams and other portents by aspirants to religious office. In many cases, it would be naive to suggest otherwise, especially where, as in Okpoko's candidacy for the kingship, there was much at stake (including rivalries at the maximal lineage level, one suspects) and dreaming appears alongside both prophecy and omens among the phenomenological armoury of the candidate. In this way, the success of the astute dreamer is akin to the success of the deft user of proverbs or coiner of sayings in Igbo society (Nwoga 1984b: 49-54), and as such will command respect and acquire authority. However, there are other ways of viewing dreaming and succession in Igboland than the strategic, and I wish to close this paper with a brief consideration of two of them.

The first is a functional view, asking the question, "what broader role might dreams of succession have in Igbo society?" A short answer is that in a situation where the dominant ideology of the society emphasises achieved rather than ascribed status, there is nonetheless in many areas a tension between achievement and ascription. While the system of graded titles is explicitly based upon individual achievement, certain other offices – notably those of Eze Nri, priest and *Onumonu* - are based upon a continuity between successive incumbents, a continuity which requires the ideology of a type of ascription. The nomination of successors via dreams "works" in as much as it avoids the necessity for any individual or any one group to be seen to be actually choosing between rival claimants to office, or indeed to choose who will emerge in the first place as a candidate. In such a situation, the successful dreaming formula is the one which best "reads" the nuances of political sentiment in the community at large, and finds the most vivid way to express it figuratively via identification of "the wishes of the gods" (or ancestors).

To some extent such a view is still "strategic", however. A rather different approach is to take the testimony of the dreamers at face value. Here, perhaps the most significant point to note is the reluctance of several of the dreamers to believe that they, rather than more powerful, wealthy or influential members of their community, were being called to esteemed office. As with other elements of the dreaming process apparently characteristic of northcentral Igbo ritual succession, this statement of its very consistency across several accounts can also be read as stemming from shared cultural perceptions of personal fate current in Igbo society at the widest level. The particular aspect of Igbo philosophy and world-view of concern in this regard is the concept of destiny and its relationship to the vicissitudes of every person's life-experience. Yet this concept is not univocally fatalistic, because it comprises a duality of perception in Igbo consciousness. On the one hand there is the predestined fate embodied in a person's identity from before birth: his or her *chi*. On the other hand, there is the unfolding fate of a person as they live their life, and more especially as they direct their energies to influence that fate beneficially through time. Such influence upon one's own destiny is effected through the agency of another constituent of male (but rarely female) personhood: the *ikenga,* the personnification of the strength of a man's right hand, his power to achieve. (see Nwoga 1984a, and 1984b: 47-8; Cole and Aniakor *op cit* 26-7; and Ifemesia, 1979).

These ontological considerations, I believe, go some considerable way towards explaining why, in personal terms, the stated reluctance to accept the full veracity or implications of first dreams of succession was followed by resort to diviners, further dreams, the discovery of omens, and the experience of prophecy. While this sequence may have, at the same time, amounted to a self-promotional strategy, it can also be seen as an "internal" confirmation of one's candidacy to oneself. Such a course would be a means of answering such questions as "Are my *chi* and my *ikenga* indeed working in concert to propel me into the priesthood/kingship/role of *Onumonu*-bearer? Is this in fact my destiny?" With the experiencing of the second or subsequent dream(s) or the occurrence of other portents, the matter is put beyond issue: the erstwhile "dreams of grandeur" would amount to an unequivocal signal of the true nature of the dreamer's personal destiny.

NOTES

The author wishes to record his appreciation of the formative influence on his awareness of Igbo cosmology of conversations with Chike Aniakor, Donatus Ibe Nwoga, and Herbert Cole in Nsukka and with Charles Nnolim and Robin Horton in Port Harcourt. Also his thanks to Rosalind Shaw for sharing thoughts (and correcting misapprehensions) on Igbo religion and society, and for editorial comments on an earlier draft of this paper.

1. *Ofo:* a staff of ancestral/lineage authority, in this case the *ofo Nri*, symbol of supreme ancestral authority. *Alo:* a senior title staff.

2. The following account is based on joint field research with Rosalind Shaw in Eha Arumona in 1984. See Ray and Shaw (1987) for further information on the *Onumonu* embodiment.

REFERENCES

ACHEBE, C., 1974, *Arrow of God* (Second Edition). London: Heinemann (African Writers Series).

COLE, H.M. and ANIAKOR, C.C., 1984, *Igbo Arts: community and cosmos.* Los Angeles: Museum of Cultural History, University of California.

ECHERUO, M.J.C., 1979, *A Matter of Identity: 1979 Ahajioku Lecture.* Owerri: Culture Divison, Ministry of Information, Culture, Youth and Sports.

EJIOFOR, L.U., 1982, *Igbo Kingdoms: power and control.* Onitsha: Africana Publishers Ltd.

EZUGWU, J.O., 1982, *Art and Social Control: a case study of Opi, Nsukka.* Unpublished BA Thesis, University of Nigeria, Nsukka.

FRAZER, J.G., 1922, *The Golden Bough: A study in magic and religion* (abridged edition).

GOODY, J. 1966, Introduction. In J. Goody (ed.), *Succession to High Office.* Cambridge University Press: Cambridge Papers in Social Anthropology 4.

HENDERSON, R., 1972, *The King in Every Man.* New Haven, Connecticut: Yale Univesity Press.

HOCART, A.M., 1927, *Kingship.* Oxford: Clarendon Press.

HORTON, W.R.G., 1954, God, man and the land in a northern Ibo village-group. *Africa,* 26(1): 17-28.

IFEMESIA, C., 1979, *Traditional Humane Living Among the Igbo: an historical perspective.* Enugu: Fourth Dimension Publishers.

ISICHEI, E., (ed.) 1977, *Igbo Worlds: an anthology of oral histories and historical descriptions.* London: Macmillan Educational Ltd.

JEFFREYS, M.D.W., 1934, *The Divine Umudri: kings of Igboland,* unpublished Ph.D. Thesis: University of London.

    1935, The Divine Umundri King. *Africa,* 8(3): 346-354.

LE VINE, R.A., 1966, *Dreams and Deeds: achievement motivation in Nigeria.* Chicago: University of Chicago Press.

MEEK, C.K., 1931, *A Sudanese Kingdom.* London: Kegan Paul, Trench and Trubner.

    1937, *Law and Authority in a Nigerian Tribe: a study in indirect rule.* London: Oxford University Press.

NWOGA, D.I., 1984a, *The Supreme God as Stranger in Igbo Religious Thought.* Ekwereazu, Nigeria: Hawk Press.

    1984b, *Nka Na Nzere: The Focus of Igbo World View: Ahiajoku Lecture 1984.* Owerri: Culture Division, Ministry of Information, Culture, Youth and Sports.

ONWUEJEOGWU, M.A., 1981, *An Igbo Civilisation: Nri kingdom and hegemony.* London: Ethnographica.

OTTENBERG, S., 1956, Ibo oracles and intergroup relations. *Southwestern Journal of Anthropology.* 8: 3-10.

    1971, *Leadership and Authority in an African Society: The Afikpo village group.* Seattle: University of Washington Press.

    1975, *Masked Rituals of Afikpo.* Seattle: University of Washington Press.

RAY, K. AND SHAW, R., 1987, The structure of spirit embodiment in Nsukka Igbo masquerading traditions. *Anthropos,* 82: 655-660.

THOMAS, N.W., 1913, *Anthropological Report on the Ibo-Speaking Peoples: Part I: Law and Custom of the Ibo of the Awka Neighbourhood, S. Nigeria.* London: Harrison.

WEBB, G., 1981, *Geographical Mobility, Status Acquisition and Personhood Among the Awka Igbo,* unpublished PhD. dissertation. University of Rochester, New York.

DREAMS, INSPIRATION AND CRAFTWORK
AMONG TUKOLOR WEAVERS

ROY M. DILLEY

University of St. Andrews

Wise and sometimes terrible hints shall in them be thrown to man
out of quite an unknown intelligence

(Ralph Waldo Emerson, 1896, on dreams)

Introduction

My concern in this paper is with the relationship between craftwork –
specifically weaving – dreams and spirit beings. These last two topics have
received much joint attention in the literature, though only occasionally have
they been linked with craftwork in particular, and with aspects of material
culture in general. The work of d'Azevedo (1973) offers perhaps the best and
most comparable approach with the one I adopt here, in which he too links all
three topics with another of my themes, that of inspiration in craftwork. Thus
he states: "The archetypical Gola artist is one who 'dreams', and whose
creative inspiration is supported by a very special relationship with a tutelary"
(*ibid*:335). Echoes of this statement will be found throughout this paper.

The association of dreams with the spirit world is widespread (see for
example d'Andrade 1961; Devereux 1969; Firth 1934; Lincoln 1935; Meier
1966; Rattray 1927; Van de Castle 1973), and as Kuper suggests it is one that
appears universal and deserving of study (1979:661, n.2). D'Andrade attempts
such a cross-cultural survey and analysis of dreams and details a number of
common dream characteristics, of which he says that there is a limited complex
centred around three of them concerned with the use of dreams to seek and
control supernatural powers (1961:321). His own explanation of this
phenomenon relates to culturally-induced levels of anxiety experienced by
individuals who, as a consequence of this anxiety, become preoccupied with
dreams and fantasy in which they seek and control "magical helpers" (*ibid*:320,
322, 326). This hypothesis is supported by data from societies set across a range
of socio-economic types. There are, however, a number of questionable
assumptions in his method which I do not have the space to discuss here. By
contrast though, I hope to set Tukolor dreams in their cultural context at the
level of structural and functional organisation, avoiding psychological
interpretations derived from conditions imputed to representative examples
from different cultural typologies. And more generally, I contrast my own view

with that apparent in many anthropological works that attempt to trace connections between culture and personality traits in the study of the cultural content and symbolism of dreams as related to innate human endowment and socialization processes. Thus, in response to Kuper's indication of the universal theme in the dream my aim is rather modest and limited: I present an ethnographic analysis of the Tukolor conception of craftwork in relation to its associations with the spirit world, and show how dreams are one form of mediation between that world and the practising craftsman.

The theme of inspiration through dreams is one that has received the attention of some writers, in particular Lincoln (1935). Quoting Laufer, he writes: "Of all categories of dreams the inspirational dream is the most interesting, because it has proved a creative force in literature, science, and art, or stimulated ambition of one sort or another" (ibid:79).[1] After a discussion of the types of culture items, including material artefacts, originating in dreams and visions, Lincoln goes on to suggest that dreams are a primary source of cultural innovation:

> Since these [examples] are drawn from all parts of the earth, one can but conclude that a large part of primitive culture is a result of the dream ...

and he continues:

> ... practically all of the culture items that originate from them [dreams] are presented by a being or spirit in animal or human form (ibid:93).

Thus, Lincoln draws together certain aspects of material culture with dream inspiration in the form of visitations from spirit beings. However, going beyond his informative ethnography, he ultimately resorts to arguments of a psychological nature to explain common themes in dreams from different cultures by suggesting that "the dynamics of motive and wish expressed in the dream would, therefore, be equivalent to reaching the foundation in human motive on which culture rests" (ibid:97). These intimations of a neo-Freudian theme, which provided much motivation for early anthropological investigations of the dream (see for example Seligman 1927, Malinowski 1927), are combined in his argument with one similar to that found in Tylor's work on dreams and the origins of religion when Lincoln states: "... the primitive mind assigns a reality value to the fantasy world equal to that of the external world, and even has difficulty in distinguishing the two ..." (ibid:98).

The problems of considering the veracity of claims about dreams as primary or secondary sources of cultural innovation are many. As d'Andrade (1961:298) adds, it is a difficult argument to either prove or disprove, for it does not take into account the process of secondary elaboration of dream experiences to which individuals might impute socially-recognised meanings or patterns of waking experience to remembered dream sequences. That a craftsman's claim of dream inspiration in craftwork may lead to cultural innovation – in that a new design may be produced, for example – is quite obvious. Yet it says as much of the possibility that he attaches socially-relevant meanings to his experience as it does of his presumed apprehension of reality. Thus I do not want to emphasise here that the expressions of dreams are central to most aspects of Tukolor cultural or social life, but instead to suggest some of the significance of dreams for the Tukolor in general and for weavers in particular, and how their reported dream experiences fit into the broader social and conceptual structures relating to craftwork. In this regard, I would echo Bastide's remarks that "Freud repersonalised the dream; now we must resocialise it" (1966:202), and his view that: "The sociological structure of the dream is then, not as with us, a reflection, or the obverse of social structure; it is an integral part of it" (*ibid:*209).

In summary, then, I take the view that the dream for the Tukolor weaver constitutes a category of thought into which he places his dream experiences – whose validity is neither provable nor necessarily objectifiable – which are closely linked with the conceptions he holds of his craft and of the spirit world. Lastly, I briefly try to show in this paper how dreams as a category of experience are a means of articulating perceptions of levels of individual skill and ability among Tukolor weavers.

In this paper I describe craftsmen's conceptions of dreams as a category of reported experience believed to be a source of innovation and inspiration in craftwork. The ethnographic data I primarily draw on concerns Tukolor weavers, though I believe that similar explanations of the significance of dreams for other Tukolor craftsmen would not be too far wrong. Furthermore, I would suggest that there are possibly similar cultural elements running through the activities of craftsmen of neighbouring peoples, such as the Wolof and Serer for example; and indeed these culture traits may even be traced to other parts of West Africa, specifically the Gola of Liberia as reported by d'Azevedo (1973). Thus there is evidence to suggest that a constellation of similar cultural elements is present across a wide range of peoples scattered across the region, though this claim cannot be substantiated due to a lack of ethnography. This is a subject that perhaps awaits further investigation. My main aim here, however, is to set in cultural context Tukolor conceptions of dreams and their relationship to the weavers' craftwork, and where relevant to highlight similarities among the Serer – a people from whom a limited amount of data was collected during the course of my fieldwork in Senegal.

Dreams, souls and Islam

Before I address my main theme of weavers and dreaming, some mention should be made of Tukolor dreams in general and their cultural uses. In common with many reports in the anthropological literature on dreams, Tukolor dreams are often associated with supernatural or spiritual agents. One common folk belief is that the soul or shadow-self *(mbeelu)* is responsible for dreams. This part of man's essential being is thought to leave the body during sleep and roam the earth at night. During the course of its nocturnal wanderings the *mbeelu* experiences another reality apprehended as dreams *(koyde)* by the sleeper.[2] However, the Tukolor are often ambivalent about the significance they attach to such dreams; for on the one hand they describe them as experience of the *mbeelu,* and yet on the other they dismiss them as meaningless in many cases. Two common proverbial sayings express this attitude: *Koydol ko fus,* "A dream is nought" and another which translates as "a dream will give much delight but it does not enrich" (see Gaden 1931).

In addition to these folk beliefs, there are formal roles of dream interpreter in which the use of dreams is institutionalised. Certain marabouts (learned Muslim clerics) and other diviners *(timoobe)* specialise in the interpretation of dreams usually induced or evoked through specific techniques and procedures.[3] Although these dreams are referred to by the same word in Pulaar, this type of dream procedure is distinguished by the Tukolor because of its institutionalised nature and its association with Islam. This distinction parallels those made by Malinowski (1927:91-4) and by Lincoln (1935:94, 189) between free individual dreams and "official" or "culture pattern" dreams which run on prescribed lines using culturally recognised symbols.[4] The distinction in the minds of the Tukolor rests on their ambivalent attitude towards the significance of the former and on their greater level of acceptance of the validity of the latter, backed by the authority of Islam and the cleric interpreters. Doubt about forms of institutionalised dream interpretation rest not so much on the possible validity of these dreams *per se,* but on whether a particular marabout or diviner is a charlatan or not.[5] Marabouts who interpret dreams use dream interpretation manuals *(deftere firtoore koyde* in Pulaar) common throughout much of North and West Africa and the Middle East; one such text found in Fuuta Toro is that by "Abd-Ghani an-Nabulsi" (d 1731).[6] These marabouts practise *listikhaar* (Islamic dream interpretation) and recognise a series of common symbols used to decode the meaning of a dream. For instance, to dream of a horse means that one will marry within the year; to dream of being bitten by a snake means one will suffer supernatural attack; to dream of a canoe voyage announces one's death in the current year. The marabout also prescribes to his clients prayers, sacrifices and alms-giving and might even hand over amulets he has prepared to avert the outcomes presaged in the dream.

A person concerned over a family or personal matter might consult a marabout who practices *listikhaar*. The client reveals his problem to him and requests that it be addressed to Allah through his intermediary, the marabout. The marabout then uses specified procedures to evoke dreams during a night retreat after the consultation with his client. He first prepares himself by performing ritual ablutions, offering up prayers and reciting his client's request that evening before he finally falls asleep. During the night it is said that a dream which contains guidance over the client's problem comes to the marabout, making it known whether his prayers have been granted or not. (Cf. Meier who reports that other Islamic mystics often gain inspiration through dreams at night, 1966:421.)

The recall of dreams evoked by other marabouts, similar to that involved in *listikhaar,* is also practised by certain learned clerics during longer retreats lasting as long as 17 days. On these retreats these clerics or grand marabouts *(sirruyankoobe)* perform *khalwa,* spiritual exercises during seclusion, with the aim of bringing about their own spiritual improvement or for the purpose of seeking direction over matters of concern. Again dreams are evoked through special procedures, and prayers are also offered up in search of spiritual guidance and teaching. A client might also consult a *sirruyanke* for direction and wise counsel before he undertakes a voyage or makes plans for a marriage. In the past, grand marabouts were usually consulted before a jihad was declared or before starting a new campaign. There are both professional marabouts practising *listikhaar* dream interpretation as well as *sirruyankoobe* performing *khalwa* on extended retreats. Their clients are charged fees for consultations which provide their income, though to employ the services of a grand marabout such fees are considerably higher.

These two examples of Islamic practice specifically involve the evocation and subsequent interpretation of dreams by the marabout, and the role of the dream here has a two-fold purpose. The first is the use of dreams in consultations with clients enquiring after specific advice or guidance in particular matters; the second is the use of dreams, in combination with prayer and contemplation, as a means of acquiring *khalwa* or religious knowledge held by *sirruyankoobe.* The source of dreams and visions claimed to be experienced by these marabouts is Allah and his angelic host. Although such experiences may be actively sought by the practitioners through physical and spiritual preparations, the marabouts themselves are ultimately passive to the reception of dreams since they are visited on them by spiritual forces not at their command. Indeed, Meier makes the point that "active modes of breaking through to knowledge" appear to be rarely used in Islam, whereas prepared but passive techniques such as dreaming are quite common (1966:422). Moreover, to return to the two roles being performed by marabouts, they can be seen as acting both as dream interpreters as well as dream evokers – two different aspects in the process of the dream. Devereux points up a similar distinction when he states: "What the dreamer assembles, the dream interpreter dissembles" (1979:20-21) through his decoding of symbols occurring in dreams. Drawing on Aristotle's conception of metaphor and dream interpretation, he considers metaphor creation and symbolic representation in dreaming to be parallel processes. By contrast, dream interpretation, viewed as a series of operations, is practically the symmetrical opposite of metaphor construction: "The poet or dreamer", he states, "increases the gap between objective reality and its verbal representation by devising metaphor, while the dream interpreter decreases it to the greatest possible extent" (*ibid.*).

In the case of maraboutic practices we see both of these processes fused, since the marabout is both the dreamer and the interpreter at the same time. However, as I will illustrate later, *mabube* weavers, who are also singers and poets involved in metaphor creation, perform predominantly the first of these aspects of the dream process rather than interpretation and exegesis of either their dream experiences or their poetic constructions.

The last point I want to highlight before I take up the theme of dreaming among Tukolor weavers is the idea that grand marabouts can acquire *khalwa* or religious knowledge through dreams during their retreats. *Khalwa* is an exclusive possession of respected marabouts, considered to be "saints" (*wayliyaabe*)[7], who are renowned for their piety and devotion. *Khalwa* forms a specialised part of a body of knowledge or lore connected with Islam, and is more generally referred to as *gandal diine* or "religious lore". This body of lore comprises that learning acquired by marabouts through the study of the Koran and other works, in addition to the lore inspired by Allah and his host through dreams, visions and visitations. Indeed, the theme of inspiration and instruction through dreams and dream-like experiences is one that lies at the heart of Islam: in this manner Mohammed himself had revealed to him by Gabriel much of the Koran (see Meier 1966; Von Grunebaum 1966). The Prophet said: "There are three kinds of vision, one comes from God, another from angels, and the third from Satan" (Trimingham 1959:122)[8]; and it is the attribution of dream and other experiences to these different categories of spirit being which constitutes major distinctions in the minds of the Tukolor.

Gandal diine or Islamic religious lore is also referred to by the designation *gandal danewal,* meaning literally "white lore". That is to say that such lore and knowledge has as its origin Allah and his angelic host *(rawhanaaje).* In contrast, the lore of weaving *(gandal mabube* – more strictly "lore of the *mabube*"), like that of the other craftsmen and musician groups, is referred to as *gandal balewal* or "black lore" whose origin is said to be the jinn *(jinneeje* or *seydaneeje).* Thus, both types of lore – black and white – are distinguished from each other according to the sort of spirit-being thought to be responsible for implanting them in the minds of men. However, there are common elements between the two in the relationship between man and spirit being, and in how man acquires lore from the world of the spirit. In the next section I move on to consider these topics in more depth as regards how the *mabube* conceive of their craft and its body of lore.

In summary, then, the institutionalised maraboutic practice of dream evocation and interpretation is linked with a body of Islamic religious lore and teaching in which the dream is a vehicle of instruction and inspiration. Divine knowledge and teaching is put into the minds of men, learned clerics, and is visited upon them by certain spirit beings acting in dreams.

Myths and dreams, lore and skill

In this section I describe the way in which *mabube* weavers conceive of the relationship between their craft, craft lore and the spirit world, and how these craftsmen mediate between that world and the community of men in the performance of their craft. I will also illustrate the connections between their occupation as weavers and their specialised roles of praise-singer and poet in regard of their relationship with spirit beings, for both the roles of weaver and poet/singer are similarly associated with the jinn, who are said to offer inspiration to the practitioners of these occupations. As was mentioned above, the designation of the spiritual source of *mabube* lore *(gandal mabube)* is socially defined and is attributed to the jinn, since its content does not fit in with the recognised, dominant religious traditions of the Muslim clergy who claim godly and angelic inspiration. Meier comments on similar distinctions in Middle Eastern Islam, and states that "according to Islamic concepts, the content of an inspiration generally indicates its source" (1966:428).

In the discussion below, I attempt to show how the concept of the dream can be seen as one of the means by which inspiration is made accessible to the *mabube* in their various occupations. But first I turn to the occupation of weaving, and here I draw both on reported experiences of dreams as well as on weaving myths in which dreams are central aspects of the narrative.

Numerous writers have considered dream and myth to be interrelated, and indeed Kuper states that "dreams are, in a sense, individual myths, and myths collective dreams" (1979:645). Quoting Burridge, Kuper also adds that "much of the content of dreams tends to become articulate in myths, and myths, or parts of myths, are retold in dreams" (*ibid.*).[9] This is certainly so for the *mabube*, though it could also be added that weavers model their own experience on the ideals expressed in myths as regards dreaming and the jinn.

Mabube weaving myths portray the weavers' conception of the origin of their craft as deriving from the spirit world. The weavers' mythical ancestor came upon jinn *(jinneeje)* weaving in the bush and after a struggle took from them parts of the loom as well as weaving lore and its associated magic. In this myth, and in other ways too, they identify their craft with the jinn. Furthermore, other Tukolor also conceive of the *mabube* as carrying out an occupation which brings them into a relationship with the jinn. and often refer to them as being "close to the jinn" ("*caagal jinneeje*", literally "next to the jinn").

Dreams feature in the exploits of the mythical ancestor, for his son Beram is said to have seen one night in a dream the loom frame, which was not originally taken from the jinn by the father since he had sufficient lore *(gandal)* to weave magically without it.[10] Puzzled by what he had seen in his dream, Beram asked his father for an explanation. The father then returned to the jinn to ask for the loom frame to be explained to him, and they named each part of the framework in turn. The father returned with this knowledge and showed Beram, an ordinary mortal, how to weave on the loom. The father, himself half-man half-spirit, did not need to resort to such technical aids and continued to weave using only the power of *cefi* (incantations and verses).

Aspects of these origin myths parallel activities performed by present-day weavers. They see themselves to be enacting the deeds of the ancestors, whose example provides a model for the explanation and elaboration of their practices and experiences, particularly in the way they regard dreams. Thus, just as Beram and his father had difficulties over the operation of the loom that were solved by recourse to the jinn, so a weaver today facing an aspect of weaving he cannot solve for himself often finds its solution in a dream visited upon him by the jinn. Weavers report that in these cases a dream might not always appear during the night, but that simply sleeping on the problem often results in the solution becoming apparent to an individual on waking. The appearance of this new idea is considered by weavers to be the result of a spirit visitation during the night. Dreams commonly figure as the source of inspiration for creating new cloth designs, in which a novel colour combination or mode of thread interlacing is seen by the weaver. And again, the implanting of this innovation in the mind of the weaver in a dream is attributed to the jinn.

The mystical aspects of weaving, which include magical formulae, verses and incantations aimed at either improving oneself as a weaver or afflicting other weavers, are also gained through dreams and visitations by jinn. The following occurrence was reported to me by an old weaver who was asked how he had obtained his *gandal* or weaving lore:

> I left my village to fetch a sheep from a neighbouring settlement. I made the mistake of leaving at midday [a time when jinn are said to be abroad, as they are at dusk and later during the night]. When I was in the middle of the bush I came to a river and there saw a female jinni washing her hair. [When in human form jinni are said to have long flowing hair and so are easily recognisable.] On seeing the jinni I could only utter *'laa'* [the first world in part of the

Muslim proclamation of faith *la ilaha illa'lah*, which is often used as a form of exclamation]. This was the last sound I uttered before I was struck dumb.

I returned home and all the household saw what a state I was in. They feared for my life. I was not, however, afraid. If I had shown any fear on meeting the jinni I would surely have died. When night fell I dreamt that the jinni visited me and she gave me much weaving lore. The following morning my power of speech had returned and I found that I could weave as never before – weaving rapidly and producing cloth of much better quality.

The old man then related to me one of the incantations he had been given, which was to be used at certain stages of weaving. In translation it goes as follows:

> There are many things in this world.
> There is man, there is woman,
> Young and old.
> Woman gave birth to both man and woman.
> As this is true,
> Threads come!

It can be seen, therefore, that there are two aspects of the weaver's craft that can be inspired through dreams: the practical and technical side of weaving, and the mystical side of it. This latter part of the craft embraces the verses and incantations used by weavers and forms part of their body of weaving lore, and it is perhaps here that most innovation is possible. Practical innovation in the craft is limited by the type of technology they used and by the method of warp-faced weaving which allows only limited design possibilities. Greater inspiration through dreams often comes in the form of verses and incantations *(cefi)* used for mystically improving a weaver's ability to weave well and rapidly, or to affect the fortunes of others.

The distinction between these two aspects of weaving is one that occurs throughout the craft, though at another level they are also connected in that greater *gandal* or lore leads to greater skill and ability. The apprenticeship of weavers is one area in which this distinction is manifest, since an apprentice gains an early knowledge of craft techniques followed by rudimentary instruction in weaving lore (Dilley 1989). Thus lore is passed on to a youth during his training, but he is not said to dream at this stage. It is only the mature master weaver or *jarno* who gains practical and mystical abilities through inspiration in dreams. As with maraboutic Islamic lore, therefore, it can be seen that expertise in weaving is passed on through study and learning at the craft as well as through spiritual inspiration in the form of dreams.

The jinn, as portrayed in myth and in reported occurrences by weavers, are usually first encountered in the bush, where they are said to dwell in cetain species of tree, termite mounds and other natural features. Weavers coming in contact with them – unless they are driven mad by the experience – often have gifts bestowed upon them in the form of *cefi* or other items of weaving lore.[11] These images suggest a spatial metaphor of bush and human settlement, which represents the conception of the origins of weaving and its source of inspiration coming from beyond the social world of men – that is from the jinn of the bush. It is the weaver who integrates and transforms these potentially threatening powers of creation into a socially useful activity such as weaving. At another level, these images suggest a metaphor of the sources of weaving inspiration that are external to weavers themselves as individual craftsmen. I will return to this topic at the end of this paper. Moreover, it is the dream that is one form of mediation between man and spirit in the performance of the weaver's craft, and through it practical and mystical teaching is passed from spirit to craftsmen. Dreams are thus a vehicle for the transmission of weaving expertise and lore from the world of spirit to the world of men.

Metaphor, dream and interpretation

The question of how esoteric weaving lore is obtained in general is seldom discussed. More specifically here, master weavers rarely discuss their dreams, nor do they try to have them interpreted since they are considered personal to them alone. Their dreams form part of each individual's stock of esoteric lore which is hardly ever divulged. The meaning of such dreams for a weaver is contained in the inspiration for new verses or incantations he receives or in the particular problem he is seeking a solution to. To the weaver the dream is an explanation in itself: it is a spirit communication which has relevance to his craft. If it is not relevant to his craft, either in the sorts of figures which might appear to him or in the ideas implanted in his mind the next day, then the dream is nought *(koyde ko fus)*. Similarly Von Grunebaum (1966:21) states that the dream in classical Islam is an instrument for the cognition of an "outside reality" which he labels "the supernatural". When dreams might suggest anything other than this for the Tukolor (as they do for us as an instrument for introspection and self-cognition) then they tend to reject their validity.

The weaver, then, is more concerned with dream/metaphor creation then with interpretation, to employ Devereux's distinction. The type of dream inspiration they receive is either of a practical/artistic nature in that new cloth patterns or solutions to technical problems may be found, or it is of relevance to their body of weaving lore with the purpose of mystically improving a weaver's abilities or afflicting another weaver. In this latter category is included *cefi*, verses and incantations with mystical power to affect the physical world, and these verses are akin to poetry in that they employ metaphor, trope, analogy and allusion. Thus, this genre of oral expression closely corresponds to weavers' poetry and praise-songs, which are also said to be inspired through spiritual agency. Dreams again form a similar medium for the poet and singer as they do for the weaver. The dissembling and interpretation of poem or song, as with the dream, is not a topic usually addressed by the *mabu* artist; it is one usually raised only by the naive anthropologist in his proving for deeper meanings, which are not always relevant to the *mabu* informant. The dream-inspired *mabu* poet or weaver places more emphasis on metaphor creation than on metaphor interpretation; indeed a not too dissimilar separation can be seen in the West between literary creation and literary criticism and commentary.[12]

Meier describes how specific Arab singers and composers received poetic inspiration through dreams, in a similar manner to *mabube* poets and singers, and that the source of this inspiration is the jinn. This source of inspiration for his art stirs a sense of religious ambivalence in the Muslim poet, one of whom Meier quotes as saying: "I do not want to bring together in my heart the words of God and those of Satan" (1966:423-5). The *mabu* weaver or poet, however, appears not to feel such a severe sense of ambivalence in the performance of his art or craft since his occupations and sources of inspiration are in one sense embraced by an Islamic cosmology, even though they may be devalued ones. Thus, the *mabu* operates in an Islamised society, utilising spirit forces interpreted as part of that world rather than as part of any other heritage. But just as the jinn occupy a lower position in the hierarchy of Islamic spirit beings, so the *mabube,* who are identified with them, occupy an inferior social position in relation to the Islamic clerics and freemen.

Meier also states that "each poet has his own demon inspirer" (*ibid:*425), who is responsible for the creativity in his art. Similarly, d'Azevedo describes Gola conceptions of artistry as deriving from spirit sources, whereby Gola singers, musicians, woodcarvers and some renowned weavers are referred to as dreamers. Moreover, their finest work, novel designs and exceptional abilities are attributed to spirit inspiration (1973:323, 328). Like Arabian poets, Gola artists and craftsmen have a personal spirit inspirer *(neme)* who puts into the minds of the practitioner patterns and pictures from which he works directly. The individual relationship between artist and tutelary is one of friendship, which models not only his work in life but also the artist's personality and behaviour. In contrast, Tukolor *mabube* weavers and poets do not regard spirit inspiration as necessarily personal or individual. Each particular *mabu* does not have a specific personal relationship with only one jinni. Instead, there seems to exist a host of jinn who might inspire him, either as anonymous beings to whom inspiration is generally attributed or as named jinn who are not individually exclusive in their acts of inspiration. A specific jinni can, however, be evoked through the power of *cefi,* and it might be said that one particular spirit was responsible for inspiring certain items of *mabube* lore.

In summary, then, it has been shown that the *mabube's* source of inspiration in their occupations is conceived of as being external to the community of men, and this is represented in myth and reported experiences in a spatial metaphor of village and bush, relating to the opposition of man/spirit. Dreams and dreaming are a means of access to the spirit world, from which the *mabube* draw inspiration for their arts. Thus, at a structural level of analysis, the *mabube* can be seen to hold magical powers of transformation, the source of which is external to the community of men. But at the level of social discourse, the externalisation of their source of inspiration serves also to articulate distinctions between individual craftsmen – a subject to which I now turn.

The creative individual

In this final section of the paper I discuss briefly some Tukolor perceptions of the master weaver as a skilled and creative individual and how these perceptions of him are accommodated within *mabube* ideology.

It has been described above how the jinn are believed to be the originators of weaving as well as the source of creative ideas in the craft. The skilled master weaver possesses his expertise by virtue of his relationship to the jinn that animate his craft. Thus personal abilities are not merely considered to reside in the individual alone, but their source is considered to be external to the craftsman himself.[13] For this reason, other Tukolor view the *mabube's* activities as acts of magical transformation in which the practitioner draws on powers beyond himself to effect the transformation of thread into cloth, word into poetry. The *mabu's* skills and abilities are, therefore, expressions of the spirit influences he controls in the performance of his craft. Camara Laye suggests a similar view of his father, a blacksmith, in his novel *L'Enfant Noir*. Other Tukolor are, then, generally ambivalent in their attitudes towards the *mabube,* whom they regard with fear in virtue of their association with spiritual agents, with scorn for the nature of the occupation they practice, and with respect for the skills they are seen to possess. Indeed, a cleric once suggested to me that the title *mabube* derived from the verb *mabaade* meaning "to manipulate deftly" or "to arrange (things) with precision". A *mabotoodo* is, therefore, one who works in such a delicate and precise manner, and this term, it was suggested, contracted to give the singular form *mabu* or *mabo* for an individual member of the *mabube.*

There are parallels here with what d'Azevedo says of the Gola of Liberia who hold similarly ambivalent attitudes with regard to the skills and abilities their craftsmen possess. Indeed, exceptional skills are seen to be permeated with the idea of supernatural power and guidance; and moreover, the Gola have no distinctive word for "creative personality" (1973:289-308). He also adds that the craftsman's product "is not perceived by others so much as an embodiment of the intention of the artist as it is of the intention of a supernatural personality" (*ibid:*337). D'Azevedo links this idea to the way in which the artist is thus insulated from public scrutiny and control. I would, however, link instead the Tukolor conception of the individual master weaver with his external creative powers to some of the concepts of *mabube* identity expressed in myth. Thus I suggest that the function of the dream as a vehicle of inspiration and learning is a means of mediating the ideal conception of their identity with the reality of individual differences in levels of skill and ability between weavers.

The theme of equality between weavers is expressed in the myth of origin of the nine founder patriclans which form the *mabube.* This theme is also reiterated in statements made by informants that members of these nine clans are equal in terms of their skills and abilities and in their access to weaving lore. This idealised conception of group identity takes no account, however, of individual differences in levels of skill and creativity among weavers. Thus, although all weavers are said to have equal access to weaving lore and the fruits that this bears, some obviously have more than others. This discrepancy between the ideal and the real is articulated through a discourse of spiritual agency, whereby although all weavers may be born equal, some must have had greatness thrust upon them in the form of spirit innovation and inspiration. Thus dreams, whether real or not as a form of innovation and inspiration for weavers through the presumed actions of the jinn, can be seen as one means of accounting for individual differences in terms of abilities, skills and creativity in the craft. By externalising the source of inspiration, the *mabube* are able to resolve the apparent paradox of ideal equality and apparent inequality through the passive functioning of dreams as vehicles of that inspiration, and thus account for the range of abilities expressed by weavers.

NOTES

1. See also Meier's article on demon inspiration in Islam describing how Arab poets and others not normally given to poetry received poetic inspiration in dreams (1966:421-9).
2. This belief about dreams is common throughout much of the world; see for example Firth (1934) and Rattray (1927:192) who notes that dreams are caused either by the visitation of denizens of the spirit world or by spirits, such as volatile souls of persons still alive which similarly are said to journey abroad during the hours of sleep.
3. This account of maraboutic practices is largely based on details reported in Gaden (1931).
4. Lincoln states of his "culture-pattern" dreams that they often involve supernatural or spirit manifestations, and are often considered as visions. This distinction between vision and dream is not particularly clear among the Tukolor since they are both considered to be of the same spiritual origin, but one occurs by day and the other by night.

5. Gaden (1931) saw the ambivalence about dreams to be a reaction of Islamised Tukolor to the popular belief in the reality of dreams based on religious conceptions of man not originating in Islamic doctrine. I would hold more to the view that the institutionalisation of dream interpretation in the figure of the marabout adds a weight to his exegesis that individual interpretation does not have. Moreover, the services the marabout performs to avert the events foreshadowed in a dream bolster his own position as a religious specialist, for interpretations are not often falsified since unrealised events foretold by him only point to the presumed efficacy of the medicines he prescribes.

6. A description of classical Islamic interpretation practices, in which this and other texts are used, is given in Von Grunebaum (1966); see also Trimingham (1959:122) on the use of this text among the Tukolor.

7. They are said to possess *barke* or *baraka* in Arabic – a gift of divine grace.

8. Similar ideas were also current in Christian thought during the Middle Ages, when demons came to play a greater part in explanation of the origin of dreams. Even later, Martin Luther was so fearful that he would be unable to distinguish divine from demonic messages that he prayed to God not to speak to him in his dreams (see Van de Castle 1973:28).

9. See also, for example, Hiatt (1979:261), O'Flaherty (1984); Kuper himself applies techniques developed for myth analysis to the analysis of dreams, revealing that both have similar internal and transformational structures.

10. Serer weaving origin myths are also focused on the acquisition (sometimes through stealth and trickery) of the craft from spirits. Again, they refer to dreams or dream-like states in which the techniques are lore of weaving are passed to the ancestral weaver at night. In one particular version of a Serer weaving origin myth I collected, a similar practical/mystical distinction I refer to later in the text above is expressed in the scene of two weaving ancestors who originally co-operated in the early stages of acquiring the craft, until one of them received weaving lore from the spirits. He then continues alone as the forefather of Serer weaving, whereas his acquaintance finds another assistant and they become the ancestors of weaving among the Manjaks (a tribe located further south in Guinea Bissau and along the Senegalese border region). To this day, the Serer point out, Manjako weaving is carried out by two weavers, one operating the secondary heddles, and the other operating the primary heddles and numerous shuttles. The Manjaks are, moreover, excluded from Serer weaving lore, which is more closely linked with that of the Tukolor (see Dilley 1984).

11. The idea of gifts being given through dreams is repeated in the legend of Pegasus and the Chimera, in which Bellerophon received from the divine Athene a golden bridle with which to tame Pegasus and thus overcome the Chimera.

12. Cf. Shakespeare's comment, put into the mouth of Bottom in *A Midsummer's Night's Dream:* "I have had a dream ; past the wit of man to say what this dream was". Indeed, Bottom, also a weaver, was inspired by his dream, in which he was served by a number of fairies, to announce that he would get Peter Quince to write a ballad of it.

13. The idea that individuals with exceptional intellectual and creative abilities are associated with forces external to themselves is not uncommon outside Africa. The word "genius" primarily refers to the tutelary spirit that guides a person through life, and post-classically it took on the reference to special mental endowment (O.E.D.). Similarly, the Arabic word *"'bqariyya"* for genius is derived from *"'abqar"*, a name of a country of jinn (Meier 1966:424).

REFERENCES

ANDRADE, R.G.d', 1961, Anthropological studies of dreams. In F.K. Hsu (ed.), *Psychological Anthropology: approaches to culture and personality.* Illinois: The Dorsey Press, 296-332.

AZEVEDO, W.L.d', 1973, Sources of Gola artistry. In W.L.d'Azevedo (ed.), *The Traditional Artist in African Societies.* Bloomington and London: Indiana University Press, 282-340.

BASTIDE, R., 1966, The sociology of the dream. In G.E. von Grunebaum and R. Callois (eds.), *The Dream and Human Societies.* Berkeley: University of California Press, 199-211.

DEVEREUX, G., 1969, *Reality and Dream: psychotherapy of a Plains Indian.* New York: Anchor Books.

1979, Fantasy and symbol as dimensions of reality. In R.H. Hood (ed.), *Fantasy and Symbol: studies in anthropological interpretation.* London etc: Academic Press, 19-31.

DILLEY, R.M., 1984, *Weavers among the Tukolor of the Senegal River Basin: a study of their social position and economic organisation,* unpublished D.Phil. Thesis. University of Oxford.

1989, Secrets and Skills: apprenticeship among Tukolor weavers. In M.W. Coy (ed.), *Apprenticeship: From Theory to Method and Back Again* New York: SUNY Press.

EMERSON, R.W., 1896, *Lectures and Biographical Sketches.* Boston: Houghton, Mifflin & Co.

FIRTH, R., 1934, The meaning of dreams in Tikopia. In E.E. Evans-Pritchard *et al* (eds.), *Essays Presented to C.G. Seligman.* London: Kegan Paul, 63-74.

GADEN, H., 1931, *Proverbes et Maximes Peuls et Toucouleurs.* Paris: Institut d'Ethnologie.

HIATT, L.R., 1979, Queen of Night, Mother-Right and Secret Male Cults. In R.H. Hook (ed.), *Fantasy and Symbol: studies in anthropological interpretation.* London, etc: Academic Press, 247-265.

KUPER, A., 1979, A structural approach to dreams. *Man,* 14 : 645-662.

LINCOLN, J.S., 1935, *The Dream in Primitive Cultures.* London: Cresset Press.

MALINOWSKI, B., 1927, *Sex and Repression in Savage Society.* London: Kegan Paul.

MEIER, F., 1966, Some aspects of inspiration by demons in Islam. In G.E. von Grunebaum and R. Callois (eds.), *The Dream and Human Societies.* Berkeley: University of California Press, 421-429.

O'FLAHERTY, W.D., 1984, *Dreams, Illusions and other Realities.* Chicago and London: The University of Chicago Press.

RATTRAY, R.S., 1927, *Religion and Art in Ashanti.* London: Oxford University Press.

SELIGMAN, C.G., 1927, Note by C.G. Seligman. In R.S. Rattray, *Religion and Art in Ashanti.* London: Oxford University Press.

TRIMINGHAM, J.S., 1959, *Islam in West Africa.* Oxford: The Clarendon Press.

VAN DE CASTLE, R.L., 1973, The psychology of dreaming. In S.G.M. Lee and A.R. Mayes (eds.), *Dreams and Dreaming: Selelcted Readings.* Harmondsworth: Penguin, 17-32.

VON GRUNEBAUM, G.E., 1966, Introduction: the cultural function of the dream as illustrated by classical Islam. In G.E. von Grunebaum and R. Callois (eds.), *The Dream and Human Societies.* Berkeley: University of California Press, 3-21.

BERTI DREAM INTERPRETATION

LADISLAV HOLY
University of St. Andrews

In most cultures, dreams are perceived as having meaning. In the post-Freudian West, they are understood as indicators of dreamers' anxieties, their repressed feelings, emotions and unconscious. Following this typically Western notion of what dreams mean, a number of recent anthropological studies have been concerned with dreams as clues to understanding the dreamers' unconscious preoccupations: one whole recent issue of *Ethos* (1981), the Journal of the Society for Psychological Anthropology, has been devoted to dreams. Most non-Western peoples too consider dreams as endowed with meanings which can be understood if the dream images (or, as some call them, "dream motifs") are properly interpreted. As they do not regard dreams as internally generated and expressive of dreamers' innermost wishes, their interpretations are not meant to arrive at the knowledge of what is in the minds of the dreamers but at the knowledge of their future, of events which they will encounter or outcomes of their actions or intended actions. In interpreting their dreams, they are not doing psychoanalysis, but semiotics.

While the notion that dreams contain encoded messages about the future and are thus semiotic systems par excellence seems to be general (and shared in the folk cultures of the West), cultures differ in the attention which they pay to dreams and in the importance which they attach to them.

Berti dreams

The Berti are not encouraged to dream and to remember their dreams. According to Lincoln's (1935) classification, their dreams are "individual dreams" – unsought spontaneous dreams occuring during sleep; they have no sought or induced "culture-pattern" dreams. Unlike various other African peoples (eg. Maragoli [Wagner 1949], Zulu [Berglund 1976]), for the Berti dreaming is a private affair and unlike many other peoples (e.g. the Mehinaku [Gregor 1981],), they only rarely tell others in the morning what they dreamt about or discuss their dreams with others. A dream remembered in the morning is rather an exception and a dreamless night is normal. When I asked informants if they had dreamt last night, on most occasions they replied that they had not, and often added that they had not dreamt for weeks. Sleep scientists have established that dreaming is a normal experience for all individuals every night and is essential to physical and mental health (Jones

1976: 24-42). There is no reason why the Berti should be an exception to the norm; it is rather that they make no effort to remember their dreams. Although they treat the dreams they do remember not as individual manifestations revealing the dreamer's psychology but as cultural representations (in the sense that the meanings of particular dream motifs are culturally shared), they show significant psychological insight in their belief that people dream mostly when they are worried about something.

Central to the Berti theory of dreams is the concept of spirit (*ruh*) which all living things, including animals and plants, possess. Although there is a clear consensus that it is nourished by water or depends on it for its existence – which is the reason why any living thing dies without it – there is no clear agreement as to where the seat of spirit is in the human body. Some maintain that it is the heart, others suggest the liver and yet others – mostly pious Muslims – believe that the spirit resides everywhere in the body. Whatever the case, the spirit is intangible and detachable from the body; during the night, when one sleeps, it wanders about moving freely to far-away places or back and forth in time, and its nightly expeditions are experienced as dreams. If one dreams, for example, of a relative who lives in a far-away place or of one who died a long time ago, this is because the spirit has been taken on its wanderings to these far-away places or times. The Berti have no explanation as to why the spirit leaves the body, but they recognise that its presence in the body is the condition of life and that a person dies when the spirit leaves the body for good, as plants or animals die when their spirit leaves them. For this reason, they avoid waking people suddenly from their sleep lest the spirit, which may be wandering outside the body, cannot return to it while the person is still asleep. The person would die on awakening. Dreams predict the future because the dreamers have no control over the nightly expeditions of their spirits.

There are no specialists whom the dreamer consults about the meaning or significance of his or her dreams. Everyone interprets their own dreams and only rarely is a kinsman, close neighbour or friend who is more knowledgeable in these matters consulted when a dreamer has an unusual dream of whose significance he or she is unsure. In interpreting their dreams, the Berti concentrate in their recollection of their dream experiences on events and objects in the dream story which they regard as meaningful signs. As among Moroccans (Kilborne 1981b:302; cf. also Kilborne 1981a), the interpretation of the dream thus focuses on specific signs rather than the encompassing story as a whole. For this reason, the recollections and rendering of dreams are brief. They are usually snapshot episodes rather than stories and emphasis is placed on signs that the dreamer sees as significant for the meaning of his or her dream. The setting of dreams is always familiar, typically one's own house, village, its immediate environment, or the local well or market place; few dreams are set in towns or distant places which the dreamers have previously visited as labour migrants. A typical actual report of a specific dream I elicited from a male informant runs: "I dreamt that I was riding a camel past a village and a dog ran out from the village, was furiously barking at me and wanted to bite me". Where the man travelled from, where he was going, why he travelled, what was the name of the village, whose dog ran after him and what preceded and followed the episode were not spontaneously mentioned and probably forgotten; the informant claimed that he did not know when I asked him specific questions along these lines. That the camel and the dog were all that he seemed to remember and spontaneously mention derives from the fact that these two animals are important keys to the meaning of this particular dream. All the other dreams I recorded were similarly brief, concrete and realistic with hardly any bizarre content or distorted images of reality.

When interpreting their dreams, the Berti select certain dream motifs, and they do likewise when they narrate their dreams. As dreams are remembered because of their possible relevance to the dreamer's future, a dream which began as a product of the individual unconscious is transformed in the process of its conscious recollection into a cultural artefact in the sense of a culturally determined set of relevant signs.

Dream interpretation

Most anthropological studies of dream interpretation, influenced perhaps by psychoanalytic insights, have emphasised the notion of what Freud called displacement: the dream represents something that does not itself occur in it. This manifests itself most often in the understanding that the dream means the opposite of what its manifest content ostensibly indicates (cf. LeVine 1982:67, 73; Tedlock 1981:313; Stephen 1982: 108). This recourse to symbolic reversal in dream interpretation seems to be indeed widespread and includes our own folk maxims, such as "to dream of a birth means death" (cf. Tylor 1974:1, 110). Two important monographs on dreams from Mayan communities in Mexico which appeared in the mid 1970s led to the conclusion that there were two other main rules governing the interpretation of the meaning of a dream. According to one of these rules, the dream is seen as a metaphoric or metonymic representation of future events, i.e. it has to be interpreted analogically to arrive at its true meaning; according to the other one, it is seen as directly representing future events, in which case it is interpreted literally (Bruce 1975:20; Laughlin 1976:9).

The Berti operate with similar rules, but unlike the Tzotzil (Laughlin 1976:9), they do not invoke them randomly. Dreams are understood as containing encoded messages. In this respect, they are semiotic systems and as with any semiotic system, certain decisions about how the encoded messages should be read must be taken in order to arrive at the correct interpretation of their meaning. These decisions themselves are rule governed. The decision as to whether to interpret the manifest content of a dream either analogically or as a direct representation of future events follows a rule which clearly gives preference to the mode of thought dependent on analogy for its operation (Freud's [1953] primary process, Piaget's [1962] symbolic thought and Levi-Strauss's [1966] concrete thinking) over the thought geared to temporal sequentiality and cause-effect relationships (Freud's secondary process, Piaget's operational thought and Lévi-Strauss's rational or logical thought). In accordance with this preference, the manifest content of the dream is interpreted as a direct representation of things to come if no signs are recognised in the dream story which would alert the dreamer to an analogical interpretation. A woman dreamt of a woman whom she had never seen before, passing through her village and shouting that there would be no rain that year. She interpreted her dream as indicating that there would be drought and when that really occurred, she had the correctness of her interpretation confirmed. On the other hand, a man who dreamt that he was sitting under a tree when suddenly a strong wind started to blow did not understand his dream as a prediction of windy weather, as wind in a dream is immediately recognised as a sign of anything undesirable in the future. Accordingly, he interpreted his dream as a bad omen and again had his interpretation confirmed when the next day boys from a neighbouring village set the dry savannah grass on fire.

When no signs are recognised in the manifest content of the dream, and this content itself is in consequence understood as the direct representation of future events, the dream is not only understood as making a prediction of specific events, but what these events are going to be is itself established solely through intratextual interpretation (Tedlock 1981:313-14) of the dream's manifest content, i.e. by focusing on the dream imagery alone. When, on the other hand, the dream motifs are recognised as signs rather than direct representations of the future, three decisions have to be made:

1. Should the meaning of the dream be understood as the reversal of its manifest content or not?

2. Does the dream predict some specific event or is its message merely of general significance?

3. Should the dream be interpreted intratextually or should contextual factors be taken into consideration in the proper understanding of its message?

Answers to these questions are determined by the character of the signs which the dreamers recognise in the manifest content of their dreams. Following

Pierce's classification, the dream motifs recognised as meaningful signs can be seen as falling into two categories: indices which stand in a metonymic relationship to the thing or event they indicate, and symbols which are linked by a metaphoric relationship to what they stand for.

Dream motifs as indices

The dream motifs which have the character of indices can be seen as standing in five particular relationships to the things they indicate:

a) as particular to general
b) as general to particular
c) as part to whole
d) as subsequent to precedent
e) as precedent to subsequent.

Indices which stand in the relationship of particular to general are the most common. They include all dream images seen as particular members of a class, and interpreted as indicating the class in general, as, for example, when one dreams of being struck by a stone and this particular kind of hostile behaviour is interpreted as indicating that the dreamer will encounter an enemy in the future. This enemy, of course, may display hostility in a different manner (especially since striking another with a stone is an unusual form of physical attack among the Berti). Further instances include the following:

Index	Referent	Note
Fight	Dispute, quarrel, theft of property, physical violence against the dreamer	
Goat	Wealth and prosperity	Ownership of goats is just one possible way among others of acquiring riches
Being shot at with a gun	To encounter an enemy	
Sword Gun	Strength or more money	The sword or the gun indicates a particular way in which one can be strong and is

| | | one particular index of affluence (ownership of a horse or fine cloths may be others) |
| Search party (*faza'*) | Fatigue | Participating in a search party is a particularly tiring activity (weeding fields, digging a well, travelling to the desert, etc., may be others) |

Some general events are taken to indicate particular instances of their occurence. For example, a gathering of people in a particular house, which may occur during a birth, circumcision, wedding, sacrifice, funeral, etc., is taken to indicate that death will occur in that house. Similarly a sacrifice which is performed on various occasions indicates death, i.e. one particular event is selected, out of many, which are accompanied by sacrifice. The market, a place where one may gain as well as lose, is taken to indicate money; a gun which may be used in different contexts (hunting, fighting, shooting during a wedding, circumcision, etc.) is taken to indicate the birth of a son, which is just one particular event out of many in which it is used; pieces of iron indicate money, coins being one particular form of metal.

In some cases, part of an event is indicative of the whole. An example is women's ululation or the men's version (*korarak*), which indicates a wedding or a search party (i.e. some of the occasions of which it is a part), and is taken to mean the occurrence of one of these events in the direction from which the dreamer heard it in the dream. Dreaming of milking cows and of a full milking vessel indicates that the cows will prosper and multiply; spilling the milk from the milking vessel indicates, on the other hand, their death. A full, round body is an index of youth and good health, and in consequence to dream of fat meat indicates a young person, while to dream of lean meat indicates an old person.

Indices which stand in sequential relationship to their referents (either as subsequent indicating a precedent or precedent indicating a subsequent) are the least common forms. An example of an event which is indicative of a precedent is a dream of a court, which indicates the occurrence of a prior offence. Conversely, to dream of grasping someone's throat, an event which in waking life would certainly lead to a case being brought before a village moot or a court, indicates victory in a court case; to dream of having one's throat grasped indicates the loss of a case.

The dream image as such stands in the relationship of precedent to the event it represents (its subsequent) when the dream is interpreted as directly representing a future event, and I would suggest that when precedent is taken to indicate subsequent, the dream is not interpreted analogically. In fact, the only difference between an anological or literal interpretation of the dream about being seized by the throat lies in the shift of the specificity of the referent. On literal interpretation, this would indicate that someone is going to grasp the dreamer's throat, while on analogical interpretation, where one possible specific referent is replaced by a different but equally specific one, it indicates the dreamer's loss in a court case. This shift is achieved through interpreting the given sign metaphorically. In the cases of the other classes of indices (particular indicates general, general indicates particular and part indicates whole), the referent of the event is either broadened (in cases of particular indicating general and part indicating whole) or narrowed down (general indicating particular) but remains in each case specific. In this respect, the interpretation of dreams whose motifs have the character of indices parallels the interpretation of dreams not containing any recognisable signs: both of these types of dreams are taken to predict specific events. There are, however, at least three dream motifs (conversation, counting money and prayer) which do not predict any specific events but are taken to indicate the future general well-being and prosperity of the dreamer. As a particular positively valued event is here taken to indicate a positively valued state of existence in general, these dream motifs could be seen as indices of the "particular indicates general" type. But as all other indices are interpreted as messages about quite specific events which await the dreamer in the future, the question arises as to whether they are, in fact, understood by the Berti themselves as indices, or whether they are rather understood by them in the same way as other general symbols which express abstract ideas of a broad and general kind. Such symbols are in consequence interpreted as good or bad omens which do not point to any particular or specific events in the future but to generally favourable or unfavourable circumstances which the dreamer is likely to encounter.

Dreams whose motifs have the character of indices are also similar to dreams with no recognised signs in that both types of dreams are interpreted intratextually by focusing on the dream imagery alone. The only exception is the dream motif of a gun, which is an ambivalent sign and can only be properly interpreted contextually. In itself, it may indicate future affluence (when it is read as particular standing for general) or the birth of a son (when it is read as general indicating particular). Obviously, in the case of a single person or one past childbearing age, it will be read as indicating future riches; in the case of a young married person it is likely to be read as indicating the birth of a son.

Dream motifs as symbols

The signs appearing in dreams have the character of symbols when they do not stand in a relationship of spatial or temporal contiguity to the things and events they refer to. Two kinds of symbols are involved in dream interpretation: 1) symbols particular to dreams and 2) general symbols, i.e. symbols which are recognised as such in waking life, where they are employed in ritual and divination.

I classify as symbols particular to dreams those objects and events which are not used as standardised vehicles of meaning in waking life. Two features can be noted about dream symbols:

1. Like indices and dreams with no recognised signs, they indicate the occurrence of particular events in the future.

2. In most dream symbols, the prediction of specific events is based on symbolic reversal in the sense that a positively valued object or event appearing in the dream indicates the future occurrence of a negatively valued event, and vice versa. It is this reversal that motivates the symbol.

Symbolic reversal is evident in the following instances:
Rain indicates locusts (rain is beneficent and locusts detrimental to crops).
Recovery from illness indicates death.
New white cloths indicate death.
Killing a snake indicates that a pregnant woman will miscarry or a child will die in a village.

Similarly, negatively valued images stand for positively valued events:
Locusts indicate plenty of rain.
Illness or death indicates long life.
Dirty cloths indicate health and long life.
Being bitten by a snake indicates pregnancy or the birth of a son.
Excrement indicates abundance of grain and satisfaction of one's hunger.
Lice indicate money.

With a few dream symbols, the symbolic reversal is not clearly apparent. Nevertheless, these symbols share with other dream symbols the arbitrary metaphoric relationship between the dream image and the future event it indicates. Thus iron indicates more children, a broken tooth indicates the death of a relative and rabbit indicates gain (a person who has dreamt of a rabbit before going to the market will gain in the market; there is a possible reverse relationship involved here in that a rabbit runs away from a person whereas gain comes to a person).

Like most indices, dream symbols are interpreted intratextually, with the exception of dreams about snakes. In general, a snake is taken to indicate an enemy. When one dreams of killing a snake, this indicates that one will win a dispute or overcome an enemy. As mentioned above, the same dream can be interpreted as indicating that a pregnant woman will miscarry or a child will die in the village. Whether one or the other interpretation is followed depends on the circumstances of the dreamer, i.e. the dream can only be correctly interpreted contextually. Similarly, to dream of being bitten by a snake indicates the loss of a dispute and the victory of one's enemy. This is an interpretation followed in the case of a dreamer involved in a dispute or court case. If that is not the case, the same dream is taken to indicate pregnancy or the birth of a son.

Whereas symbols particular to dreams are not used as vehicles of meaning in waking life, general symbols have the same significance in waking life and in dreams. Unlike dream symbols which indicate particular events, general symbols signify the future occurrence of good or bad states of affairs; dreams whose motifs have the character of general symbols are thus interpreted in general terms as good or bad omens. Berti symbolism resorts to numerous symbolic vehicles: colours, animals, specific objects and specific qualities. In each of these categories of symbolic vehicles, symbols are seen as standing for abstract ideas and values of a broad and general kind. These values in themselves are either positively or negatively valued and in consequence, when general symbols occur as dream images, they are interpreted as predicting the occurrence of desirable or undesirable events and states of affairs.

	Auspicious symbols	*Inauspicious symbols*
Colours	White Green (vegetables, green things, e.g. green cloth) Red	Black
Animals	Horse Donkey	Cow Camel Dog Goat
Objects	Milk Water Rain Grain Stone (it is a good sign if one dreams of climbing a hill as hills are rocky and stone is a symbol of endurance and longevity)	Fire Wind
Qualities	Wet	Dry

When a dream image contains two or more symbols, they either reinforce one another and strengthen the prediction, or one of them modifies the meaning of the other. Colours in particular function in this respect as modifiers. This indicates their overall importance as vehicles of symbolic meaning which obviously derives from the fact that they are more abstract and in their imagery more removed from what they stand for, and hence more powerful symbols than other vehicles. For example, a dream of a horse is a good dream; the horse is an auspicious symbol which indicates long life and a good future (e.g. a good rainy season); it stands in particular for strength, authority, power, wealth, children, a wife. The future of the dreamer is seen as particularly good if he has dreamt of riding a white or red horse. To dream of riding a black horse, on the contrary, is a bad omen: the significance of colour as the vehicle of symbolic meaning modifies, and on interpretation overrides, the significance of the other symbolic vehicle.

It is also the action of the dreamer in relation to the symbolic vehicle that is taken into consideration in the interpretation of its particular meaning. For example, anything dry is taken to be inauspicious, and to dream of a dry river bed or a dried-up well is a bad omen. If one dreams of having fallen into a dry well from which one had not been rescued, the dream is interpreted as a prediction of death. On the other hand, if one dreams of having fallen into a dry well and having been pulled up from it, the dream is taken as foretelling a good future. Similarly, a dog is an inauspicious symbol, since it is an indication of hunger, a bad harvest and poverty to see a dog in one's dream. This message of a bad future is strengthened if one dreams of having been bitten by a dog. On the other hand, to dream of having killed a dog indicates a good future, well-being and prosperity.

I have already mentioned the similarity of interpretation between dreams whose key motifs have the character of indices and dreams with no recognised signs. Dreams whose key motifs have the character of general symbols differ from dreams of the first two types in that they are taken as predictions of the general state of the dreamer rather than predictions of specific events. Dreams whose key signs have the character of symbols particular to dreams are the only dreams where the manifest value of the key sign indicates the opposite value of the specific event which the sign is taken to predict; in other words, they are the only dreams whose manifest content is the reversal of what it is taken to predict. The mode of interpretation of the four recognisable types of dreams is indicated in the diagram below.

The art of dream interpretation

The crucial variable underlying the decision on whether the dream means the

no signs
(literal interpretation)

signs
(analogical interpretation)

indices

symbols

dream
symbols
(reversal)

general
symbols
(no reversal)

foretell specific events

foretell general state

"snake"
"gun"

ambivalent: recourse
to extra-dream context

"conversation"
"counting money"
"prayer"

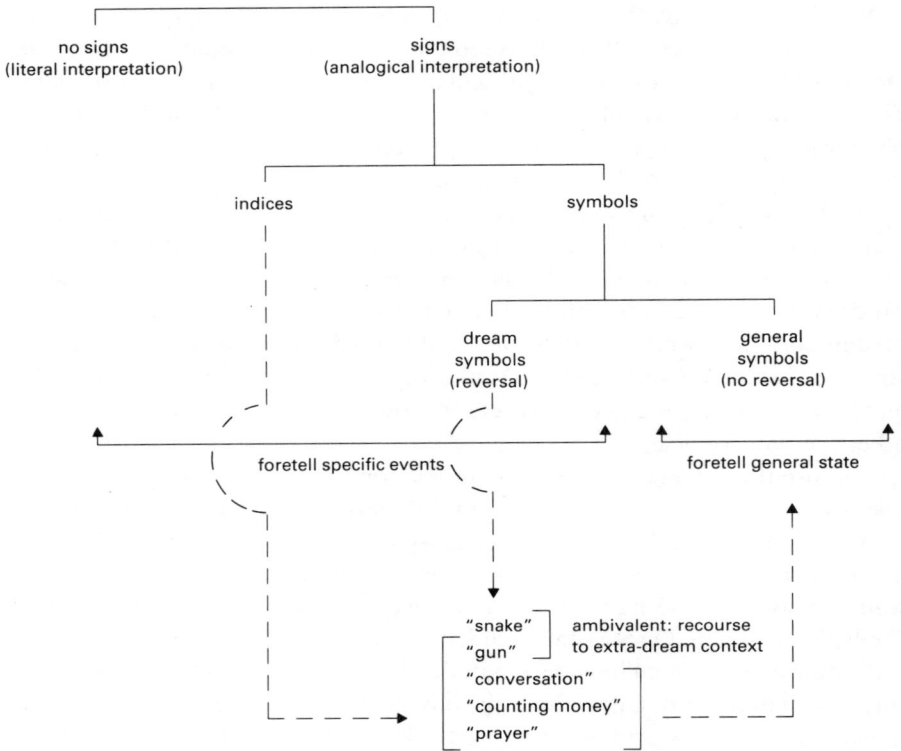

Berti Interpretation of Dream Motifs

same or the opposite of what its manifest content indicates and whether it
predicts a specific or a general event is the appropriate classification of signs as
indices, general symbols or dream symbols. Not all Berti are equally interested
in interpreting their dreams, or equally good at it. Whereas most of them can
suggest what their dreams mean when the dream motifs are recognisable signs
whose significance is known virtually to any adult, only some are able to
properly interpret dreams in which the signs are ambivalent, and the context of
the dream becomes crucial to its proper interpretation. The art of
interpretation among particular individuals varies according to two
dimensions: the extent of the knowledge of signs and the extent of the
awareness of the significance of context. Obviously, people with only limited
knowledge of signs are able to see only some dreams as meaningful. The more
extensive knowledge of possible signs a person possesses, the more dreams he
or she is able to interpret as meaningful and the more likely he or she is to be
able to decide whether to interpret a particular dream analogically or as a direct

prediction of future events. For example, a dream image of a goat can be classified either as an index of wealth or as a general symbol where the goat stands for the devil (*shetan*), and as such has strongly inauspicious connotations. Similarly, the dream image of iron can be classified either as an index of money or as a dream symbol indicating more children, while the dream image of rain can be classified either as a dream symbol which indicates locusts or a general symbol of future well-being and prosperity. In these and similar cases, it is the context of the dream which determines how a particular sign should be properly classified and in consequence the dream properly interpreted. Sensitivity to context thus comes into force when the classification of dream signs is problematic. There are basically three kinds of context to which attention can be paid: the dreamer's personal circumstances, the time of the dream and the location of the dream.

The dreamer's personal circumstances, particularly his or her age and marital status, will ultimately determine whether dreaming of iron, for example, should be interpreted as indicating money or more children. The time of the dream will determine whether dreaming of rain indicates the appearance of locusts or the general well-being and prosperity of the dreamer. A dream occuring shortly before the onset of the rains is likely to be interpreted in the former way, the same dream occuring during any other time of the year in the latter. The location of the dream is particularly significant in the case of bad dreams, such as those about black things: cows, camels and other motifs which have the character of inauspicious symbols. The Berti consider wilderness to be a place ridden with dangers in opposition to the village, which is seen as a place of safety and generosity. Dry river beds, areas with tall trees and hills and rocky outcrops are considered to be particularly dangerous as they are places favoured by devils (*shayatin*), but other places may be potentially dangerous as well. Men who sleep in the open, for example when on pasture with sheep and camels, move to a different location after the occurrence of a bad dream which has alerted them to the dangers of the place in which they have been staying. A dream of a goat would under these circumstances be interpreted as a bad omen; the same dream in one's own house may rather be seen as indicating future riches for the dreamer.

I have already mentioned that different symbols may appear in the same dream, either reinforcing or contradicting one another. This fact would be taken into consideration by a skillful interpreter, whereas a less skillful one may have his or her attention drawn to only one of the symbols and disregard, or be unaware of, the modifying influence of the other. The same obtains when symbols are combined with indices. Most people would understand a dream of meat as indicating death. Meat is, however, not only a dream symbol but also an index of age: lean meat indicates an old person, as a dried out body is for the

Berti a clear sign of old age or illness; fat meat indicates youth and good health. By paying attention to the quality of the meat one has dreamt about, a skillful interpreter is able to be more specific in his prediction of what kind of person is likely to die than one who concentrates merely on the symbol of meat alone.

The rules according to which the Berti operate when interpreting their dreams can be formulated in the following way:

1.   Dreams are interpreted intratextually; contextual interpretation is resorted to only in the case of a few ambivalent signs.

2.   Dreams are interpreted as predicting specific events in the future; only dreams whose signs have the character of general symbols predict the general future state of the dreamers.

3.   The manifest content of the dream itself predicts both specific future events and the general future state of the dreamer, irrespective of whether the manifest dream motifs are interpreted literally or analogically as either indices or symbols; only in the case of symbols particular to dreams is the symbol the reverse of what it stands for.

Needless to say, these rules are unconscious in as much as grammatical rules are. I appreciate that this may be to reiterate the worn out parallel between language and culture. But when it comes to language and dreams as semiotic systems, the parallels are striking. Although language has to be rule- governed in order to function as a semiotic system, most of what its speakers are consciously aware of – in the sense of being able to paraphrase – is the meaning of words and utterances. Most of what the Berti are consciously aware of when interpreting their dreams is the meaning of dream signs. But as it is only through recourse to grammar that one is able to recognise the meaning of received linguistic messages, it is only through recourse to the rules of dream interpretation that a Berti is able to recognise the meaning of messages received in dreams. In this paper I have tried to indicate what these rules are.

REFERENCES

BERGLUND, A.I., 1976, *Zulu Thought – Patterns and Symbolism*. London: Hurst.
BRUCE, R.D., 1975, *Lacandon Dream Symbolism*. Mexico: Editiones Euroamericanas.
FREUD, S., 1953, *A General Introduction to Psychoanalysis*. New York: Permabooks.
GREGOR, T., 1981, "Far far away my shadow wandered ...": the dream symbolism and dream theories of the Mehinaku Indians of Brazil. *American Ethnologist* 8:709–720.
JONES, R.M., 1976, *The New Psychology of Dreaming*. Harmondsworth: Penguin.
KILBORNE, B., 1981a, Pattern, structure and style in anthropological studies of dreams. *Ethos* 9: 165-185.

1981b, Moroccan dream interpretation and culturally constituted defence mechanisms, *Ethos* 9: 294-312.

LAUGHLIN, R.M., 1976, *Of Wonders Wild and New: dreams from Zinacantan*, Smithsonian Contributions to Anthropology No. 22, Washington DC: Smithsonian Institution Press.

LE VINE, S., 1982, The dreams of young Gusii women: a content analysis. *Ethnology* 21: 55-77.

LEVI-STRAUSS, C., 1966, *The Savage Mind*. Chicago: University of Chicago Press.

LINCOLN, J.S., 1935, *The Dream in Primitive Cultures*. London: Cressett Press.

PIAGET, J., 1962, *Play, Dreams and Initiation in Childhood*. New York: W.W. Norton.

STEPHEN, M., 1982, "Dreaming is another power!": the social significance of dreams among the Mekeo of Papua New Guinea. *Oceania* 53: 106-122.

TEDLOCK, B., 1981, Quiche Maya dream interpetation. *Ethos* 9: 313-330.

TYLOR, Sir E.B., 1974 (orig. 1871), *Primitive Culture*, 1-11. New York: Gordon Press.

WAGNER, G., 1949, *The Bantu of Northern Kavirondo*. London.

DREAMS AMONG THE YANSI

MUBUY MUBAY MPIER
Centre d'Etudes Ethnologiques, Bandundu

That dreams occupy a prominent place in the life of the Yansi is evident from a stroll around a village in the early morning, as people are arising from sleep and recounting and discussing the dreams of the night. Before some undertaking, such as going on a hunt or going to the farms in the forest, people will recall their dreams to assess their chances of success. When someone is ill their dreams, as well as those of kinsmen, are carefully examined. All of which suggests that dream experiences are for Yansi as important as, perhaps even in some circumstances more important than, those of waking life.

In an earlier work (1974), I analysed how dreams are perceived by the Yansi and compared their ideas with the scientific conceptions of psychologists. As a result of that comparison I arrived at the conclusion that there is no fundamental difference between the dream conceptions of psychologists and those of the non-literate person, but there is a difference of emphasis because the psychologist through his "how?" question looks for a profound and comprehensive description of dreaming, while the ordinary person through his "why?" question is looking only for the meaning or implication of the dream. In the present work I attempt to deepen our knowledge of the cultural conceptions of the dream among a particular people, the Yansi of Zaire. The objective is to show how the Yansi define and use the dream, and in seeking to find meaning, what general considerations they take into account in order to assist in this search. In short, the aim is to discover the science of dreams according to the Yansi and to find out how this science engages with their everyday life.

The study of a subject such as the one embarked upon here cannot be realised without recourse to those methods which are based on the expression and the understanding of the people concerned, for it is a matter of describing a phenomenon which exists in the intimate experience of each person and which therefore cannot be understood except through their interaction and social relations. This is why the method of case histories and in-depth interviews has been supplemented by participant observation. Specifically, I have been present on several occasions under different circumstances at dream interpretation sessions, particularly during the formalities of dispute settlement and informally during everyday conversations. I have thus accumulated information from personal experience which has allowed me to see the phenomenon which we are studying from the inside. It is a way of seeing which elucidates the subject under study.[1]

The Yansi inhabit the lower Kwilu and Inzia Rivers in Bandundu Province in the Republic of Zaire and are part of the great Central Bantu culture area which extends across central Africa from West to East. It will be useful to outline the main elements of Yansi society.[2] Typically three fundamental features define the structure of Yansi society: the system of stratification, the system of kinship and marriage and the *lebui* priesthood. The population is stratified into members of the aristocratic clan (*kingoma kimwil*, "drum nobles"), free members of other clans (*nsaan*) and individuals belonging to clans in various other ways (pawns, wards, descendants of slaves). Autonomous chiefdoms are composed of five or six nucleated settlements, but because the matrilineal clans are dispersed the influence of chiefship interpenetrates chiefdoms, and a chief with the appropriate personal qualities will be recognized as an arbitrator among several contiguous chiefdoms. There is a stated preference for marriage with the daughter's daughter (*ketiul*), but in practice the maternal grandfather cannot marry his grand-daughter and instead allocates his daughters' daughters among the men of his clan, usually his matrilineage, his sisters' sons. Grandsons (*mutiur*) are an equally important category of persons among Yansi, and in particular the *mutiur* of the aristocratic clan play a signficant role in the relationship between the nobles and the commoners (*nsaan*). From among the *mutiur* of chiefs are drawn the men who alone can handle the corpse of a dead chief and control the wild animals which his death is said to release.

In addition to chiefly power there is a spritual power called *lebui* which is held to be responsible for the fertility of the land, the forest and the general well-being of the people who dwell in it. *Lebui* is manifest in several material embodiments which are in the custody of persons from the five commoner clans who control the custodianships. The majority of deaths are attributed to breaches of the interdictions of the local *lebui*. The territories "controlled" by the custodians of *lebui* are not coincidental with those of the chiefs. The embodiments of *lebui* are part of the general class of more or less powerful objects called *nkidh* (in Kikongo, *nkisi* and in English usually glossed as "fetish" or "medicine") and a complement of the concept *mun* (*ndoki* in Kikongo, "witchcraft").[3] In search for the causes of personal setbacks, attention turns to the possessors of *nkidh* and *mun*, and in this search dreams are highly valued.

The Yansi have a special and appropriate vocabulary concerning dreams.[4] It will therefore be worthwhile to begin by considering this terminology because language is one of the best bridges by which one can cross into the heart of the culture of another people. In Yansi the dream is referred to by the collective noun *ndoey*, a word which also refers to the beard. The singluar form *londoey*, which in fact is seldom heard, refers to one hair in a beard. A dream, then, is also a kind of collectivity, and to refer to several dreams the plural form *mandoey* has to be used. This plural carries, however, a pejorative connotation and is often used when speaking about the dreams of people who indulge excessively in describing their dreams, or to refer to bad and frightening dreams which frequently recur. The experience of dreaming, of having a dream, is described by two expressions, *apwo ndoey,* literally to sleep a dream and *a lor ndoey,* literally to divine, to guess, to foretell a dream. The Yansi therefore do not have an equivalent to the English verb "to dream". The expression *apwo ndoey* seems to be used by adults more than by the young, who seem to prefer the expression *a lor ndoey*, though I do not know why this should be so.

A number of expressions are used which are equivalent to the English expressions "to recount a dream" or "recall a dream". Firstly, *a sami ndoey*, literally, to recount, to announce, or to tell a dream; *a swo ndoey*, literally to show or reveal a dream; *a taa mandoey*, literally to count dreams, to itemise or list a series of dreams.

At funeral assemblies where people gather and attempt to identify the immediate cause of death, which is usually believed to have occurred because of the breach of some magical interdiction (not necessarily by the deceased but perhaps by one of their kin), those who lived as members of the same household as the deceased are asked, "*Taa mandoey!*", "List your dreams!". They are then expected to set out all the dreams which may have a bearing, whether direct or indirect, on the death which is the reason for the assembly.

Several expressions would seem to be indicative of the Yansi notion of dream interpetation. For example, *a bumi ndoey*, literally to turn a dream. The verb *a bumi*, to turn, to turn round, is used in a sense which connotes turning round in order to reveal an otherwise hidden aspect. The symbolic quality of a dream is a consequence of its nature as something inverted. The act of interpreting a dream, or as we might say of decoding the symbolism, is rendered figuratively in Yansi as a turning action which reveals the hidden facet which is the content, the meaning, the message. If someone dreams of the death of an infant in the village, then the dreamer can anticipate success in hunting in the forest. Conversely, a successful hunter and possessor of a hunting fetish (*nkidh*) is vulnerable to accusations of being the cause of the deaths of infants if the latter seem to be abnormally excessive. *A bel ndoey* means literally to pick over a dream, and refers to the careful interpretation of a dream in which no detail and possible symbol is neglected. Its content is then completely elucidated. This expression is used of specialists in the interpretation of dreams, particularly when commending them, and distinguishes between simply turning over, or turning out, the dream in order to discover its gross meaning and the techniques of "picking over", or "combing out", or careful dissection in order to reveal with precision the complexity of meaning. *A kori ndoey* means literally to open up a dream. The same verb *a kori* is also used in connection with proverbs and riddles. To grasp or understand the meaning of a proverb or a riddle is rendered by the expression *a kori kengan* (a proverb), and *a kori soo* (a riddle), to open a proverb or open a riddle. The verb used here implies something closed, and which encloses something desired, but which cannot be acquired except after an act of opening, in this case the opening of a dream.

Ndoey ndeag is an expression used to distinguish an important dream. It is used when speaking about a dream which appears to have important consequences for people. The *ndoey ndeag* is also a dream which will come true. It is to be contrasted with *ndoey mutwe*, "a dream of the head", a dream which happens only in the head and has, therefore, no real significance and whose message is not of general importance. Sometimes *ndoey mutwe* is called *ndoey ndoey*, a dream dream.

True dreams are those where one sees in a dream what later is concretely realised. To say of someone that he dreams true dreams, the Yansi say *nze nde mutwe ndoey*, "you have a head of dreams", that is, through your head events to come or which have passed announce themselves. Typically such persons are owners of a *nkidh* ("fetish" or "medicine"). While all *nkidh* have consequences for people other than the owner, most are primarily charged with protecting the individual interests of the owner. A few, such as the great named clan fetishes or representatives of the land fetish *lebui,* are of very general interest. *Nkidh* are kept by the owner at the head of the bed so that their power may direct and shape the owner's dreams. It is evident from Yansi attitudes that such people are as much feared as they are sought after. They are feared because they can recount dreams which herald misfortune, tragedy and anxiety, but sought after because since they can dream about what is to occur, they can also dream the solution to vexing problems and because they can, by foretelling good fortune, allow people to anticipate contentment. The attitude at any one time to such dreamers is a function of the state of the person who needs to listen to the dreamer.

Conversely, ordinary people may experience true dreams by virtue of those people encountered in dreams. A dreamer will see someone in a dream and be informed by that person of his state of health, his problems, and of the intentions of the person in the dream towards the dreamer, or perhaps towards one of the dreamer's kinsmen. Yansi are very sensitive to such dreams. Certain categories of person, when seen in dreams, bring about real anguish or real jubilation among dreamers. Thus to dream of someone who has the reputation of being a witch (possessor of *mun*) is a cause of anxiety. I have heard reports of a dreamer who almost physically attacked an elder with such a reputation because he was seen in a dream. To dream of one's mother's brother is a source of great uneasiness because the maternal uncle is attributed extraordinary power by Yansi, and it is believed that if the maternal uncle appears in a dream it is invariably in order to threaten and to bewitch.

There is also a person called "the dream teller" (sami-ndoey). It is a distinction given to those storytellers whom it is believed are able by the power of their performances to stun their audiences into a state of dreaming. Their extraordinary character, the audacity of their performances, brings about such astonishment in the listeners that this state is compared to dreaming.

Proverbs can be regarded as a condensed form of the thought of a people, and may therefore be used by the investigator as a privileged source of information on aspects of their culture. However, Yansi proverbs in which the key word is "dream" are rather rare, to judge by the few that I have discovered. Nevertheless, one that is frequently heard is ndoey pwo tol, "to recount a dream is come out of sleep", that is to say, one cannot recall a dream, one does not know one is dreaming, if one is still asleep and unaware. During an assembly called to deliberate on a dispute or at an official tribunal, it is usual to ask of a witness to say what it is that they know about the issue. If the witness has no insight into the problem, in order to assert his ignorance he may say, "a sami ndoey pwo tol!", meaning "I cannot speak of something of which I am unaware [without the danger of lying or misleading]."

The expression "ndoey lor mbua" (the dream of a dog) implies that although the dog can dream of good or bad things nobody can know of this, because it does not have the power of speech and is unable to recount its dreams. In Kikongo there is a similar expression for the same idea: "what the dog sees and knows stays in its heart and dies with it." This proverb is used to speak about those who are unable to keep secrets which are confided to them. Thus it is said that they should keep secrets in the way that a dog keeps its dreams, since the dream of a dog is a well-guarded secret. Alternatively, it is used to speak of those who seldom talk but who listen. It is also used to speak of those who, despite the importance of their thoughts, do not know how to express them, perhaps because they cannot, as in the case of children, or perhaps because they have only an imperfect command of the language.

Although a mentally handicapped person can dream and recount their dreams, no one attributes any importance to these accounts. Such utterances are considered to be an effect of madness. Someone, after having vainly tried to convince another about an experience of his, may say discouragingly that perhaps his experience was a fool's dream (ndoey nkin).

Yansi will sometimes say that a person dreams only of what they like and that what is seen in the dream is what has been preoccupying that person during the day, during waking life. Yansi elders, who, as such, are attributed with some wisdom, know that when they hear recalled dreams, certain of them are only the desires or the apprehensions of waking life. Such dreams are regarded in much the same way as *ndoey mutwe* and are not interpreted with much care. Such a view prefigures that of Freud, who declared dreams to be no more than the realisation of suppressed desires. According to Freud such realization is important since it allows for the discharge of psychic emotions accumulated by the presence of such desires, tensions which can prevent adequate and sufficient sleep. Dreams intervene, therefore, as the protectors of sleep. Yansi elders, however, concede this function only to some dreams, which are for them in many ways the least important of dreams. Indeed they cite this function of a dream in order to discount it.

Anyone telling a seemingly astonishing account of some experience may be asked "*yen ndeag e ndoey?*", which may be translated as "Is that real or a dream?" Such a question shows that a difference is recognised between dream and reality, but these are not symmetrically exclusive categories for Yansi. Where we would use the term "reality", the Yansi uses the term *ndeag*. *Ndeag* refers in the first instance to language, speech or discourse and is extended metonymically to refer to what is talked about, particularly current affairs, matters of discussion and reflection, and manifestly this will include dreams. But the experiences of dreams are not appreciated as dreams until one moves from being asleep to being awake, and the Yansi proverb already cited ("one cannot recount a dream until one has emerged from sleep") expresses this hierarchical relationship.

The dream as a phenomenon is regarded by Yansi as extraordinary. The Yansi adopt several diverse, even contradictory, attitudes to the dream. The principal ones are an attitude of admiration, an attitude of fear, an attitude of attraction and an attitude of indifference. The attitude of admiration is most evident in the conversations of the elders. Gathered in the shade of a tree to deliberate upon a dispute, or in a house, or perhaps casually engaged in making ropes or basket work, they recount their dreams. During these conversations perhaps one of them will exclaim, "God is strangely entertaining! He has even made these things we call dreams". The dream, though difficult to define, is nevertheless an object of admiration. Yansi say it takes wings from a bird and gives them to a man; it paralyses the legs of a man standing before a lorry which is bearing down upon him at great speed; it gives a beard to a small infant; it puts the living and the dead into face to face relationships. Dream life is marvellous: the dreamer is transported to a world which is inaccesable in waking life.

The Yansi are very sensitive to the fact that a sense of unease, even dread, persists after waking from a frightening dream, and that this sensation is not assuaged by knowing that "it was only a dream!". That the Yansi give credence to the message of the dream is shown by the fact that during waking life they remain afraid of those who have frightened them in a dream. It is a matter of urgency to know the meaning of a nightmare or violent dream in order to identify the object of fear. Here is an example of such a dream recounted to me. "I saw and heard my late husband talking to one of our dead grandchildren. 'Let me... I want to show him my anus because he can't see any more... No let me...'. Then he departed angrily saying to my son, 'You had the chance.. I was going to show everything'. But with these words I woke up trembling and sweating with fear." After having recounted her dream, the dreamer elaborated in the following way: "My husband is dead but before he died he called for my son, E., who works in Bakuvu and whom he loved the most of all in the family. To his great disappointment he didn't come back. He sent many letters but he never returned and so he died harbouring ill feelings towards him. Today, in the dream he tried to show him his anus. That is very serious because it means he wants to curse him. It was fortunate, very fortunate that our grandchildren were there to prevent him doing that. But my son E. is still in grave danger because his father still harbours a grudge against him." The dreamer was obviously frightened by the message brought to her in this nightmare. But she took comfort in the ending because their grandchildren (*mutiur*) had intervened.

Dreams which provoke fear engender anxiety, and although this is obviously felt by the dreamer, among Yansi it will spread out among his kinsmen. The anxiety which results frequently makes the dreamer and close kin exercise caution in all their subsequent activities that day, perhaps even extending to the next day. Sometimes certain dreamers will refuse to work at all, or at least will do only light work during the day. As for the nature of this anxiety, it is above all an anxiety about death: it is death, or a sickness which can bring about death, which is feared and which the dream message announces.

In certain circumstances dreams are sought after. People wish to have dreams as commentaries upon their current circumstances. These could be as follows: before some important activity, before going hunting in order to find out whether it would be worth while, before making a journey and so on. Dreams are also looked for before, during or after a ritual. For example twins, unlike other children, need to be ritually integrated into the clan. For this purpose the chief of the clan brings together the women and the most powerful elders of the clan for the ceremony at a time fixed in advance. In order to identify the day for the ceremony the clan elders pass the night out in the open under the stars. In the morning all the dreams of the night are recalled and carefully interpreted to learn how the dead are disposed towards the ceremony, for they are supposed to participate with the living whenever the clan comes together. Moreover, during the ceremonies the dreams of the elders constitute a test of success or failure. In litigation and judical processes, dreams are attended to in order to learn the likely outcome, or when people are waiting for the results or outcome of some undertaking which has been embarked upon, or when someone is seeking to know in advance the possible result of some project. For example, a hunter waits for a dream to tell him whether game has been caught in his traps if he is undecided as to whether to visit his traps or to attend to some other pressing matter. In general in all crucial situations the Yansi pay particular attention to the discussion of dreams. This is expressed as a desire to know whether non-human forces oppose or are favourably disposed to the purposes and outcomes of their actions. At the same time to talk about crucial social circumstances is to talk about the psychic tension experienced by individuals. The dreams which are desired are aimed precisely at the alleviation of this tension. A catharsis is achieved after a dream reflecting the circumstances and the subject of tension, whether it is in favour of the dreamer or not. Indeed in both cases anxiety seems to be diminished in the individual suffering from tension by the mere fact that they have had a dream commenting upon the object of tension, which is taken as indicative of the intervention of a non-human force, even if intervention can only be established after the interpretation of a dream. In other words from the perspective of the individual, the active pursuit of dreams is a means of reducing psychological tension as well as provoking discussion of the resolution of social conflicts.

Some dreams, mainly those of infants, are a matter of indifference to Yansi. Other dreams have themes so removed from everyday life that they seem to have no significance at all. Everything depends upon the social situation of the dreamer and his household. In effect in normal situations dreams are considered to be insignificant, but in a situation of crisis they are interpreted with great care. For the individual no dream is entirely without significance.[5] No dream can be neglected because the dream which is ignored perhaps announces the dreamer's death. Yansi say, "We are men, we die in the dream". In practice the dreams which are given the greatest public attention are those experienced when the clan is facing a crisis, such as when restoring to a place of honour a fetish which has been abandoned and therefore has been provoking sickness, or when the clan must decide whether or not to emancipate a slave lineage, or when deliberating on the distribution of bridewealth received. Moreover, on these occasions special attention is accorded to the dreams of certain persons distinguished because of their social position in the clan and the transitional or mediatory nature of their being. Thus the dreams of a clan chief, of fetish owners, of diviners, of guardians of clan fetishes, of twins, of pregnant women and of ill persons are considered with particular care.

Three glosses have been given for Yansi expressions for dream interpretation: 1) "turning a dream the right way round" (a bumi ndoey); 2) "opening a dream" (*a kori ndoey*); 3) "picking over a dream" (*a bel ndoey*). The dream is not directly comprehensible. It has to be "turned the right way up", it has to be "opened up", it has to be "picked over" in order to apprehend the message, and it is through these essentially social procedures that Yansi secure the guidance which they have need of in order to give their lives direction. Not surprisingly Yansi describe the people who can interpret dreams as persons with intelligence, maturity, patience, experience and knowledge of tradition, and it is no less surprising that in practice they turn out to be the clan elders. In a village there is always a small number of old men, elders who have a reputation for knowing how to interpret dreams. It is to their houses that people will go to seek to find out the meaning of their dreams. It frequently happens that a dream is the object of discussion among several old men in order to better interpret it. The interpretation of one person is perhaps flawed and will therefore give a false meaning to the dream. Such dreams are often those which happen at a critical moment for the clan, lineage or village as opposed to those concerning an individual. During my own childhood in a Yansi village I was able to establish that my father was very solicitous as regards the interpretation of dreams. An elder by the name of Mungwon was similarly inclined, but I also noted that the latter, though much older than my father, came from time to time to our house, told my father of a dream and compared his own interpretation with that of my father.

According to Yansi the most propitious time to interpret a dream is the instant which follows its appearance. Mainly in order to avoid forgetting the dream, spouses recount to each other and discuss their dreams in the morning. If one has had a dream which seems particularly significant, he or she will wake the other and recount the dream. A brief and simple interpretation is made. This will take place at any time during the night. Over and above this, many people recount their dreams in the morning before setting out to work. The importance of the morning interpretation of dreams lies in the fact that if someone identifies some bad augury he or she will refrain from work in the forest beyond the safety of the village. On the other hand, if the signs are propitious then one can anticipate finding, for example, traps full of game or success in a fishing expedition. On certain days, particularly Thursdays, when hard work is prohibited, people confine themselves to light work in the village such as basket weaving. They gather in the shade and chat during the work, and it is here that dreams are recounted and interpreted. Dreams are rarely interpreted in the evening. Discussion of dreams is avoided at this time of day, according to Yansi so that they will not repeat themselves.

Each time a dream is told a determination through interpretation is made first of all as to whether it is a good or bad omen. For example, to dream that one is mourning the death of an infant signifies that one will be successful in hunting, and kill game. Therefore it is a good dream. To dream that an ancestor comes and offers a goat is a good dream because it signifies that the ancestor comes to offer a present and in practice this will turn out to be in the form of fame. On the other hand to dream that one has been arrested by soldiers is a bad dream as it signifies that one has fallen into a trap set by sorcerers. To dream that one has been wounded by a buffalo indicates that one is being attacked by a sorcerer. The wound inflicted by the buffalo means that the sorcerer has successfully inflicted an injury and in short foretells a sickness, and is therefore a bad dream. In another category are dreams which begin by being "good" but end with a bad message, or vice versa. The Yansi say that the dream has "become bad" or that the dream has "become good". For example, a dream which begins with the dreamer being arrested by soldiers but ends with his escape from them indicates that the dreamer has been caught by a sorcerer's trap and escaped, and so they have not succeeded in injuring him. One informant reported the following dream, "I entered into a small backwater and a crocodile caught me by the head. I shouted at my son who was waiting on the bank to pull me by the legs. My son succeeded in pulling me from the throat of the crocodile, but, although I was seriously injured, I was able to return to the village." Another informant provided the following commentary upon the dream. "The dream is bad because you have been caught by a sorcerer but it became good when you were pulled from its throat. The sorcerer was partly successful because although you returned to the village you were injured. This is not serious. The essential thing was to have been rescued from the clutches of the sorcerer."

Clearly Yansi do not consider dreams to be a source of information about the psycho-dynamics of an individual. Rather they are taken into account in giving meaning to the actions and interactions of self and of others. Dreams do not determine Yansi courses of action, although that may seem to be the case because dreams recalled are used to modify and to give a sense of direction to a certain course of action. It is important to remember that the Yansi ideas about dreams, their attitudes and sentiments about them which have been outlined in this paper, are an integral part of a much wider and extra-dream configuration of elements of which the most prominent are *mun* (witchcraft) and *nkidh* (medicine). Dreams are not only evidence of these extra-human forces in human relationships, but also, according to Yansi, a means of acquiring knowledge about them whereby their powers can be rendered effective or ineffective according to a person's interests.

NOTES

1. This study has benefitted from investigations made into dreams among the Yansi by Mundala Mpangande (1980; 1981) which comprise two volumes in typescript preserved

in the archives of CEEBA.

2. The most useful sociological studies of Yansi are those of G. de Plaen (1967; 1968; 1974) and E. and G. de Plaen (1967). Also valuable is the work of R.P. Swartenbroeckx (1948; 1964; 1969) and P. Malembe (1967). R. de Beaucorps' (1933) monograph is rather partial and superficial.

3. *Mun* is comparable to the Tiv notion of *tsav* (Bohannan 1957) and Lugbara *ole* (Middleton 1964) in so far as it is a morally ambivalent dimension of the power to sanction attributed to men of influence and authority such as clan elders. See also Batukezangu (1972) and MaMpolo (1976) on *ndoki* and MacGaffey (1977) on *nkisi*.

4. All the terms used here are from the Yansi dialect of the Kmobo chiefdom, one of the chiefdoms of the Nsala-Mbanda grouping. These form a Yansi grouping inhabiting the Mushuni region on the left bank of the river Inzia.

5. "Each dream yields up a meaning. A dream which is not interpreted is a letter which has not been opened" (Fromm 1952; 103).

REFERENCES

BATUKEZANGU, Z., 1972, *Bandoki*. Kinshasa: Ed. St-Paul.

BEAUCORPS, R. de, 1933, *Les Bayansi du Bas-Kwilu*. Louvain: Editions de L'AUCAM.

BOHANNAN, P., 1967, *Justice and Judgement among the Tiv*. London: Oxford University Press.

FROMM, E., 1952, *Le Langage Oublié*. Paris: Payot.

MALEMBE, P., 1967, La Société politique Yansi. *Cahiers Economiques et Sociaux* 5: 221-235.

MA MPOLO, M., 1976, *La Liberation des Envoutés*. Yaounde: Ed. CLE.

MacGAFFEY, W., 1977, Fetishism revisited: Kongo *Nkisi* in sociological perspective. *Africa* 47: 172-184.

MIDDLETON, J., 1964, *Lugbara Religion*. London: Oxford University Press.

MPANGANDE, M., 1980, Reves Yansi. Unpublished in Archives CEEBA, 84: 1-64.

1981, Songes et presages. Unpublished in Archives CEEBA, 87: 1-58.

MPIER, M.M., 1974, Conceptions Culturelles et Scientifiques des Rêves. Unpublished Thesis, University of Zaire, Kisangani.

PLAEN, E. and G. de, 1967, Mariage et tension sociales. *Cahiers Economiques et Sociaux* 5: 415-453.

PLAEN, G. de, 1967, Note sur les funerailles d'un chef Yansi. *Cahiers Economiques et Sociaux* 5: 203-220.

1968, Role social de la magie et de la sorcellerie chez les Bayansi. *Cahiers Economiques et Sociaux* 6: 203-235.

1974, *Les Structures d'Autorité chez les Bayansi*. Paris: Presses Universitaires.

SWARTENBROECKX, R.P., 1948, Traite des migrations Yansi: quand l'Ubangi vient au Kwango. Bayansi ou Babingi? *Zaire* 2: 723-755.

1964, Les institutions matrimoniales des Bayansi du Congo. *Bull. Soc. roy. Belge. Anthrop.* 75: 97-105.

1969, La magie chez les Yansi du Congo. *Bull. Soc. roy. Belge. Anthrop.* 80: 187-226.

INGESSANA DREAMING

M.C. JĘDREJ
University of Aberdeen

For the people of the Ingessana Hills in the Republic of the Sudan the dream is a dimension of experience which has an important institutional aspect. Dreaming has been appropriated and represented socially and culturally in a manner which shares many characteristics with non-industrial societies, both ancient and contemporary, but which also has features which are, as one might expect, particular to the Ingessana themselves. The subject of this paper is then what Malinowski (1927:93) has called "official dreams". Dreams are an intensely subjective experience and they can only be reported, never observed. Yet in the Ingessana Hills great public undertakings involving people over large areas and the production, distribution and consumption of considerable quantities of goods regularly proceed as a consequence of dreams. This is not because Ingessana confuse subjective and objective realities so that for them life is "a long dream" (Tylor 1865:137), but indicates that people take into account dreams as well as the events of waking experience. The problem, as Shweder (1982) has pointed out, is not that non-literate peoples have remained "childlike" by retaining an inability to distinguish between events experienced in dreams and events experienced while awake. Instead, having as children learned, like children everywhere, to distinguish the events in dreams as unreal and subjective in contrast to the objective real world, some, depending on their society, then confront an adult world where an explicit theory of dreams (or at least certain dreams) as external perceptions prevails not in ignorance of the facts of waking experience but apparently regardless of them. There is nothing peculiar to dreams about this kind of ambiguity, which is quite comparable to Mauss' analysis of the gift. According to Ingessana dreams contain, as ever, messages, but these are not communications from different localities within the architecture of the dreamer's personality but communications from components of a cosmology in which the dreamer is situated. It is unlikely that this cosmology has ever been formulated explicitly by the people but since, like other communications, the supposed senders will in the process convey information about themselves, it may be possible to construct a cosmology by inference from such contextual and marginal data.

Like the Greeks before Aristotle, Ingessana talk about certain significant dreams as the consequence of the activities of supernatural beings impinging upon the dreamer (Dodds 1951:104-117). When ordinary people (*jok bark*) dream they sometimes see images which, according to Ingessana, doctor-diviners (*kaik*) and *cak* (people with what we, like the Ingessana, describe as "second-sight" or "second eyes") can see while awake. In addition, such extraordinary people have dreams which no ordinary person ever has. Many of the stories ordinary people tell about events and encounters in their lives are remarkable because they seem to confirm the existence of a boundary, a boundary which we draw in terms of experiences in the external world of reality and the internal world of the imagination but which for Ingessana is located between different kinds of people. The following story arose in the course of a conversation among a group of men about hunting, a favourite topic and preoccupation. "I suddenly came across a buffalo standing in the undergrowth. I fired at it and struck it but it didn't fall there. It ran off a short way and then fell and died at the entrance to that fearful temple at Mathelk which I hadn't noticed. I left the buffalo alone and called to Ngalow [the name of the custodian of the temple] and said to him 'One of your cows in down.' So I left it to Ngalow. Ngalow never brought me a piece of the meat and I have never spoken to him since about the affair." This incident is not only about the speaker's prowess as a hunter and the cultivation of that reputation but about Ngalow who, as the teller indicated by referring to the buffalo as a "cow", is able to see beyond the limits of the speaker's vision. Though related as an account of a waking experience it also has for Ingessana powerful dream references since what is frightening about the temple is its association with *nengk*, ghastly creatures which bring illness and death and demand livestock, especially cattle, from their victims, and which ordinary people only see in dreams. Such recollections and often told stories of singular events experienced while alone, usually hunting or herding among men, share formal characteristics with the reports of dream experiences. It is possibly here, in the distillation processes of remembering-forgetting, that dream experiences and waking experiences flow together, each qualifying the other with its own properties.

So it seems that the difference in the content of recollections of waking experiences and experiences in dreams is in part attributed to the different capacities of certain kinds of dreamers rather than to the nature of dreams.[1] This is why ordinary people, when they find themselves to be suffering and believe they are under attack from the supernatural, recount their dreams to a doctor-diviner since he will be able to recognise what may appear obscure to the dreamer. The doctor-diviner's interpretation of a dream appears at first to each dreamer as an elaboration, but it is also a reduction of the manifold of actual dreams to the dream of *nengk*. The doctor-diviner has a kind of code of equivalences which enable this procedure, but since almost everybody seems to be aware of its basic elements this knowledge is not the principal source of his authority. The doctor-diviner is authoritative on what the dream signifies has to be done by the dreamer because he is able to see while conscious (*den ok*, literally, watching the situation) what an ordinary person can only see in dreams, and then obscurely. Drawing boundaries between waking and sleeping experiences in this way means that there can be a complete interpenetration of these realms in terms of cause and effect.

The Ingessana word for dream is *caal,* but in conversation one usually hears the plural *caalk* and people talk about seeing something "in dreams". Jung's remarks that "one does not dream, one is dreamed. We undergo the dream, we are the objects" (Jacobi 1942:70), express well Ingessana dream notions of passivity, of being acted upon rather than acting. Indeed this is taken to an extreme in the common expression of being "consumed by dreams" (*nams i caalk,* literally, "eaten by dreams"). So if the dream extends vision beyond the limits of ordinary consciousness, then these limits are, to some extent, manipulated by those beings occupying privileged positions beyond the limits of waking vision. Moreover, not only are people the passive objects of dreams, but the content of the typical Ingessana dream makes it clear that the dreamer is also a victim or a child or a messenger or a subordinate or a combination of such relationships.

This essay will first of all describe the kinds of dreams and associated institutions which are typical of ordinary people and of ritual office holders. There is, however, a very important set of rituals carried out by a cult-group which is not associated with dreams in the sense so far described but which nevertheless is highly relevant to an adequate understanding of Ingessana perceptions because, most obviously, the cult group involved is referred to as "dreams" (*caalk*). We are familiar with the Tylorian view that people of "primitive cultures" mistakenly attribute objective reality to their dream experiences but here, it seems, are a people who apparently perceive certain features of objective reality as if they were a dream. There is an appealing psycho-analytical interpretation which would begin by noting the ribald "joking" behaviour and the association with wild animals which are typical of the cult group. This suggests an obvious Freudian dream symbolism according to which theory it would be argued that for the people of this culture, secondary mental processes (characterised by logic and rationality) had made little progress in repressing primary mental processes so far from being confined to manifestation in dreams, the latter also appear in other modes of human activity. This explanation is at least better than the homonym argument, namely that there really are two distinct concepts denoted by apparently similar words, but since it involves the reduction of social phenomena to the psychic make up of individuals, though intellectually interesting, it is not satisfactory. This is a difficult problem, but an attempt will be made to synthesize the results of the present analysis into what must remain a tentative configuration of cultural categories which lays emphasis on the relationships between the categories and concepts, since it is ultimately these relationships which define the categories rather than what might appear to be the essence of the realities so designated.

Of all the dreams that an ordinary Ingessana may undergo, the dream involving *nengk* is the dream that is the most feared but also the most widespread of socially significant dreams. The word is the plural of *nenget* and is a compound derived from *na en* which means "the one that is frightful". When Ingessana are asked to describe *nengk* the first thing that is said of them is that they are *engk*, frightening. Ingessana say that any awful image in a dream is *nengk* or the work of *nengk*. Not only does the appearance of these creatures fill one with fear, a fear which persists even after awakening from the dream, but they also threaten sickening personal consequences for the dreamer. This is how it was explained to me by one renowned doctor-diviner. "At night a *nenget* will come to you and show you a cow (*nenget la rimdun to*, the characteristic phrase heralding the sacrifice of a cow) and before it goes away it will broadcast sorghum seed around the homestead. Unless you sacrifice a cow, the *nenget*, by the seed it has planted in the homestead, will take (the lives) of your livestock or even your wife and children and yourself. So you will send for a doctor-diviner and tell him of the dream. That it is *nenget* will be confirmed by the diviner casting three pieces of tobacco and interpreting how they fall. So the diviner will go around the homestead digging out with his special staff (called *cer*) the *jerg i nenget* which he is able to see. Sometimes he will also have to pull seeds out of the body of some afflicted person in the homestead. A cow is 'cut' (*wiir*) (its throat is cut, that is, it is sacrificed) and then the elders deliver orations addressed to the *nengk* asking them to depart now that they have been given what they demanded."

It is also common for a dead kinsman or woman to appear with the *nengk* in a dream and though nobody thinks of their own dead father or mother as a *nenget,* ordinary people sometimes talk in general as if the "souls" or "shadows" (*kuthek*) of the dead become *nengk,* and therefore the English term "ghosts" might be a suitable gloss.[2] In such cases the sacrifice will proceed as before except that in addition to the cow a smaller item of livestock will also be killed, but inside the homestead in front of the hut of the household head. Cows sacrificed for *nengk* are killed outside the entrance to the homestead. Dreams involving dead kinsmen are linked less with illness and material misfortune than to disputes and bad feelings among the descendants of the dead person and the sacrifice of an animal marks the conclusion of a settlement and the re-establishment of amicable relationships.

In general *nengk*, though normally invisible, are not remote but seem to lurk around and from time to time erupt into the affairs of people. A few homesteads are particularly associated with *nengk* and have a reputation for extraordinary happenings. For instance, I was told of one such homestead which was found in the morning after a *caalk* group ritual had taken place there to be completely encircled with bowls of oil. This was attributed to the *nengk*. In the same homestead the women have to leave the kitchen after sunset in order, they say, to allow the *nengk* to do their work. Such *nengk* are called *Jok Calofan* (Calofan People). One man told me that the *Jok Calofan* came to him in a dream and warned him not to visit that particular homestead. The reputation of this homestead was explained to me as a consequence of the previous household head having come from the household of a man, now dead, who had been notorious for his dealings with *nengk* and other mysterious creatures. According to Ingessana he had a "dirty body" (*iinge ruii*).

The response of Ingessana is twofold. As has been mentioned, individual household heads will from time to time sacrifice and occasionally, perhaps once a year, a locality will come together to drive *nengk* out of the area. The promotion of such events will involve long and difficult discussions and negotiations. A husband/father/son-in-law may have to be persuaded of the need to sacrifice, or he may have to convince his household. The household head will want to secure the participation of senior elders and many kin and affines, neighbours and strangers. There are problems of timing and coordination with other events. Into these proceedings the recollections of recent dreams by adult members of the afflicted household will be introduced and some recounted to doctor-diviners, since it is through dreams, or rather the discussions to elucidate a consensus on their meanings and significance, that crucial details are specified, such as the colour and markings of the animal which must be sacrificed. If the household head does not have such an animal, then delicate negotiations with kinsmen who have the appropriate animal take place through a third party who will be a senior kinsman.

As regards the sacrifices, their structure may be presumed to be appropriate to what are considered to be the attributes of *nengk* and the desired relationship between them and people. In this respect two points are especially worth remarking upon. First of all these sacrifices ought to be and generally are occasions when unusually large numbers of people will congregate in a homestead and consequently there is a deliberate and evident heightening of social interaction and an awareness of the presence of people. There are no formal limits on the kinds of people who may attend such gatherings and indeed there is an established place for strangers. Moreover, people gather into sub-groups according to age and do not divide into kin groups. There is then not only a reassuring expression of solidarity with the troubled household but also it seems as if flooding, as it were, the space of the homestead with people thereby drives out by weight of numbers what is inimicable to people, the *nengk*. Secondly, the dominant formal theme of the ritual symbolism is separation. The *nengk* seed is removed from an afflicted person and cast out; the sacrificial animal is taken from the interior yard of the homestead to the entrance outside and there, as a climax to the ritual, its throat is cut. The Ingessana phrase meaning "to sacrifice a cow" translates simply as "to cut a cow" (*wiir to*). Finally, in long and elaborate orations the elders tell the *nengk* to depart and leave the people of the homestead alone. In sum the whole procedure simultaneously disengages the threatened inhabitants of the homestead from the intrusion of *nengk* and integrates them into the society of humans.

The other type of response to excessive activity by *nengk* is a collective attempt to drive them out of the locality. This is a feat of considerable organisation, since each parish and section over a large area of the hills must coordinate their actions. In each parish the horn of the war leader (*sen i kung*) is blown to call the men to the traditional meeting place. Tactics are agreed by the elders and executed by the war leaders, where again the horn is used to issue instructions. Several doctor-diviners accompany the group of well-armed men and the party moves through the locality in a disciplined and efficient manner, stopping occasionally to discharge volleys of stones in the direction of targets, i.e. *nengk* and other fearful creatures visible only to the doctor-diviners. When the party reaches the boundary of the local group territory it meets with the waiting war party of the adjacent territory. The elders of each group deliver orations, then the war party of the adjacent locality takes up the action and continues driving the *nengk* until they meet up with the next group, and so on until the *nengk* are driven out of the hills. But all this can only give temporary respite since the *nengk* slowly and insidiously return to infest the hills again.

However, it is clear that there is some differentiation among *nengk*. Those called *Jok Calofan* have already been mentioned, and are described by the people of Tao (Jok Tao) in the south western section of the hills as the children of a particular *ninget* called Ngarema. Ngarema inhabits a temple located among the people of Aselk, a subsection of Tao, and is described as the wife of another *ninget* called Mufu inhabiting a temple at Mathelk, an important ritual centre for Jok Tao. They are not driven out of the locality, but this cannot be because they are considered particularly desirable. On the contrary Ngarema, Mufu and a third called Melesongol are obviously feared, or rather to be accurate people speak with some awe and fear of the houses, which I have called temples, that they are supposed to inhabit. An outbreak of coughing and symptoms rather like influenza among people and to which deaths are frequently attributed is supposed to originate from the temples. People say that the sickness among them is because the "door of the temple has been opened". People passing by will keep these houses at a distance, cease conversation and increase their pace until they have passed them. Considerable social distance is maintained between ordinary people and the men in whose homesteads these temples are located, who are regarded as in some sense the custodians of the temples, though even they may not be able to enter the temple. Usually only one person, a doctor-diviner of remarkable reputation, may do so. Ordinary people have not even seen these beings (Ngarema and Mufu) in their dreams, only their offspring and other anonymous *nengk,* but men such as powerful doctor-diviners are said to be able to see them, usually, according to Ingessana, when they are on the road between their respective abodes as they travel to visit each other. One doctor-diviner told me that they were not human in appearance and Ngarema, whom he had seen, could not be described because the image seemed to reflect like a mirror.[3] They ride on horses and make a distinctive metallic sound as they move, though this may be the tack and not the horse or its ghastly rider. There are a number of other remarkable features and associations, but rather than clarifying a mysterious entity, these seem only to deepen the mystery. To begin with, such a being is also referred to as *tel* and the temples may be referred to as *we i tel* (house of *tel*) or *we madden* (big house). This is interesting because the term *tel* can be glossed as "god". It is used in a number of contexts where the Arabic "Allah" or English "God" would be used. *Tel* is the omnipotent creator of the world and therefore is the ultimate cause or reason why things are as they are or happen in the way they do. *"Gar i tel"*, say Ingessana where we might say "God only knows". A woman will say of the children she bore *"Tel* gave me boys only". When someone dies they are "taken by god" (*baks i tel*). The word *tel* can also refer to the sun, so that midday is *tel tal tao* ("the sun standing straight up"). Most curious of all, however, is a statement made to me by an old man, the descendant of a line of custodians of an extremely important *we madden*, in which he was contrasting and promoting the nature and origins of the *we madden* for which he was responsible with the temples of Ngarema, Mufu and Melesongol. The latter he said are *nengk* and "their ancestor is the ground squirrel" *("ek methenii sej") [xerus erythropus]*. Of all creatures, why the ground squirrel, raises the classic anthropological classificatory problem. There are some interesting and suggestive features. This small rodent is a human familiar and a nuisance to farmers because of the damage it does to seeds and crops. It is also fearless and its bite can be lethal to humans, probably because of the pathogens it transfers through the wound. It is typically seen standing up on its hind legs looking quizzically around. However Ingessana do not otherwise hold the creature in any respect, and kill them and eat them whenever they get an opportunity.

These remarks about the term *tel* lead into the issue of the dreams of non-ordinary people, in particular doctor-diviners and those people with second sight called *cak*. A man who is a *cak* may pass this attribute to one of his sons, which will be revealed by some indicative event in his life such as a fever when the child becomes delirious, or perhaps out in the bush the child will suddenly cry out in fear as if it had seen something frightening. The doctor-diviners will then make him into a *cak* by a procedure described as "washing" where particular attention is payed to the joints of the limbs. This is not unlike the procedure whereby a man becomes a doctor-diviner. Some people who suffer from pains in the joints and who have dreams in which doctor-diviners appear may have to be made into doctor-diviners in order to prevent their limbs becoming stiff and crippled. *Cak* are otherwise undistinguished persons, though one I knew had taken upon himself responsibility for the dry season water hole. That is to say he would instigate action if he thought that it was being misused, especially by people watering herds, or that the shallow wells needed rebuilding. His authority for doing so derived from a dreamlike experience when, it is said, his bucket while he was taking water from the water hole was seized by a *manyil*. Now *manyil* is another supernormal creature but, unlike *nengk*, does not seem to feature in the dreams of ordinary people nor extra-ordinary persons, but they are on the other hand familiars of people such as *cak*, and doctor-diviners and some elders attribute them with special powers and abilities according to the particular *manyil*. A *cak,* for example, is able while asleep to leave his body and go out on the back of a *manyil* and travel over great distances instantaneously. *Cak* were particularly valuable for reconnaissance puposes when raiding and warfare was endemic since, after such excursions, they would report upon what they had seen. It is tempting to say that this is an instance of dreaming but my notes do not say for certain that Ingessana used the word *caalk* (dreams) in accounts of these abilities of *cak*. They did, however, say that *cak* may dream of "being shown a cow by god" (*tel*) in deliberate contrast to an ordinary person who only dreams of being shown a cow by *nengk,* and it also seems to be deliberately ambiguous as to whether the *cak* actually see the face of god or whether they only see god's cow, that is to say, the cow being demanded in sacrifice. These dreams of *cak*, which will be reported as experienced by several *cak* at the same time and be the subject of widespread public interest, occur during those periods of serious misfortune such as famine or epidemics of sickness among people or livestock which are on a scale that affects the whole population of the Ingessana hills. As a consequence of these dreams a delegation of elders proceeds to Jebel Gule, which is beyond the hills and an old provincial capital of the divine kings of the Funj, and there they secure from the ruler "the cow of god". This sacrificial animal would then, if it really is the cow of god, say Ingessana, start walking towards the hills of its own accord with the people following behind and it will, still unguided by men, perambulate through the hills by a traditional route until it comes to the temple at Kamol in the centre of the hills. Whatever may have been the position in the past, this sacrifice is now seldom carried out, and the last occasion was probably about sixty years ago.[4] This being the case, the role of *cak* as dreamers has clearly much diminished.

The final category of persons whose dreams have, and continue to have, enormous social implications are the dreams of the men who are the hereditary custodians of certain temples. The Ingessana calendar is punctuated by three festival days. These festivals are called *san*, a term which also means beer, and each is named. Among Jok Tao the festivals are *San i Poinj, San i Sak* and *San i Bal*. In other sections of the Ingessana Hills population the names and timing can vary. Among the Jok Gor two of their festivals have become partly assimilated with Islamic festivals. *San i Bal*, which takes place soon after the beginning of the early rains and not long after the seeds have been planted in the farms, is the most elaborate in its involvement of various life promoting rituals, and also announces the period during which the final ceremony in the establishment of any marriages may occur. The name *bal* refers to the musical instrument, a kind of whistle, which along with another woodwind instrument called *singer* are played on these occasions but are then put away after the *San i Poinj* and may not be played until *San i Bal* comes round again. The *San i Poinj* announces the season typified by the music of the lyre and the songs and dancing which it accompanies. The period between *San i Sak* and *San i Bal*, which occurs among Jok Tau during the latter half of the dry season, is a period of quiescence characterised by the absence of a specific cultural activity rather than the presence of some feature.

However, the festival days themselves are dominated by the lineage ancestral rites. On the day of the festival no work is done and as Ingessana put it "the *jeza* mat comes down". In most, but not all homesteads, the household head has a large mat woven from dom palm (*jeza*) fronds. This mat hangs, rolled up, in the hut of the household head. Inside there are some old staffs and throwing sticks which belonged to ancestors who were temple custodians (*aurek*) or doctor-diviners along with perhaps some other relics of dead kinsmen. On the morning of the festival all the *jeza* mats throughout the section are brought down, unrolled, and spread out on the ground in the hut of the household head. The relics are laid upon it. Beside them on the mat are placed a bowl of oil, a bowl of porridge, a bowl of beer (*san*, hence the term for festival) a length or two of cloth and a block of tobacco. The household head, having thus prepared everything, murmurs an invitation to the ancestors to partake of this offering which is for them. The mat is also brought out on wedding ceremonials and at burials, when the dead person is bound into the mat to be carried to the grave. But a relic is brought back from the grave to be lodged in the *jeza* mat which is suspended in the hut. Ingessana say that this is the deceased's "shade" (*kuuth*).

Now, while the household head remains where he is there occur some interesting changes in the personnel of the homestead: any affines and matrilateral kin depart and are replaced by agnatic kin. Thus his wives will be replaced by his sisters and he will be joined by his younger brothers with their sons and daughters. Similarly sons-in-law will be replaced by his sons and their children. In short, the domestic or household group based on a husband and wife is replaced by a patrilineage of shallow depth. The food, beer etc., on the *jeza* mat has, since early morning, been respectfully ignored – save to keep children and animals out – but in the middle of the day the patrilineage will gather in the hut. Each will first of all anoint themselves with oil, putting some on forehead, chin and breast. The oldest woman will give everybody some of the beer and porridge, the children before adults. The tobacco is ground up and distributed to the adults for snuff. The beer is drunk slowly and the people gently converse. Later others from neighbouring homesteads will visit and some will likewise go out, taking the opportunity to see old friends and kin not usually encountered. When the sun goes down the household head "puts up" the *jeza* mat until the day of the next festival, the patrilineage dissolves and the household reconstitutes itself. Clearly these rites are in the nature of a communion: the dead and the living join together in commensality for the duration of a special day which has been set apart from other days. In every detail this rite can be contrasted formally with sacrifices prompted by the dreams of some afflicted person. Yet the timing of these festivals in each section is also regulated by dreams, in this case the dreams of one particular person.

Among Jok Tau two of the festivals, namely *Sak* and *Poinj*, are regulated from Mathelk by the dreams of the man who has the *we i sem*, the temple of the *semk* cult group, in his homestead and who is known as *bao i semk* (father or lord of the *semk*). He will be approached in a dream by his father and others among his ancestors who were his predecessors, that is those who, when they were alive, were responsible for identifying the precise day of the festival and regarded as the custodians of the temple. In the dream they will say to him: "announce the festival tomorrow"'. He will then give the special horn (*cil*) to a young man who will early in the morning of the following day set off around the section blowing the horn. Since every one has been expecting this announcement of the festival, they know that this means that in the morning the *jeza* mat will be brought down. In fact it can be rather more complicated than this account, which is the one given by the man who has this responsibility, suggests. In March 1984 the *bao i semk* was quite old and rather senile and the senior men around him were becoming uneasy as the time of the *San i Sak* festival approached and days went by without the old man saying anything. Eventually one morning about seven of them and the old man entered the *sem* temple, having first bared their upper bodies and tied lengths of cloth around their waists, and attempted, it seemed, to make sense of any recent dreams of the old man. After some discussion a fire was laid in the temple and a bowl of water taken inside and then they emerged saying, "the matter is settled: the festival will be announced tomorrow". No one could now enter the temple until after the day of the festival. The third festival and the one which initiates the cycle, *Bal*, is regulated quite differently. According to the old man, "Ancestors do not come to me. An egret will come and alight and stay in that tree beside my homestead. Everybody around will see it. And so I will give the horn to the messenger to announce the festival".

In general then, for the people of the Ingessana Hills dreams are occasions when ordinarily invisible beings, *nengk* (ghosts), *meithet* (ancestors) and *tel* (god) make demands, issue warnings and instruct, while certain extraordinary persons credited with what is expressed as special sight are able outside dreams to penetrate consciously beyond the normal spectrum of visibility to see the ghosts. The messages from dreams are also oracular in the sense of stating what has to be done, and interpretation pronounces on the intentions of the senders. The ultimate concern in all cases is the material well-being of the members of a household, the inhabitants of a territorial section and, in rare instances, the entire population of the hills. The rituals demanded by these beings through dreams restore the relationship between them and people. In the case of the ghosts the relationship has become too close and their eruption into the affairs of humans causes disease and death. On the other hand, the ancestor and gods must be regularly attended to in order to secure the health and well-being of people and livestock and to maintain the fertility of the land. In the former case, the rituals are directed at severing an unwelcome association and focus on the ritual killing of an animal and in the latter on a communion of ancestors and gods expressed in the sharing of porridge.

But Ingessana are not merely concerned with the material aspect of life and there is an important ritual institution devoted to promoting the restoration of the "souls" or "shades" (*kuuthek*) of children. Indeed, the typical ritual of the group of people charged with this responsibility is described as "restoring the souls of children" (*liimen kuuthek i nyulk*) or sometimes "bringing back to the children their souls" (*war nyulk kuuthek*). The cult group which carries out these rituals is called *"caalk"*, "dreams". The rite will be carried out when the parents of a child who has suffered some frightening experience which has disturbed the child approach the local leader of the cult and ask her (this person, called *taun*, is always a woman) to restore the child. They arrange a day and the *taun* tells them to prepare beer for that day. Word is passed around the local members of the cult, who say "there is somebody to be buried", which signifies, typically of the cult, quite the opposite: that someone is, on the contrary, to be saved from the grave. On the appointed day other parents in the neighbourhood bring their children and gather in the homestead of the patron of the ritual, who need not necessarily be the parents of the original child.

The events of the day fall roughly into three phases: initial dance, rite and then concluding dance. The cult group arrives and they begin their singing and vigorous dancing around the homestead, brandishing their characteristic switches. There is a great deal of commotion and much horseplay involving references to sexuality, defecation, breaking wind and other bodily functions among the cult group members and between them and onlookers. When the *taun* arrives she throws a handful of millet at the entrance to each hut in the homestead and places her equipment in the middle of the yard. The second phase begins when the child is taken to the place where they had the frightening experience. The child is made to sit on the spot and is then covered with ashes by the *taun*. The child is stood up and then sprayed with water, and immediately everyone runs back to the homestead. Once inside all the children are assembled around the *taun's* equipment. The main elements of the rite involve the *taun* putting ash on the left legs and arms of the children, making them smell a mixture of burnt chicken feathers from a chicken which has been plucked alive and a species of cress which the *taun* chewed. The children are then picked up and held upside down over gourds containing separately beer and ashes. They are then stood right way up and the *taun* sprays them with mouthfuls of beer from a special double gourd owned by the *taun*. A chicken which has been immersed in beer is circled over and around the children and this too sprays them as the bird flaps about. These operations completed, the rest of the cult group members resume their singing, dancing and horseplay. A similar procedure is also carried out for twins every lunar month until they are weaned. As in the case of the children, Ingessana explain that this is done to restore the souls of the twins (*liimen kuuthek i waik*) so that their soul will not abandon them, "run off into the wilds", as one person put it and which, it seems, the souls of twins are more likely to do than those of ordinary children. It is also significant that representatives of *caalk* act as mediators and messengers during the negotiations between two kin groups arranging a marriage and have a necessary role to play in the formal procedures of bringing a man and woman together as husband and wife.

The licensed deviance which is a feature of *caalk* conduct is reputed to extend beyond their very public interpersonal ribaldry and even the startling exhibition of carved phalluses which some of them wear hanging between their legs, to grossly sacriligious acts such as defecating on the sacred monolith upon which the revered *semk* cult pray. On other occasions some of their number are dressed in masks said to represent hyenas. In addition the *caalk* have no centre or temple as do the *semk* with which they are contrasted. Instead, their members are distributed throughout society and indeed beyond, since significantly *caalk* or *caalk*-like institutions are known by Ingessana to exist among neighbouring peoples such as those of the Mughaja hills to the west and south. Yet despite such features which put *caalk* origins symbolically beyond Ingessana society and even perhaps human society, they are in practice central to the vital interests of the people. It is perhaps because *caalk* embody characteristics from beyond the limits of Ingessana society that they are able to restore to persons, in particular children, the intangible aspect of their being which in certain circumstances is likely to detach itself and, as they say, "run off into the wilds".

The question posed at the beginning of this account was what, if anything, is the connection between *caalk* (dreams) and *caalk*, the cult group. There is also another problem concerning the appropriateness for Ingessana of taking dream recollections into account when considering and negotiating acceptable courses of action in dealing with the contingencies of life. The answers to these two problems are closely related.

The first and most obvious inference which can be drawn is that *caalk* are mediators: ghosts, ancestors, gods and other non-mortal beings communicate with people through dreams; a vocabulary of dreams and dreaming is used to attribute acceptable intentions to departures from normal conduct and thereby links the otherwise unaccountable actions of individuals to what is the norm, what is expected and acceptable; the *caalk* cult mediates between husband and wife and their respective kin groups and between people and the non-mortal aspect of their being. The conduct of the representatives of *caalk*, which would be intolerable in other people, is accounted for by their nature as *caalk* and is, of course, a typical case of "joking" behaviour.

Secondly, beyond the formal congruence a difference of orientation or trajectory has to be recognised. Mediation involves both conjunction and separation, and this is elaborated in the institutionalisations of *caalk* in different but related ways. In the settings in which *caalk*, the cult group members, materialise as agents of mediation, the general concern of the people involved is with a conjunction and their actions are directed towards this end. By contrast the irruption of ghosts and the like into the affairs of people represents an unwanted conjunction, and dreams are both part of this intensification of the relationship between people and ghosts and indicative of it. The contrasting orientations to identical structural relationships is vividly represented by the spectacle in waking life of the benign old grandmother, the *taun* of the *caalk* group, casting seed around the homestead as a benediction and the dream image (*caalk*) of the frightening and vicious ghost casting malevolent seed around the dreamer's homestead.

Finally, this contrasting orientation also manifests itself in the two contrasting modes of *caalk*, dream and cult group, modes which themselves are wholly consistent with the different aspects of their mediating functions. *Caalk*, the cult group, the dreams of waking life, are concerned with conjunction, but their origin and mode as "strangers" sets them apart from Ingessana society, a distancing which allows them to act as conjoining mediators. *Caalk*, the dreams of sleep when interaction with others is at a minimum are the locus of unwanted conjunctions, but are also the means of knowing how to bring about a desired disjunction and separation. But these *caalk* are not "strangers"; they may not even be shared with some adjacent other, but originate with and are inseparable from each person as an individual.

NOTES

The information reported here was obtained during various periods of field research between 1971 and 1973 with support from the University of Khartoum. A further period of fieldwork was made possible from January to March 1985 by a grant from the ESRC. Relevant ethnography on the Ingessana can be found in Jędrej 1975, 1979, 1983 and Okazaki 1985, 1987.

1. Consequently Ingessana display a range of ambivalent and puzzled attitudes to persons such as doctor-diviners which, of course, corresponds to the puzzlement and intellectual vertigo with which we amuse ourselves thinking about the reality of dream experiences and waking experiences. And just as there are the hard-headed among us who suspect a clever trick and know (hope?) by common sense that the world is not somebody's dream, so also among Ingessana common sense normally prevails but, who knows, perhaps somewhere or at some times doctor-diviners do not just perform clever tricks.

2. Okazaki (1987) has rightly warned of hastily translating the word *"kuuth"* as "soul" and thereby imparting unwarranted Platonic ideas. According to Okazaki *kuuth* does not refer to some essential component of a person but figuratively to something like a remembered image of the whole person.

3. "For now we see through a glass, darkly; but then face to face: now I know in part; but then shall I know even as also I am known." (I Corinthians 13:12)

4. See Jędrej (1983) for details of this ritual as described by several informants and for some speculations on the linkages with the Funj kingdom of Sennar.

REFERENCES

DODDS, E.R., 1951, *The Greeks and the Irrational*. Berkeley: University of California Press.

JACOBI, J., 1942, *The Psychology of C. G. Jung*. London: Routledge and Kegan Paul

JĘDREJ, M.C., 1975, The social organisation of the Ingessana. *Sudan Notes & Records*, 56: 108-119.

1979, Cults of the dead among the Ingessana. *Anthropos*, 74: 40-46.

1983, The Funj bull: myth, history and ritual. In R. Bridges (ed.), *An African Miscellany for John Hargreaves*. Aberdeen: Aberdeen University African Studies Group.

MALINOWSKI, B., 1927, *Sex and Repression in Savage Society*. London: Kegan Paul, Trench and Trubner.

OKAZAKI, A., 1985, Living together with "Bad Things": the persistence of Gank, notions of mystical agents. In M. Tomikawa (ed.), *Sudan Sahel Studies*, 1. Tokyo: Institute for the Study of Languages and Cultures of Asia and Africa.

1987, Man's shadow and this man of shadow. *Sudan Sahel Studies*, 2.Tokyo: Institute for the Study of Languages and Cultures of Asia and Africa.

SHWEDER, R., 1982, On savages and other children: a review of *The Foundations of Primitive Thought*, by C.R. Hallpike, *American Anthropologist*, 84: 354-366.

TYLOR, E.B., 1865, *Researches into the Early History of Mankind*. London.

DREAMS AND VISIONS IN NINETEENTH CENTURY YORUBA RELIGION

P.R. McKENZIE
University of Leicester

Dreams and visions seem to be a most attractive way to approach the inner areas of religious experience and their relationship to the outward structures of religion, especially when the latter are being subjected to severe stresses from the impact of powerful new ideas and values.[1] On the other hand this is an area of considerable theoretical complexity. Consequently this paper restricts itself to reporting on the results of investigating some preliminary questions concerning dreams and visions among Yoruba in the middle of the nineteenth century upon whom the early efforts of Christian missions impacted. The most likely place to begin would be among the personal papers of contemporary Yoruba CMS Catechists held in the CMS Archives, and in this material I found some 28 reports of dreams and visions. Some of them are rather brief and fragmentary; others are reasonably detailed. They have the advantage of being early, from people during the transitional period when colonial rule had not yet been imposed over the whole of Yorubaland, and traditional religion and society were still largely intact. Many of the catechists themselves came out of traditional cult groups and many of their relatives were still followers of the deities or *orisa*. On the other hand, what the catechists wrote in their journals and letters was in the main addressed to those who assumed that traditional religion was very largely a matter of darkness and superstition.

The dreams which the catechists were told by Yoruba and which they recalled in their journals and letters can be grouped easily around four significant themes: first of all we find the traditional Yoruba use of dreams in dealing with contingencies attributed to the gods. Dreams were then available to deal with the impact of Christian missions. Secondly there are dreams associated with crises of religious identity, thirdly a series of explicit accounts of conversion in which dreams feature and lastly visions of sick and dying early Christian converts.

The first of the traditional group of dreams and visions is a vision by a follower of the goddess Osun. It is uneschatological in character and serves to reinforce devotion to the *orisa*. Told to Samuel Johnson at Ibadan in 1875,[2] it is preceded by an account of how the narrator had been promised to his father before birth after the father had offered sacrifice near the river Osun. Years of neglect of religious obligations then ensued until in Ibadan, at the brink of death and nearly penniless, he suddenly had a vision of the goddess Osun entering his house with a train of followers. Those about him saw nothing. The *orisa* accosted him by name and sharply reprimanded him for his neglect of her. She assured him he would become well if he resumed his worship of her. He did so and his fortunes improved.

Also linked with the cult of Osun is a dream of evil omen. Samuel Doherty, on a journey from Abeokuta to the Ibarapa country in 1876,[3] encountered a priestess of Osun who asks him as an *alufa* or priest to make an amulet for a woman relative whose son's marriage dream she regarded as a bad omen in the context of a situation of hostility involving another man. No further details are given, but the dream seems to be a traditional dream of evil omen, as does another recorded earlier by Samuel Pearse at Badagry relating to the cult of Ifa.[4] Pearse encountered a senior Ifa diviner or *babalawo* making sacrifice for a woman who was the victim of a terrifying dream. Little is said about the dream itself; much about the ritual containment of its baneful effects. But it is "traditional" as a communication from spirits (*orisa*), a revelation which has to be interpreted and counteracted. The sacrifice to expiate the evil omen consisted of *agidi* (maize food) covered with oil and the blood of a fowl, with feathers and cowries embedded in it and a final sprinkling of *iyerosun* or Ifa powder. She was to take this to a crossroads where three ways meet, describe three circles in the air with it and leave it there. She did so, then returned and received the *babalawo's* blessing. The latter added the prediction that despite the continuous dry weather it would rain before three days. On the appointed day it rained and the woman as commanded went out into the rain. The evil omen was finally washed away, and her confidence in Ifa doubly reinforced, by the sacrifice and rain.

Another type of traditional religious experience is the predictive vision, of which there are two vivid examples. The first is associated with *orisa* Sango, while the second does not name the *orisa* concerned. A former devotee of Sango told Daniel Olubi at Ibadan in 1872[5] how he had been caught up in the Ibadan-Ijaye war of 1860-65, which ended in Ijaye's destruction. Taken prisoner, he prayed to Sango for release. Then he had a vision in which he was told he would be rescued after five days, and so it turned out. He came back to Ibadan still with the fetters on by which he had been fastened.

The second predictive vision gives more details, but without naming the *orisa* concerned.[6] A man noted for his previous exploits in war and kidnapping related how during a campaign he climbed a large silk cotton tree to get a squirrel. The creeper he was using as a rope to climb the tree with broke. He could neither get down again nor could others help him to get down. It was on the third night up the tree that he had the vision. A man appeared to him and said he would be released in the morning. The next morning, a storm blew up and moved the branches of a nearby tree close enough for him to catch hold of one and so make his way down. Many of his companions were deeply impressed at his deliverance, which they ascribed to the *orisa*. They then proceeded to ask a blessing from them.

Two traditional shamanic visions are also recorded. The first is mentioned by C. N. Young at Ondo in 1875.[7] It occurred in the course of a festival for Obatala. Women were beating the drums with great skill. All night long praise songs and dances took place around the image of the deity. Later a great shout announced that "the *orisa* has got into one of their number, who ... fell ... to the ground ... crying and uttering serious words in a voice ... which startled all of them with much fear". The possessed one later told them that she had been to the spirit world and had been instructed by Obatala to warn everyone of the evil that would befall them if they did not perform the appropriate sacrifice. The impending evil was mainly that those who had asked the deity for children would be deprived of them.

The other vision involved a *Himmelsreise* and a *Himmelsschau* but raises a question concerning the traditional character of its underlying cosmology. First the vision and then speculations as to its *Sitz im Leben*. Samuel Johnson relates in 1875[8] that the friend of a *babalawo* fell gravely ill, sent for his relatives but died before they arrived. His body was wrapped in cloths according to custom. But before the internment his corpse was seen to be moving. It was unwrapped and they found the man had come to life again. In the event he lived for many years. When he recovered he explained how he had seen a great high God "enthroned in a spacious place, from top to bottom in white. On his right is the God Orisa-nla and on his left the God Ifa, both his counsellors. Behind him is a pit where all the condemned are cast into; and before him and in active service are the Gods Ogun and Sopona. Ogun is armed with 4000 short swords...He goes out daily on earth to slay, for his meat is to drink the blood of the slain. Sopona also has 4000 vials about him; his also is the work of destruction, bringing in his victims, and disappears immediately for others and so continually. As for Sango he is a very mighty God, and when he is about to go (to) the world he is cautioned by Ifa and Orisa-nla to deal gently with their own special devoted worshippers."

Although we are not told about the particular consequences of this vision for the dreamer or his relatives, this complex vision reflects in general the unstable conditions of the late Oyo empire. There is a decided shift away from the microcosm of the individual *orisa* cult towards the macrocosm of the high god Olorun, the synoptic Ifa cosmology and a special stress upon the "hot" deities Ogun, Sopona and Sango. There has been a measure of consolidation, but the great *orisa* are still powerful actors in a scene of great danger to mortals who are threatened with kidnapping, disease and war. The figure of the high god may have been enhanced as a result of contact with Islam and Christianity, and there is also some mention of the fate of evil doers. However, the scene is essentially a traditional court and is not strongly eschatological. It is still compatible with the traditional metempsychosis put to C. N. Young by an Ondo man when he declared that when anyone dies "he has to enter the womb of women".[9] The notion of "another world" was not developed before the arrival of missionaries.

Although this vision is a traditional form and in a sense typical it also evidently expresses a transition, in particular the historical changes which Yoruba society and its religious tradition underwent during the period of these dreams and visions from 1852 to 1879. We may expect the transitional mood to be at least as prominent in the second group of dreams and visions: crisis dreams and dream warnings of those on the fringes of contact with Christianity. These dreams are traditional in the sense of still being accorded a powerful, revelatory and transformative virtue.

The following is an account of the dreams of an Ijaye captive in 1862 who was later redeemed by his brother in Ibadan.[10] The slight contact he had with Christianity had, however, served only to increase his devotion to his *orisa*: Osun, Ibeji and Ifa. But he recalled how on successive nights he had two dreams. In the first dream "there was a large fire...and his *orisa* (Osun and Ibeji) with himself were chained ready to be burnt. A captain with his soldiers well-armed came and ordered that they should loose him. He was taken out of their hands by force and his *orisa* alone were cast into the fire. The heat of the fire was so intense that he clung to the man for shelter." He awoke trembling and had no further sleep that night. The following night he dreamt that "the man came again and told him that as he is set free he must never again fall down before these *orisa*". He had no peace until he disposed of his images; then he visited a mosque but was not allowed in, but at the church at Kudeti (Ibadan) he was welcomed.

William George, a schoolmaster at Abeokuta, reports a predictive dream by a traditional religionist with scarcely any previous contact with Christianity. He went to an outlying village to conduct a service in 1879.[11] The owner of the house where the prayers were said related the following dream: a man came to him in white apparel, asked him to kneel down and pray, and then went away. This householder, a follower of the *orisa*, found his dream fulfilled to the letter when William George came. It was incomprehensible to him as he was not a "book man".

The next two dream reports are different in so far as they involve an active role for Olorun, the sky deity, and hence represent a cosmological shift towards a Christian concept of deity. At Badagry in 1862 an "enquirer" told Samuel Pearse[12] that Ifa had directed him to learn to read under the orders of Olorun. In so doing he had begun to neglect his *orisa*, but "many a time I had frightful dreams such as would induce me to consult and do sacrifice to my Ifa, but I was determined always to place myself under Olorun's protection". He asked for God's direction regarding his *orisa* who, especially in the case of Esu, had greatly helped him. Then the Lord heard his prayers and showed him how to dispense with his Esu. "In my dream I had seven such images before me, all of which I was ordered by a voice to bury in the ground. I bravely did so, and then I awoke ..." (His images were in his other house, in Lagos.) In this case the traditional dreams in which Ifa is fighting him are resolved by another dream where the voice, attributed to Olorun, now prevails.

The other dream is reported from Otta: James White recorded that the Apena of Ilogbo told him that he had become a church attender after a dream in which he saw a house like James White's.[13] In his dream he was questioned by a person who asked him if he knew his true identity. He answered that he did not know. Then the other answered him that he was Olorun and that the Apena should serve him. Here Olorun appears in a dream very much like an *orisa*.

From the dreams of those with very little prior contact with Christianity we now have to turn to those that are explicitly conversion dreams. The first dates back to 1856 at Otta, where it was recorded by James White.[14] A Sierra Leonean woman told of a dream she had had in which her three deceased children appeared to her to authorise a change from previous ways. They pleaded with her that she should no longer trade on Sundays and should give up her traditional religious practices or else be lost in the world to come. In her dream she was staggering on rough ground in a "dreary wilderness", making her way through thorn bushes. Her children found her, took her by the hand and brought her to a fine path. She interpreted this as God speaking to her, and obeyed the divine call. Members of one's own family appearing from the spirit world to advocate a change from one path to another is a very traditional theme.

A dream with somewhat similar features led another person at Otta to remarry the wife he had divorced.[15] Samuel Otana had a dream in which three men appeared to him "in sacerdotal robes". They reprimanded him for putting away his wife. He took this as a sign of divine disapproval. In this case no eschatological motif appears. The following year at Badagry a woman told Samuel Pearse of her conversion dream.[16] The theme this time is not the two paths but two groups. One company are calm and serene, with bright and cheerful countenance, the other troubled and confused. "In her dream she was standing alone viewing and considering this sight when a strange person appeared to her and said: 'Layemi, this is the word you are told'." And pointing to the traditional believers he added: "These are all idol worshippers." She started back with fear and then awoke determined to renounce her *orisa*. This is a clear conversion dream, rather traditional and non-eschatological, but with obvious facility in the teachings of the catechist.

The future life appears strongly in the dream of one Israel at Oshielle in 1874.[17] Israel was a centenarian long resistant to the new faith. The dream which directed him to change was largely eschatological. There was revealed to him, we are told, "the different states of mankind in the future life".

A series of shamanic and eschatological conversion visions were described to James White by a carefree, mercurial and widely known literate specialist in drumming. The visions coincided with a strange illness and were followed by a profound character change.[18] When Tifa, which was his theophoric name, fell ill he was attended by relatives who gave him traditional medicines, sacrificed to the *orisa*, and by divination discovered that he had offended against Ifa and Owo, a local river deity. He said to James White: "Baba, I am seeing strange things. It is no dream. I see them as clearly as can be though no one else sees them. My heavenly father has given orders to some being to fetch me. He has bound me with fetters and is ready to take me away. But on saying I am not prepared for this summons ... Father commanded me to be set at liberty. I am let loose, but go I must, for the messenger is standing by me and is waiting for me."

He was later transferred to the schoolmaster's house where he continued to have visions. He now expressed a wish to be baptized. He even told James White that God had baptized him and named him Michael. "I see him also", he said "plucking (out) my heart, putting it into a vessel and cleansing it" – images consistent with shamanism and recalling Islamic legends of the Prophet's childhood. Tifa or Michael also described visions of heaven, of God, angels, devils, wicked men and hell, mingled with Biblical and traditional imagery. He told people that God's anger rested on Otta because of the people's hardness of heart. When he returned home he was locked up by his exasperated relatives. He proclaimed God's judgment against them and began to fast, being supported by "heavenly sustenance". Recovering his health he became "quite a different man"; he was now zealous, sober and affectionate. He invited the king and chiefs of Otta to attend church, he gave up his Ifa and Osu, his household *orisa,* and above all (regretfully) his drums. The emphasis upon visions with the associated illness in the account thereby indicates the intense and prolonged inner conversion struggle of this young man.

As well as appealing to the traditional authority of dreams, these conversion dreams and visions also contain references to traditional cultural and religious elements. A divine figure appears, whether an angel, messenger or Olorun himself, and authorises the change to a different path or group. In the next and final group, that of converts' dying visions, we would expect Christian theology and eschatology to feature more explicitly than before. And such indeed proves to be the case. But we are fortunate to have for comparative purposes a record of a purely traditional dying vision which makes clear the contrast. In 1862

Akibode, the *babalawo* at Badagry, tells Samuel Pearse about the last days of his brother Omoni.[19] Omoni told his brother first of all that he had received a pardon for what he had done wrong. Then came a vision of a large body of people coming to attend his funeral. He wanted them all to be fed liberally. At the end he sat up, repeated the name of his brother and added: "My spirit is going, going up, going up". He repeated this three times, then lay down as if to sleep, and died.

By contrast, Joseph Ikono who died old and sick at Abeokuta in 1873, had, we are told by Pearse, a clear vision of Jesus.[20] Unable to speak, he raised his hand in a gesture of salutation, put a hand over his face in prayer, shook hands with his children and others, then breathed his last.

David Williams also reports two more dying visions in the same year. A young woman who was ill and dying had what seems like a vision of a large rock from which water flowed.[21] She wanted people to take her out and wash her in it. Then in a state of ecstasy she declared she was going to Christ. She removed her wedding ring, gave it to her husband, commended him to God and asked that he be provided with a wife who would give him children (as she had not been able to do). The vision of another dying young woman was of two Yoruba messengers who were sent to bring her home. But in this case they were singing the hymn *Jesu afe pade* (Jesus we love to meet). This she too sang, prayed, said *Amin*, and died.[22]

The following year the convert Eliza Afrezi died at Badagry.[23] Although clear in mind, she was infirm and blind from extreme age so that she was in the habit of being spat on as a witch as she went along the street. Towards the end she became aware of the presence of Christ, followed by a vision which caused her to cry out: "My eyes are open, my eyes are open", in a state of ecstasy. She too sang a hymn, one composed by Maria Ekidan: *Olugbala iso li oba mimo* (O Saviour thou art the holy king).

The theme of rejection and deliverance from suffering is repeated in the vision of a sick convert in Abeokuta in 1870, who saw evil spirits surrounding him.[24] They did not touch him but they frightened him. Then another company of men was seen coming to pray for him, after which the evil spirits ceased to appear.

Perhaps the most detailed record of a vision is by Matthew Luke at Palma in 1878.[25] It is worth noting in passing that Matthew Luke himself had a predictive dream earlier the same year: he was told in the dream that he was in his last year at Palma. And so it proved when the next year he was moved to Leke.[26] The dying vision he records was of a convert who had experienced persecution in Abeokuta in 1867. "She found her feet lifted up as if she were under the cross; she had gone with Jesus to the judgment hall and had been pleading his innocency with wicked men that rose up to condemn him, saying, 'This innocent man who raised the dead... you are going to kill'...But they did not listen to me, and so they killed him. The drops of blood are as if he is just slain, they dropped on my sin-stained garment and I am clean." This vision, like the previous one, does show strong identification with Jesus as *Olugbala* (Saviour). The eschatological element which is present here becomes even more pronounced in the case of Hannah Pearse of Otta (reported by James White) whose dying vision depicted God, angels and heaven in detail.[27]

The Yoruba catechists not only judged at least some of the dream experiences which were recounted to them as significant, but it is also evident that they accorded importance to their own dream experiences, some of which were also recorded. Dream recollections were used here to articulate and realise the personal experiences of profound social and religious changes which disrupted precisely that by which one's individual identity could be secured among one's fellow men, the traditional terms through which people share in ultimate human values. Traditional Yoruba recollections of dreams seize upon the interlinked themes of neglect of social obligations, estrangement from the gods, and the threatening isolation of sickness or captivity or a journey, and by giving expression to them, seek to transcend them. Dreams are used to achieve a social and personal integration by appealing to precisely those elements which threaten integration, and so can be elaborated and adapted to the needs of deep religious change experienced at the personal level as a crisis of identity or recognition of conversion. The period from 1852 to 1879 was a time of profound religious change in Yorubaland. What emerges is the fact of the living traditional substratum, out of which enquirers and converts emerge, and part of which they retain along with new symbols and new religious experiences issuing from a new faith with its eschatologically-oriented cosmology. This intermingling of the traditional and the new was to be strongly discouraged in order to stress the distinctiveness of the new way. It re-emerges only in the following century with the rise of the independent churches.

NOTES

1. See for example Sanders 1985; Lewis 1971:138; Idowu 1967:18 and Lienhardt 1976.
2. Church Missionary Society Archives, Birmingham University Library. CA2, 058, Jnl. 13/11/75.
3. 035, 19/5/76
4. 076, 28/5/63
5. 075, 2/12/72
6. 019, 17/8/70
7. 098, 13/4/75
8. 058, 29/2/75
9. 098, 6/8/79
10. 019, 18/12/77
11. 041, 7/2/79

12. 076, 16/9/62
13. 087, 27/9/70
14. 087, 25/4/56
15. 087, h.y.e. 25/9/65
16. 076, 30/4/66
17. 037, 5/8/74
18. 087, h.y.e. 25/9/65
19. 076, 7/4/62
20. 090, 12/1/73
21. 090, 7/3/73
22. 090, 13/10/73
23. 076, A.L. 13/10/74
24. 029, 3/6/70
25. 064, 9.e. 30/9/78
26. 064, 31/1/78
27. 087, h.y.e. 25/9/65

REFERENCES

CHURCH MISSIONARY SOCIETY ARCHIVES. Birmingham University Library.
IDOWU, E.B., 1967, The Study of Religion: with special reference to African Traditional Religion. *Orita.* 1, 3-13.
LEWIS, I.M., 1971, *Ecstatic Religion.* Harmondsworth: Penguin.
LIENHARDT, R.G., 1976, *Divinity and Experience: the religion of the Dinka.* Oxford: Clarendon Press.
McKENZIE, P.R., 1976, *Inter-religious Encounters in West Africa.* Leicester: Dept. of Religion.
SANDERS, N.K., 1985, *The Epic of Gilgamesh.* Harmondsworth: Penguin Books.

PRIVATE DREAMS AND PUBLIC KNOWLEDGE IN A CAMEROUNIAN INDEPENDENT CHURCH

RICHARD T. CURLEY
University of California, Davis

Introduction

The starting point of any anthropological analysis of religion is the idea that religion is a social phenomenon. Following Durkheim (1915), anthropologists have emphasized the collective nature of religious experience and have studied how religion draws from and shapes other forms of social life. As fruitful as the Durkheimian legacy has been, there are a number of problems associated with it. The problem to be addressed in this paper is the relationship between the individual believer and the religious group, or, to put it differently, the conjunction of private religious experience and the shared knowledge of a community of believers. A dogmatic adherence to the Durkheimian admonition to omit consideration of the self from the study of religion leads at some point to the problem of recognizing that religion involves particular ways of perceiving and knowing the world and that this must include taking account of the consciousness of the believer.[1] In calling attention to "moods and motivations" (1966:8-12) Geertz has suggested that religion is, in part, a matter of the psychic states of individuals. But individual religious experiences such as dreams become proper grist for the anthropological mill when they are communicated to others, acted upon, and interpreted in a particular social context. Here I would concede that Durkheim may have the last word on this topic, for it is fundamentally sound to argue that although dreams may arise in the individual psyche, the anthropologist must study them in their capacity as social facts rather than as clues to the workings of the mind.

In doing research on the Camerounian branch of an evangelical Christian church called the True Church of God, I listened as people recounted their dreams in church services and in other settings, and I became interested in the place that dream narrations occupy in the public life of the church. The purpose of this paper is to discuss the topic of dreams with respect to the larger question of the relationship between the individual and the religious movement. I will discuss the place of dreams in the social relations of the congregation, but I will focus on the process by which the experience of dreaming and the contents of individual dreams became incorporated into the collective life of the sect.[2] A new member of the True Church of God is expected to narrate a dream which becomes an important part of the individual's public identity in the church and establishes the credentials of the dreamer as one who has contact with God. But the dreams of individual members also comprise part of the collective knowledge of the Church and provide religious experiences for the entire congregation which are continually being renewed as dreams are recounted and interpreted.

The church and its membership

The True Church of God was established in eastern Nigeria in 1953, and there are now about 5000 members belonging to 125 branches. The church is independent, although it professes to be closely allied to other evangelical churches in Nigeria. The headquarters of the church in Nigeria is moderately successful in maintaining a centralized authority which appoints pastors and oversees the activities of the various branch churches. The data in this study were collected during the observation of two small branches: one in Tiko and one in Victoria, consisting of 65 and 73 adult members respectively.[3] Most of the members are Igbo who were born in Nigeria but who migrated to western Cameroun to seek work. Since the Camerounian government has rather strict policies pertaining to the employment of Nigerian citizens in any government controlled enterprise, Igbo who reside in Cameroun generally work as traders or in the transport business. Those who are well established control Igbo lineage associations which are closely linked to commercial activities and provide a means for newcomers to find housing and employment. For various reasons, many Igbo newcomers are unable to participate in this system of patronage, and these people often find themselves at the bottom of the urban social order with very few prospects for employment and little reason to return to Nigeria. When some personal crisis or health problem affects them they may present themselves to the True Church of God and, in the eyes of the members of the church, they become candidates for conversion. The church is not ethnically exclusive, however, and five of the adult members are not Igbo. It is considered desirable to have non-Igbo in the congregation because of the fear of discrimination or some kind of government action against Igbo and, more importantly, because the church places a low value on ethnicity, which it sees as something associated with a tradition-bound, pre-modern and "pagan" West Africa.

The sect demands a great deal of its members. They are expected to conform to strict rules which embrace most aspects of life. Church attendance averages 14 hours per week for each adult member, and sanctions are applied to those whose attendance seems to be lagging. Members are expected to contribute at least 10% of their incomes to the church and to donate labor each week to the maintenance of the church building and gardens. Family relations are regulated, with husbands and wives being expected to maintain a strict division of labour within a framework of mutual respect and equality. Children are disciplined severely, perhaps because of the recognition that it is difficult to maintain control over children as they reach adolescence, and many of them drift away from the sect. The church also controls marriage by requiring parents to send their daughters to the bishop's residence when the girls are about 16 years of age. The unmarried girls are expected to serve the church leaders for a year or two until they are married. Young men who are looking for a wife must write to the bishop requesting one of the unmarried girls, and the bishop usually responds by arranging a marriage. Prospective marriage partners have little choice in this matter, and the bishop is expected to use his judgement in arranging the marriage. There are also rules pertaining to eating, fasting, bathing, sleeping arrangements, wearing clothes, and personal comportment. The sort of music one listens to and the company one keeps are also included in this comprehensive set of rules which enfolds the member in a totalitarian community. There is undoubtedly a draconian quality to participation in the True Church of God, but one must also note that there are compensations and rewards for church membership which greatly soften the discipline and regulations. Church members perceive the community as a virtual utopia which has helped them to solve many of the pressing problems of daily existence and will assure their admission to the afterlife. They believe that they are working to construct a perfect community based on equality and mutual concern (Curley 1983:24).

There is one feature of the church which deserves special attention because it bears upon almost all aspects of the life of the participants. This is the rule that enjoins members from seeking medical care of any sort outside of the church itself. A central tenet of the church is that the prayers of its members, under the direction of a church official, have the magical power to heal any injury or sickness (Curley n.d.). This means that traditional African healing techniques as well as western medicine are to be assiduously avoided. This requirement means that the individual puts a great deal of trust in the church and is dependent on the collective faith of the congregation. In extreme cases one's very life is in the hands of the church community, and the most emotional of the church's public events take place when a seriously sick person is being prayed for.

There is little systematic theology in the True Church of God apart from a lively interest in the Old Testament, which forms the basis of many of the preacher's sermons and remarks. All of the adult members own Bibles and read them enthusiastically, although some have only a minimal reading ability. There is no formal biblical instruction, and the exegetical comments of the church leaders are often idiosyncratic and inconsistent. Rather than knowing the bible, church members are expected to have a fervent commitment to God and a willingness to follow the rules of the sect. Indications of commitment are sought when people first present themselves to the church as supplicants or as potential members.[4] Energetic dancing and singing, generous monetary contributions, audible prayer and frequent attendance are all taken as signs of commitment, but these in themselves do not serve as qualifications for membership. It is expected that a convert will undergo a critical and dramatic experience which offers clear proof that the person possesses a religious faith which is strong enough to bring him into direct contact with God. The dramatic experience comes in the form of a significant cure or a particularly vivid dream, and most new members experience both shortly before being admitted.

Dreams and the transformation of the individual

There are two contexts in which dreams are important in the True Church of God: in religious conversion, when the newcomer experiences a formative dream, and in the regular activities of the church in which people reconfirm their faith by recounting recent dreams. Elsewhere I have described how the conversion dreams help to endow the sect with legitimacy as a true community of believers, whereas the reconfirming dreams are part of a thinly veiled form of competition between men who are vying for positions of leadership in the church (Curley 1983:31-36). In the present study I am interested in the way a conversion dream aids in transforming an individual into a member of a collective community. A person who is attending the True Church of God and who is recognized as a candidate for conversion soon learns to await a vivid dream which will indicate that he is having a direct experience with God. Moreover, he or she will hear of the conversion dreams of other church members, since these are often discussed in conversations with friends. The potential convert will be encouraged to try to remember any particularly interesting dreams and to report them to the church as soon as they occur.

In addition to awaiting the dream, the person who is considering conversion engages in other activities, the most important of which is likely to be undergoing a cure. The duration and intensity of the curing will vary depending on the severity of the ailment. In the case of a serious ailment the candidate may move into the church compound and attend services three or four times each day, or several members of the church may pray constantly over the person, even maintaining an all night vigil. The candidate may also undergo instruction at the hands of the pastor or one of the church elders. This usually entails some Bible reading and lengthy discussions of the rules of the sect. One of the most noteworthy features of the conversion experience is the social immersion of the candidate into the church community. Members of the church prepare meals for the candidate and perform numerous other services.[5]

When the convert recounts a dream there is typically a tentative quality to the narration lest the narration prove to be unacceptable or inadequate proof of the piety of the individual. The dream can be tried out on two or three trusted friends within the congregation. This preliminary audience plays an important role in the acceptance of the conversion dream. If they are impressed by its contents, the dream will be retold and discussed. Some church members explained that during the period of their conversion they recounted several dreams until one of them was proclaimed as evidence of direct contact with God. It is at this point that the dream becomes publicized, news of the experience rippling outwards through the congregation. The preacher takes advantage of the next well attended church service to announce that the individual has had contact with God through a dream, and after the preacher has made some comments, the initiate is asked to stand and publicly recount the dream.

Candidates learn to expect a significant dream, but do they look for certain standard motifs in the dream? Observers of other African religious movements have found that the dreams follow a formula and may even be stereotypic (Fabian 1966; Sundkler 1961:273). I collected accounts of the conversion dreams of 35 of the members of the True Church of God, and there, although there are some common symbols, there is considerable variation in these dreams. Some of the recurring symbols are death and rebirth, light, bodies of water, religious symbols such as the Bible and baptism, physical afflictions, dead family members (particularly children), forests, mountains, and, above all, scenarios in which the individual was able to overcome some seemingly insurmountable obstacle. Dreams are not deemed unacceptable if they are lacking in any of these symbols, nor are the contents subjected to scrutiny for the purpose of eliminating those whose dreams do not fit into a standard mould, as in the Zulu Zionist churches (Sundkler 1961:274). The principal criterion of the acceptability of a dream narration is whether it contains sufficient evidence of a direct communication with God. This is decided informally and impressionistically on the basis of the dramatic impact of the dream narration on others. Nor is there much effort to intepret the dream once it has been narrated and accepted as evidence that the candidate has communicated directly with God. The dream is essentially regarded as self evident.[6] What is deemed important is its impact rater than any esoteric message that it might convey.

Turning to an example of a person who experiences such a dream when joining the church, we can consider the way in which the dream facilitates the acceptance of the individual into the church. John is an unmarried man of about twenty two who lives alone with his mother in a small rented dwelling about one hundred yards from the church. He is atypical of the church membership in that he is not Igbo but is a Camerounian from the Bamenda, or Grassfields, area. John attended a Roman Catholic mission school in Bamenda until the age of thirteen, when he quit and assisted his father on the family farm. His father beat him regularly for being lazy, and at about this time John's mother became mad. She was incapable of looking after herself and was barely coherent. John reported that he was unable to put up with the way his father mistreated the increasingly sickly woman, and John left the family home and took his mother with him to try to find work in the coastal plantations. His employment on the coast was short lived, and he had to quit working because he was not strong enough to do plantation labor and because he was experiencing headaches. He had given up attending the Roman Catholic church, and, essentially destitute, he continued to live with his mother while doing odd jobs.[7] His headaches became worse, and he began to have fevers. Living close by the True Church of God, he learned of its reputed ability to cure, and he approached one of the church members in the marketplace one day. John was introduced to the preacher and was soon regarded as a good prospect for recruitment. He was given a copy of the Bible and began to attend church meetings two or three times each day. He worked around the church grounds, and several of the more stalwart members read the Bible with him and explained the rules of the church. John asked the preacher to try to cure his illness and help his mother. He reported that he had been turning pale and that "his blood was vanishing", so the congregation continued to pray for his recovery. After a month of being prayed for, John's conditions failed to show any signs of improvement, and in the meantime his mother's condition deteriorated.

As for his religious commitment, John was obviously likely to be a dependable member of the sect, but his piety had still not been demonstrated in any dramatic way. It should also be noted that John is not a forceful personality. He is young, small of stature, inarticulate, shy, unmarried, and without any kinsmen to offer him assistance. These character traits did not mean that he was undesirable to the church as a prospective member, but his passiveness made it difficult for him to demonstrate the sort of visible religiosity that is sought in the convert. John was often asked whether he had experienced any interesting dreams and was told that he should expect God to come to him in a dream.

About five weeks after he began attending the church, John approached two of the men who had been coaching him and reported that he had experienced a dream in which he had been walking near the church one night when the devil leapt out from behind a tree and threw him to the ground. The devil proceded to bind his hands and feet and left him lying on the ground for three hours. At daybreak some members of the church found him and released him. After John recounted the dream to the two men they discussed it and reported that it was an encouraging sign but that he should continue to await a dream of greater import. Later, when people came to discuss this dream, they said that it was insignificant in that it did not particularly indicate that God was in communication with John. Indeed, the power of the devil over John was taken as a troubling sign, and furthermore, the release of John in the dream was effected through human rather than supernatural agencies.

Six days later John reported a second dream to the same two men. The devil appeared to him again and beat him badly. After subduing John, the devil forced him through a narrow opening of a tree into a hollow space inside. At this point John became an infant, and he was sure that he was inside his mother's womb. There was no way for him to get out, and he was stricken with terror at being pent up in the small space. But after hearing a loud cracking noise and seeing a flash of light, he felt himself being released as the tree split in two. The trees around him were on fire, and then God appeared to John and explained that he had seen fit to release him but that he would let John burn to death if he did not confess his sins. The dream concluded with John asking God to reveal what his sins were and then being given a list of all the sins which he was to confess publicly.

John reported that he woke up at this point and asked his listeners if they thought that he should make a public confession. The dream aroused a great deal of interest and was reported to the preacher, who told John that he should confess his sins publicly the next day at the Sunday service. By the next morning everyone in the Church had heard the dream; nevertheless, the preacher asked John to stand and recount it once again before confessing his sins. The public recounting of the dream was highly successful. The preacher and others pointed out that John had come into contact with God and that he was henceforth a new man. In fact, the dream attracted much more attention that the public confession of sins, which was somewhat anti-climatic.

There is no formal ceremony which marks official admission to the True Church of God. Once the congregation has accepted that God's power has acted upon the individual then it is expected that the newcomer will become an active member of the community and follow its rules. Although the candidate is challenged to experience either the dream or the cure, it is not really a test designed to eliminate the unworthy or insincere. It is assumed that anyone who has shown enough interest to seek out the church is likely to join. Moreover, the sect is very small and needs members. It proselytizes actively and is not likely to weed people out. I have never heard of a person being deemed unacceptable because his dreams were not sufficiently convincing, although many, like John, are encouraged to come up with better dreams.

After settling into the life of the church, John seldom reported dreams. He did not present the reconfirming dreams at Sunday services as many other men did, but this is to be accounted for both by his shyness and by the fact that he was not competing with other men for recognition. He remained impressed with his own conversion dream and made frequent reference to it. As time went on, other people were less keenly interested in the dream that John had at the time of his conversion, but it was mentioned several times at Church services by the preacher and several elders. On two occasions the image of John in the uterus was cited in sermons as an indication that people who are not in the True Church of God have not really been born. The image of the burning forest was also recalled during a sermon on hell, and John was asked twice to confess his sins because this had been part of his instruction in the original dream at the time of conversion. John also referred to it in conversations with the ethnographer and other church members. Depending upon the flow of the conversation, one or another feature of the dream would be highlighted, but it was apparent that the dream had made a lasting impression on John and, perhaps more importantly, entered into the way in which he was regarded by the rest of the congregation.

The dream and the church

The narration of the dream is a public rendition of a private experience. The person who begins to attend the True Church of God soon hears of the dreams of church members and learns that individuals gain recognition for their dreams. As his interest in the church grows he may anticipate a conversion dream, and, in doing so, enters into a process of negotiation with the congregation as to the nature of a successful religious experience. Thus, the conversion dream is significant for the individual because of the attitudes towards dreams within the belief system of the True Church of God and also because of the social relations of conversion, i.e. the conversion dream plays an important role in incorporating the individual into a new community. The salient belief, as we have already noted, is that the individual must strive for evidence of a direct contact with the supernatural. In that respect the search for a dream constitutes something of a vision quest – an affirmation to the prospective convert that his interest in the Church was well founded, and that he has taken the right course of action in joining the group.

It is worth noting that, of the five conversions which I observed, all of the converts expressed some apprehension concerning the anticipated dream. Interest in the conversion dream seemed to be less among those who were undergoing a cure for a serious illness. In one case, when a man had been injured in an automobile accident and could barely walk, he sought the assistance of the church after the local hospital had been unable to do anything for him. In another instance, a woman began attending the church while she was experiencing something of a medical crisis after six months of intestinal pain. She was vomiting blood, and the congregation responded to the urgency of her case by holding several all night prayer vigils. Only a modest amount of effort was put into encouraging these two people to anticipate dreams, for it was expected that they would be cured suddenly and visibly, and that the cures would constitute sufficient proof that the converts were in direct contact with God. These individuals reported dreams after they had been cured, but the accounts of the dreams were received with less interest than the fact that they seem to have been cured miraculously. Curing and dreaming, then, constitute parallel paths to conversion. Most people experience both the dream and the cure, and both became a part of the person's identity within the church. Either the dream or the cure might be emphasized at the expense of the other, depending upon the particular case. Those persons who do not come to the church with a serious physical ailment which can be cured in some dramatic manner are more likely to experience a particularly strong dream that will later be presented to the congregation at large. These people are likely to complain of somewhat vague symptoms – often psychosomatic in nature, like John's headaches and fever. Curing will be a part of their admission to the Church, but in such cases, the dream takes on greater importance in the process of conversion.[8] Interestingly enough, several members of the church pointed out that there have been many instances in which sick people have attended the church and after being successfully cured lose all interest in the church and are never seen there again. In mentioning these cases, the church members emphasize the value of the dream as a surer sign of religious faith than the cure. The dream, they argue, originates in the mind and is willed by the individual, whereas the physical cure is induced by external agents, the prayers of the faithful. In other words, the dramatic cure is as much an indication of the faith of the congregation as a whole as it is an indication of the piety of the individual. The conversion dream, however, is a personal experience which begins not with the congregation but with the individual. This is not really a tenet of the church, but it may help to explain why converts are expected to have a dream at the time of conversion even if they have experienced a cure.

The apprehension of the individual who is awaiting the dream is undoubtedly related to the desire to meet the expectations of the congregation. The True Church of God has a strongly developed sense of the boundaries which demarcate it from the rest of the society. The attitudes towards those who are not members of the church range from indifference to animosity. Members of the church often harangue people in the marketplace for their ungodly behavior, and the local population sometimes responds with considerable hostility. People who belong to the mainsteam Christian churches are viewed with contempt, and outsiders are generally seen as sinful and dangerous. The person who is undergoing conversion is in an uncertain position. To a certain extent converts stand apart from the rest of the outside world because they have made a step away from the larger community towards the church. Their inclinations and interest in the church are valued by the congregation, but they are still tainted by their association with the outside world and its habits. While the convert is learning that a dream is expected he or she is also becoming increasingly dependent on the church community. The obligation to reciprocate builds up as the convert is fed and cared for by the congregation, and these material transactions are instrumental in facilitating the entrance of the person into a new set of social relations. It is difficult to tell from the data at exactly which point in the process of conversion the individual is likely to report a dream, but I did not hear of any instances in which the dream was reported within the first three weeks of joining.

Turning from the social position of the convert to the place of the dream in the teachings of the church, we have already observed that there is little formal instruction associated with admission into the church, nor is there any official admission procedure. There is a simple baptism during which the convert renounces his past, but the ceremony is generally a minor part of the Sunday service and may be scheduled long after the person has come to be regarded as a member. The teachings of the church do not specify the exact point at which the individual has entered into the fold except to reiterate the church's overall emphasis on the individual's direct involvement with God. The requirement that one demonstrate one's faith would seem to be in clear continuity with the missionary tradition in West Africa, which has constantly called attention to the "reality and fate of the individual soul" (Fernandez 1982:283). In criticizing the spirit of individualism which permeated the missionary enterprise, the Ghanaian church scholar, K. A. Dickson asked, "are we in danger of preaching with too great an emphasis on individual involvement ... the doctrine of justification by faith is, for example, the most missionary of doctrines" (Dickson 1969:43, cited in Fernandez 1982:283). Apart from the fact that the requirement to demonstrate one's faith is a legacy of colonial missions, the difficulty with such a demonstration is that it requires some clear criterion as to how one makes the demonstration in such a way as to convince others. The convert to the True Church receives some advice from his instructors and listens to enough narrations of conversion dreams to learn how to present the narration. In doing so, he puts forward a new formulation of self, one that conforms to the church's view of itself as a community of "saved" individuals.

If there is a requirement to conform to certain levels of intensity in dreaming we might expect that there would be some standardization of the contents of dreams, but their contents are actually quite varied.[9] The most frequently recurring motif involves the dreamer performing some kind of miracle. Sometimes God is standing by or appears in the dream as the evident source of superhuman power, as in John's dream. In many occasions, however, there is only a vague allusion to God as the source of power, and the narration seems to emphasize the strength of the dreamer. For example, in one dream a woman saw her three children fall into a swift stream, and she saved them from drowning by jumping in and swimming after them. This narration made an impression on people partly because in her preamble she stated that she was unable to swim. As far as the congregation was concerned the meaning of this dream was self evident, and the preacher and other leaders did not undertake any interpretation. The narration seems to be based on the assumption that God was responsible for her heroic act, but this is only implied because God does not actually appear in the dream. This particular example also includes the second most popular motif in the conversion dreams, a reference to water or a body of water, which is present in about one third of the dreams. The other common elements such as birth, death, fire, light, and various features of the landscape might best be interpreted psychoanalytically rather than anthropologically, but it is highly likely that these symbols recur because the people have heard them recounted in the narrations of other church members. In other words, the private experience of the dream, in its very details, may have been suggested by public performances within the community.

I suspect that if the leaders of the church engaged in a more systematic interpretation of the dreams, and if the dreams were used for divinatory purposes, the amount of standardization and patterning would be greater, or at least that more attention would be paid to the meaning of specific elements within the dream. My data suggest that the branches of The True Church of God which I studied in Cameroun attached greater significance to dreams than do other branches of the church, and that dream narrations became a more important part of the conversion process in the late 1960s. I do not have much information on the use of dreams in other branches of the True Church of God, but members of the Tiko and Victoria branches suggested that they pay more attention to dreams than do the members of other branches. If their interest in dreams is really recent, and if other branches of the church lack that interest to the same degree, then there may simply not have been enough time for the church to have devised a formal procedure of interpretation whereby specific meanings are assigned to various symbols. Indeed it would be reasonable to assume that in many independent churches dreams become the object of an increasingly analytical interpretation as time goes on and as the sect becomes more routinized. Such a development would have the effect of strengthening the authority of church leaders who can come to be regarded as capable of clarifying the esoteric contents of dreams. What seems to be of most interest within the True Church of God is the acceptance of the dream narration as the indication of a spontaneous profession of faith.

The Church's acceptance of a dream narration at face value without endeavoring to interpret its symbolic content or to use the dream for divinatory purposes raises several issues with respect to the place of the individual in the church. In a tightly organized community, regulated by comprehensive normative rules, and calling for a great deal of group activity, the conversion dream stands as one of the first emotionally charged experiences which the individual has within the church community, the other being the cure. In narrating the dream, the individual continues to negotiate with the congregation regarding the validity of this dream and the depth of his or her religious faith. The convert learns that the community expects him to have intense religious experiences, but that these experiences are not to be kept to oneself. The religious experiences, like the rest of oneself, become the property of the community. This is instructive to the convert during the early phases of church membership. The intensive solicitude which is extended to prospective members usually lasts about a month, and when it winds down the individual must play an active part in the church. The new church members must now be prepared to pray for others, make burdensome monetary contributions, and adhere to the strict rules of the church. The acceptance of the conversion dream, together with the curing experience, informs the newcomer that he or she possesses the requisite spiritual qualities to live up to the expectations of the church. Church sermons and the remarks of church members are replete with discussions of "unworthiness", "sin", and "failure".

Even the most faithful adherents find it difficult to live up to the church's expectations, and church members walk a thin line between the states of "grace" and "evil". Lapses often occur, and the preacher metes out harsh punishment – banishing people for various periods of time, fining them, demanding public confessions and statements of contrition, and insisting that they fast or go without water. The prospect of living up to the requirements of the church is daunting to many converts. Most of the people who approach the church as potential members are deterred from joining by the strictness of its rules. "It is very difficult and painful to watch them", a man told me after he had been attending for two weeks. The conversion dream and its publicizing help individuals recognize that they have passed a turning point, the creation of a new person who has left behind the chaos and loneliness of disbelief to join the companionship of God and the community. Armed with such a reformulation of self the individual is better prepared to face the challenges of church life.

This account of the convert as an individual who is in an uncertain position suggests that conversion resembles the rites of passage so amply documented in the literature of anthropology. The symbols of illumination, death and birth, and miraculous feats are similar to many of the symbols which have been widely reported in connection with initiation (La Fontaine 1985). The most prominent feature of the social backgrounds of those who join the church is the absence of a network of kinsmen. Most are labour migrants from Nigeria who face economic hardships and discrimination, and the True Church of God offers such individuals an all-encompassing community. They are free to enter if they possess the requisite religious faith, and the quest to demonstrate that faith involves a period of considerable uncertainty and anxiety. The liminality of the convert is not unlike the liminality of initiates in many other societies (Turner 1967). As they strive towards a resolution of this liminality during their incipient membership, they begin to undergo a profound change in the way that they view themselves. The change is dramatized in the dream experience and in the subsequent public narration of that experience. I am suggesting, then, that the conversion dream marks a kind of turning point for the individual in both an intellectual and social sense. Armed with a new religious faith, the person begins to experience the world differently, and that experience is shaped by a new social world into which he enters.

The conversion dream continues to be important for people as long as they remain in the Church. Of the people who attended the Tiko branch, the most long-standing members were a husband and wife, Abel and Mary, each about sixty years of age, who had joined the church together about eight years before my research. The preacher of the church and 12 other members knew something of the conversion dreams of these two oldest members. When asked to recite the conversion dreams of Abel and Mary, people told several different versions, and one of the accounts clearly confused the conversion dream of Mary with that of another woman. Only once did the preacher refer to the conversion of Abel, whereas Mary's was not mentioned in any sermon. Several times during conversations about Abel and Mary people referred to their conversion dreams, but their recollection was somewhat hazy. Yet Abel and Maria themselves were both animated while recounting the dreams that they had experienced upon joining the church. They stated that the dreams had marked the beginning of their commitment to the church. Others were also emphatic in describing their own dreams of conversion, and stated that the dreams had constituted an encounter with God. The occasional references to the dreams on the part of the older members and the more frequent references on the part of newer members indicates that interest in the dream may wane as time goes on, but the dream continues to remain a part of their own identity within the church.

The dream and communal knowledge

It is clear from the account of John's dream that the dream is not merely a matter of the individual demonstrating sufficient piety, but what is important is that the dream provides a visible link between the individual and the community at large. First there is the matter of the expectation itself – something that is communicated quite early on to each newcomer. Listening to church members recount their dreams the convert presumably learns the elements of a successful narration and, more importantly, learns what constitutes a valid religious experience. For example, hearing accounts of miraculous feats performed by people who are much like oneself impresses upon people the transformative power of religious faith. Similarly, the portraits of danger and punishment that befall the non-believer and such symbols as death and birth that run through the narrations of dreams demonstrate not only the faith of the individual narrator, but more significantly demonstrate the validity of the True Church of God. We might add that the dream narration comes very close to being a sanctified message in the sense in which Rappaport has discussed sanctification (1974:1979). The dream is believed to convey a kind of truth which is unaffected by human thought and is free of distortion – a pure truth emanating directly from the supernatural. Moreover, the act of narration is regarded by the members of the church as an occasion in which it is most unlikely that the speaker would distort the truth or fabricate. I have never known anyone in the congregation to raise a doubt regarding the truth of a dream narration. This attitude towards dreams gives the dream a kind of intellectual weight – a greater truth value than would be the case if a speaker, for example, were to tell a tale of his own prowess or rebirth without couching the account as a dream.

It remains for us to examine the place of the conversion dream in shaping the collective religious experience, for in recounting a dream the individual dreamer makes an important contribution to the collective knowledge of the congregation. Each narration invigorates the congregation as a set of people who are in direct contact with God. The narration presents a vivid and unquestionably true account of wondrous events taking place under the eye of God. We might suggest that the role of dreaming in the True Church of God is similar to the role played by spirit possession in many other African traditions. The possession trance and the ideology of spirit possession offer a demonstration of the immediacy and power of the supernatural realm that is thoroughly convincing to those who are inclined to believe. The possession trance allows the individual who is experiencing the trance to communicate a sanctified message. In many religious traditions, possession experiences help to redefine and reinterpret the supernatural world and its relationship to the real world, imparting a remarkable creativity of thought and adaptiveness to the religious tradition. In a similar manner, the use of hallucinogens in religious movements allows the individual to add to the collective religious experience by recounting particularly vivid or unusual episodes (Aberle 1965). Fernandez describes how Bwiti members ingest the psychotropic *eboga* during initiation before experiencing visions of encounters with the supernatural (1982:470-493). These religious experiences activate the religious consciousness of the individual and enable that consciousness to add to and enhance the prevailing religious ideology. The experiences confirm religious conceptions, in Geertz' words, "clothing those conceptions with ... an aura of factuality" (Geertz 1966:24).

The contents of the dreams of conversion in the True Church of God are generally simpler than many of the supernatural encounters believed to be associated with possession and the ingestion of hallucinogens. The narrations are not as dramatic or as convincing as most trance sessions, and they may therefore be less effective. It may be that as sanctified messages they are less sanctified than messages which are revealed in the more highly elaborate performances of religious experience like trances or the *eboga* sessions of Bwiti. Still, the dreams constitute an important form of religious experience for the members of the church. The narrator of the dream is changed by the narration and changes, ever so slightly, the prevailing view of the supernatural and its relationship to man.

Conclusions

In examining the conversion dreams of members of the True Church of God we have shown that the public and the private aspects are each identifiable, but that they are thoroughly intertwined. The emphasis which fundamentalist Christianity places upon individual salvation would appear to place a certain onus on the individual who might wish to join the church. The person is obliged to seek a religious experience which should put an end to a past life of sinfulness and despair and signal the opening to a new life of piety and intense communal life. This religious experience involves the person being singled out by the supernatural, and it takes place in the most private of settings, the time of sleep. It also carries the message that the individual can overcome obstacles, and it offers the person a set of images which help to mould a somewhat inchoate religious message into a clearer form. The dream brings the religious message into the person's own life by assuring the dreamer than he or she is an actor in the drama of sin and salvation that the Church continually enacts. In this sense the dream experience is a process of individuation: it helps to give form to a new identity.

The identity which is formed, however, is that of a person who is merged in a strongly collective community. Indeed the prevailing dialectical process within the True Church of God is the problem of combining individual salvation, personal faith, and the need to have a highly personal relationship with God, on the one hand, with an interest in promoting an egalitarian disciplined community, on the other hand. This is a struggle between individualism and *communitas*. We have seen that the dream itself arises out of the church's requirement for a demonstration of individual faith, and the dream is soon communicated to others. It is stimulated by the group, and after it is publicized it becomes the property of the community. In affirming the religious faith of the individual, the dream also affirms the religious faith of the community as a whole. The memory of one's own dream reminds the church member that he or she is in contact with the supernatural, and the collective dreams of the community remind the entire congregation of its faith and, thus, of the truthfulness of its message. Each new conversion dream offers the congregation a vicarious religious experience which infuses the community with a new and fervent vigour. In this way the dreams of conversion play an important role is resolving the tension between individual and community.

Recent trends within social anthropology have re-examined the Durkheimian assumption of social life as something which provides us with a means of transcending the self and rendering irrelevant the biologically and psychologically driven individual. Michele Rosaldo has characterized this trend as the insistence that "meaning is a public fact, that personal life takes place in cultural terms, or better yet, that individuals are necessarily and continually involved in the interpretive apprehension (and transformation) of received symbolic models" (Rosaldo 1984:140). Like all religious traditions, the True Church of God offers its adherents a set of meanings that enables them to interpret their private experiences and see that their lives can be rendered intelligible by cultural precepts. The church persuades its congregation and the occasional outsider that if they have religious faith and that if they practise that faith within the church they will thrive both physically and spiritually. But this cultural system requires the continual revitalization of its message. Like all cultural systems it is based on lived experience, and dreams of conversion are among those lived experiences which continually revitalize the message.

NOTES

1. Changes in the consciousness of individuals are well documented in the extensive literature on the role of trance, conversion, and hallucinogens in religious traditions.
2. In an earlier paper I discussed the place of dreams in the social organization of the True Church of God and concentrated on the ways in which dreams are used instrumentally as individuals compete with one another for prominence and key positions in the congregation (Curley 1983).

3. Research on the True Church of God was carried out during 1975 in Tiko and Victoria, Cameroun. I am grateful to the Committee on Research of the University of California at Davis for a grant which made fieldwork possible. I also want to thank Jim Racobs for a number of helpful suggestions.

4. Some non-members believe that the sect has a magical ability to cure. They attend because they are seeking medical treatment even though they may have no interest in joining.

5. Such practices are widely known in the study of religious conversion. For example, members of the Unification Church of the Rev. Sun. Myung Moon shower the potential member with kindness and gifts, a practice which they have aptly termed "love-bombing".

6. The True Church of God does not have any system of interpreting dreams in a formal way. Occasionally a preacher or a senior member may comment on a dream, but little effort is put into trying to interpret the dreams as events which may reveal a deep truth about human nature, the supernatural, or future events. The practices of the Church are reminiscent of the treatment of dreams in Tikopia, where "stock attributions of meaning are few" (Firth 1934:74).

7. Converts to the True Church of God tend to come from the orthodox missionary traditions, viz. Roman Catholic, Presbyterian and Baptist. In this respect, the sect resembles the Aladura churches of Nigeria (Peel 1968; Horton 1971:91).

8. By allowing some people to prove their piety by means of a dream, the church is increasing its pool of potential members. It need not recruit solely from among those who are sick with obvious physical symptoms.

9. In discussing the sameness among dreams in the Zulu Zionist traditions, Sundkler comments, "Dreaming in accordance with pattern becomes ... a group integrating force of surprising strength" (Sundkler 1961:273). In a more recent study, Kiernan paints a different picture of Zulu Zionist dreams, discussing a number of different types of dreams and visions and implying that the dreams are not as standardized as Sundkler believed (1985).

REFERENCES

ABERLE, D., 1965, *The Peyote Religion Among the Navaho*. Chicago: Aldine.

CURLEY, R.T., 1983, Dreams of power: social process in a West African religious movement. *Africa* 53(3): 20-38.

    n.d. Pushing Ahead: Development as a Metaphor in a West African Independent Church; manuscript.

DICKSON, K.A. & ELLINGWORTH, P. (eds.), 1969, *Biblical Revelation and African Beliefs*. London: Butterworth Press.

DURKHEIM, E., 1915, *The Elementary Forms of the Religious Life*. New York: Macmillan.

FABIAN, J., 1966, Theories of dreams in the Jamaa movement. *Anthropos* 61(2): 544-560.

FERNANDEZ, J., 1982, *Bwiti: an ethnography of the religious imagination in Africa*. Princeton: Princeton University Press.

FIRTH, R., 1967, The meaning of dreams. In *Tikopia Belief and Ritual*. London: George Allen and Unwin.

GEERTZ, C., 1966, Religion as a cultural system. In M. Banton (ed.), *Anthropological Approaches to the Study of Religion*. Association of Social Anthropologists Monographs, 3, 1-46. London: Tavistock Publications.

HORTON, R., 1971, African conversion. *Africa* 41(2): 85-108.

KIERNAN, J.P., 1985, The social stuff of revelation: pattern and purpose in Zionist dreams and visions. *Africa* 55(3): 304-317.
LA FONTAINE, J.S., 1985, *Initiation: ritual drama and secret knowledge across the world.* Harmondsworth: Penguin.
PEEL, J.D.Y., 1968, *Aladura: a religious movement among the Yoruba.* London: Oxford University Press for the International African Institute.
RAPPAPORT, R., 1974, The obvious aspects of ritual. *Cambridge Anthropology* 2(1): 3-69.
  1979 Sanctity and lies in evolution. In *Ecology, Meaning and Religion*, 223-246. Richmond, California: North Atlantic Books.
ROSALDO, M.Z., 1984, Toward an anthropology of self and feeling. In *Culture Theory: essays on mind, self and emotion.* Cambridge: Cambridge University Press.
SUNDKLER, B., 1961, *Bantu Prophets in South Africa,* 2nd edition. London: Oxford University Press for the International African Institute.
TURNER, V. 1967 *The Forest of Symbols.* Ithaca: Cornell University Press.

DREAMS IN AFRICAN CHURCHES

SIMON CHARSLEY
University of Glasgow

Dreams as data

Regardless of the varying cultural perceptions of the nature of dreams, including those of our own culture which has characteristically attempted in recent times to attach them to physically measurable manifestations (Webb and Cartwright 1978), the student of dreams is faced with accounts. These are constructed in particular circumstances, at particular times and for particular purposes. Different accounts given of what is claimed to be the same dream may sometimes be obtained (e.g. Evans-Pritchard 1937: 142-44), but there is no way in which one can go behind accounts to their hypothetical origin.

As long, therefore, as such accounts are taken unthinkingly as approximations to something different which is the real object of study, to hypothetical dreams as dreamt, there is confusion at the roots of any enquiry. There is not, harping back to a Tylorian idea of dreams as somehow a natural source of culture (Tylor 1871), something potentially outside culture here. Nor is it merely, as Bourguignon (1972:415) puts it, that cultural dogma "influences not only the *reporting* of dreams ..., but also, as far as we can tell, the subjective experience of these states". We have to deal, and can only be dealing, with linguistic performances inevitably imbued with the meaningfulness and values of a particular culture. There is no way in which even the most positivist of observers can conceive of a culturally neutral, or "scientific", account of a dream, because it is at best observable by one person only and then in a manner so unlike normal observation as to raise doubts as to its nature (Malcolm 1959).

When it comes to the interpretation of dreams, that they may mean more than their tellers understand is a common idea. What is equally conspicuous as soon as any body of dream narratives is examined is the extent to which interpretation is already embedded in their very construction. This goes beyond the need to understand the culture and experience of speakers if the significance of their words is to be appreciated. The associations and fans of meaning of key terms used in giving accounts commonly build interpretive implications into the accounts themselves. Firth (1934:168) exemplifies this well in his discussion of an ominous Tikopian dream of a shark in bad condition. He writes: "The association here between the gaunt appearance of the fish – 'with ribs showing' is the idea conveyed by the term *maki* in the original; the same word is used as a substantive, denoting epidemic disease – and the appearance of a sick man is very clear, especially when reinforced by this simile used by the narrator himself". I have myself considered the general interpetive context and the particular use of the term "heart" in the shifting of meanings which are standard components in interpreting (Charsley 1987), and I return to this below. An implication which ought therefore to be drawn from the recognition that accounts are the only data available is that they are bound to include a measure of what may be called "primary interpretation". It may indeed be that it is the exceptional permeability of dream accounts to such primary interpetation which leads humanity so often to see them as potentially meaningful.

A further crucial implication of the realization that narratives are the data concerns sampling. There is no way in which what may or may not occur at the hypothetical point of origin in sleep can be sampled. There is no way, for instance, of assessing whether there are more ancestral or non-ancestral dreams (c.f. Kiernan 1985:307), or whether sex plays a greater or lesser part in one people's dreams than in another (c.f. Gregor 1981), or whether African dreams have more manifest content than Euro-American (Lee 1958; c.f. Lincoln 1935:99). One can establish frequencies within a set of dream-narratives, but the conditions of their collection cannot then be ignored when it comes to explaining such frequencies. The implications for research methods in most anthropological settings are daunting. For any explanation to be possible, narratives will have to have been collected in a manner to allow a serious estimation of the circumstances and purposes involved in their telling. They cannot be treated simply as a sample of the "dream-life" of a group, people or culture.

The distinction frequently made between free and stereotyped dreams offers an important case in point. Though it is rarely mentioned in the literature, individuals may certainly believe themselves to have the same dream repeatedly. They may also believe that is is possible for different people to dream the same dream (Evans-Pritchard 1937:138). It is clear that there are often well known and standard categorizations of dreams, but it is also clear that many observers have been too ready themselves to categorize and to declare the existence of stereotypes, as if "dreaming the same dreams" were an unproblematic reality. There is a long tradition in anthropology of distinguishing between induced "culture pattern" dreams and individual, spontaneous dreams (Lincoln 1935:22). It has even been tempting to contrast cultures or contexts with stereotyped dreaming to those without (e.g. Charsley 1973:249). Whilst attempts to induce dreams are clearly something which may or may not occur, examination of dreams as accounts suggests that, as far as stereotyping is concerned, the classic distinction is largely the product of uncontrolled research and a failure to grasp the way in which interpetation is integral to the data.

From Africa, Hunter (1961) and Field (1960) provide evidence of the way in which narratives, though in reality varied, may be seen in terms of stereotypes because they are already marked at first telling by an immediate understanding of what they represent. The examples of dreams of *izulu* which Hunter provides in the course of her study of the Pondo of South Africa allow the reader gradually to realize the variability of the narratives which are being identified, mainly by the conviction of the tellers themselves, as dreams of this apparently stereotyped kind. The *izulu* is described initially as a common witchcraft familiar, a lightning bird which appears in the form of a beautiful young man and becomes a woman's lover *(op.cit.: 282)*. Dreaming of an *izulu* indicates that the dreamer has such a lover or is getting one, to her ultimate distress. However it emerges that neither the lightning bird nor the beautiful young man necessarily appear in such a dream. Out of the two it is said indeed to be always the latter, but at the same time rivers, green fields and pumpkins may be identified as "equivalent to" the *izulu (op.cit.: 285)*. A later series of examples of such dreams complete the collapse of the stereotype. There was a dream in which a visiting woman had killed a flying bird *(op.cit.: 327)*, and another in which the dreamer had heard someone saying that she would be bewitched with lightning and had later dreamed of lightning flashing around her head *(op.cit.: 490)*. A third was a dream of being chased by a man. How, the anthropologist wanted to know, did the woman in this last instance know it was an *impundulu* (another term for the same thing)? "If you dread a person then you know it is an *impundulu*. You do not fear if it is only an ordinary human being" *(op.cit.: 491)*. Field, from the very different context of her ethno-psychiatric study in Asante, Ghana, provides documentation of a similar phenomenon. An initial statement of a stereotyped dream – "people in fear of retribution for sin commonly dream that the deity, in the guise of a long-haired priest, is chasing them with a club and sometimes knocks them down" (1960:131) – is followed by examples which show a variety of chasings, a variety of weapons, and indeed a variety of creatures, from the deity himself to cows and snakes *(op.cit.: 176, 204, 217, etc)*.[1]

Lee (1958), a psychiatrist attempting a systematic analysis of Zulu dream contents on the basis of a large sample and his experience in medical practice, provides, unwittingly, impressive evidence of the same variability of dream narratives. He wishes to emphasize the small number of "main content headings" under which the Zulu dreams he collected could be classified. His technique of research, asking a sample of people what they dream about rather than for particular dreams, also seems calculated to maximize any stereotyping present. Given his intention and his method, what is impressive, however, is that he still requires almost fifty headings, and even the more definite of these embrace such a variety of individual dreams as to suggest the difficulty in sustaining even as complex a scheme as this. As in all systems of classification or of attributing meanings to dreams, the diversity of objects and events presented in all but the very briefest of narratives is necessarily discarded, to be replaced by a concentration on a relatively small set of items deemed significant.[2]

While therefore there may certainly be indigenous classifications of dreams, and the primary interpretation inherent in narratives frequently displays an awareness of them, attention to instances leads to a melting of stereotypes. A characteristic of dream narratives seems to be that they are as varied as the ideas and experience of those who tell them. Indeed, it may well be that there is here something of the essential character required for a narrative to be accepted as a dream at all. Too close conformity to any stereotype would jeopardize credibility.

Dreams in African Christian contexts[3]

> Dreams and visions are like dew on gossamer shining in the early morning sun in a clearing in the African bush. They are made of the most fine and delicate stuff, and they reveal the hidden hunger for beauty and holiness and a sacred rhythm of life (Sundkler 1960:31).

The impression is sometimes given that significant dreams are ubiquitous in African independent churches, indeed that they are ubiquitous in African Christianity and in African cultures even when not influenced by Christianity (e.g. Mbiti 1976; Shorter 1978). It is apparent that, if Africa is viewed as a whole and contrasted with Euro-America, the attachment of significance to dreams in Africa is considerable, possibly at times even justifying Sundkler's romantic image quoted above. The general impression needs, however, to be severely qualified. It arises from a tendency to seize upon any occurrence of dreams, of whatever kind and in whatever context, as exemplifying a supposed African preoccupation. Dreams may be of ancestors or of witches; they may be the ordinary dreams of ordinary people or the one momentous dream of an heroic leader; they may be what legitimizes cult membership or what must be left behind in "paganism" by the true believer. Such variety requires distinctions, not aggregation. There is a further problem too: it is only too easy to notice those contexts and studies in which dreaming does occur, to be impressed and to accept them as representative, whilst negative instances are ignored. A report which fails to focus on dreaming does not, it is true, mean that dreams are necessarily insignificant in that particular context[4], but neither does their mention imply high significance. In either case, the interests with which observers approach their study intervene. The evidence suggests, when reviewed, not ubiquity but a variable and patchy ocurrence.

Zulu society, in South Africa, is conspicuous for the attention which has been paid to dreaming within it. Interest was already clear in the nineteenth century, in the texts published by Callaway (1868-70; 228-52 and *passim*; c.f. Berglund 1976:25). Both traditional Zulu dreams and the dreams of Christian converts were already appearing. Much more recently Berglund (1976: 97-102 and *passim*) and Lee have emphasized the vigour of the pre-Christian tradition of dreaming which was still apparent in the 1950s and '60s. On the Christian side, Lee writes: "Patients of mine who claimed, as good Zionists, to dream often of *'ingelosi'* angels, on being pressed further, described these angels as ancestors wearing long white robes and, occasionally, wings!" (1969:152; c.f. 1958:279-80. Also note 1 above). The pioneering study of Christian dreaming is, however, Sundkler's (1961). He writes from long experience in the Christian field in Zululand and with a particular interest in the religious life of the Zionists. His preoccupation is first with call dreams, either those of founders or to membership of an already established church, and then with the routine telling of dreams which was a part of some churches' pattern of worship. He stresses the stereotyped nature of such dreaming, seeing it as revealing the control exercised even over the psyche of members by their church: *"They dream what their church expects them to dream"* (1961: 273; his emphasis). This is a perspective which has of course to be challenged in the light of the discussion above. More recently Kiernan, on the basis of research conducted between 1968 and 1970 in an urban setting, reports an apparent return to ancestral dreams as the main form, with an incipient opposition between such dreams on the one hand and visions and interpretation on the other. The former belong to ordinary members, the latter to the leadership and those aspiring to it: they are "the prerogative of prophecy" (1985:305). Unlike Pauw (1975:297, 304), he notes that dreams were not part of the standard set of contributions to Zionist meetings in an urban Zulu setting in the late 1960s (1985: 317). The same more restricted relevance is suggested by West's (1975) survey of independent churches in Soweto, Johannesburg; dreams of any kind are marginal in his account.

Even therefore in South African Zion, the classic ground of African church dreams, the apparent ubiquity of preoccupation with dreams falters when the range of evidence begins to be inspected. Sundkler in the mid century felt that the dammed force of such a preoccupation was one of the factors making for the departure, apparently inexorable, of African Christians from missionary churches and for the rise of a more truly African Christianity in the form of the Zionist movement. His sense of the direction of history led him to what can now be seen as an over-emphasis on a particular religious form (Zionism) and on one always somewhat variable feature of it (dreams). Though the Zionist movement has undoubtedly swept on, other forces have been at work too, and their varied effects are apparent in West's study.

Elsewhere in Africa the positive instances of dreams to which reference is made throughout this chapter are certainly to be found. It is striking that the KiKongo newspaper *Minsamu mia Yenge* was already publishing Christian dreams as early as 1894 (Janzen 1985:231). But, as Sundkler himself recognised, there are negative cases too. He offers the Balokole of East Africa as an exception to the general pattern he sees. That movement operated with the idea that dreams were from Satan; they would therefore be removed from the minds of the saved (Sundkler 1960:25-31). Much more generally, in the many churches in South Africa which he termed "Ethiopian", lacking the pentecostalism and the religious enthusiasm of the Zionists, dreams have never had great prominence. Even amongst churches similar in many respects to the Zionists, there have clearly been many in which dreams have not been important: Barrett was able in the 1960s to survey six thousand independent churches in some detail with no more than occasional passing mention of dreaming (Barrett 1968: 149, 178, 274).

It is clearly misleading to think in terms of an alternative between acute preoccupation or total absence in whole societies or even whole churches. The reality is that of patchy interest in dreams and of variable uses made of them. Amongst Kenyans in Uganda in the mid 1960s, my own choice of a particular church for detailed research rested not on its typicality but on the unusual extent to which it offered interesting matter for study. Part of this was the prominence, unmatched in most other churches locally, of dream-telling in its meetings. Daneel (1974) offers quantification of the same kind of variation from an area of rural Zimbabwe in the same period. He found likewise that in only a few particular churches had dream-telling a regular place in services. Though call dreams attracted attention in some, in all churches a majority of the members denied ever having experienced any such dreams before joining, or any church-related dream subsequently. The highest proportion, 38% of members of one particular church within what he describes as a "casual sample", said that they had been persuaded through dreams to join, whilst 29% had dreamed relevantly after joining. Far commoner was the idea that dreams are a channel through which God communicates. At a rather constant half of all members of all churches this was by far the commonest of mentioned means of communication, far ahead of "His word (Bible) and preachers". Most of this half, however, had clearly not themselves experienced such communication. With the possible exception of what Daneel calls "Spirit-type churches", the other half to whom even the possibility of such communication did not appeal have also to be remembered (Daneel 1974:139-41, 183-85).

Further, there is no necessary connection between traditional and Christian concerns, even if familiarity in parts of Africa with the idea of dreams as ancestral or spirit communication sometimes provided the historical base for an acceptance of Christian ideas about communication from God. Sundkler is notable for his determination to relate current Christian practice to the indigenous background, to *"the pattern of dream activity in heathen Zulu morality"* (1961:265; his emphasis). But for any church in which knowledge of the Bible is stressed, the models it provides are directly relevant and can hardly be missed. Shorter examines their full range in both the Old and New Testaments (1978:283-84), and Turner (1967, II:122) documents the sophisticated awareness of these in the 1938 constitution of the Church of the Lord (Aladura) in Nigeria. In my own East African field it seemed to be the dreams associated with Joseph in the book of Genesis which were best known and most frequently caught the imagination. Joseph's own dreams of future lordship over his family in Genesis 37 are not attributed to God, but their truth as an immediately interpretable account of future events is clear. Subsequently, in Chapters 40 and 41, the dreams interpreted by Joseph in Egypt are shown unequivocally as coming true. In the case of Pharaoh's dreams, Joseph's interpretations contain the reiterated assertion that God has shown Pharaoh in the dream what he is about to do. No more than a literal-minded readiness to identify with the Old Testament is therefore required for dreams, whatever the indigenous background, to be taken as potential "letters from God", as it was expressed in the "Independent African Church" I studied (Charsley 1973:248-49).

A classification of dreams

As has been emerging, the circumstances in which people are thought to have such meaningful dreams and the contexts in which they tell them are varied. Four main possibilities with organizational relevance can be distinguished: dreams may be connected with the founding of churches; they may be connected with the origination of features of their cultures; they may be connected with acquiring membership of particular churches; and they may be a standard contribution by members to the ongoing life of the church. Partially outside this organizational framework lies a fifth possibility. Dreaming may be an element in the development of special powers, particularly those of prophets and healers. Such a classification cuts across the commonly perceived category of "call dreams" (e.g. Daneel 1974:142-53), which has been used somewhat indiscriminately to apply to the dreams of founders, of those regarded as possessing special spiritual powers, and of ordinary members joining and sometimes receiving the Holy Spirit. For any sociological understanding it is important to distinguish between possibilities with such very different significances. Observed instances should not, however, be expected always to fit neatly with any such classification. In particular the nature of dreams must not be forgotten. It is interpretation and events subsequent to their first telling which determine their ultimate significance.

1. Foundation dreams

These are the unusual and momentous tales or myths, the "canonized dreams" (Daneel 1971: 289-90) to which the founding of new churches is attributed and in terms of which they are explained and legitimated. Such dreams have often looked explicitly to the Bible, as in John Masowe's dream of being dead and told to pray to God. He was then told by voices that he was John. This he took to refer, in what may well have been primary interpretation, to John the Baptist, though the forty days he then spent in the wilderness refer more directly to Jesus (Dillon-Malone 1978:12; c.f. Sundkler 1961:110, 270-71). More often such dreams seem to be associated with a liminal period of sickness and recovery from it. The leader of the Action Church among the Nzema of southwest Ghana is reported as claiming a series of three such dreams. The first and last were directly related to the Bible, but the third was more oblique. In it he dreamed of bananas of a particular kind, "long hands", growing from his hair. Someone came and told him not to eat them but to eat another, short kind. He later came to understand that "The banana bunch was the symbol of the new church. Eat the short one means found the new church" (Lanternari 1976:224-25).

To the extent that there is an established order, such dreams, once accepted, provide the charismatic break needed to accomplish the transition from allegiance to old truths to commitment to new. J. B. Sadare, for instance, a pioneer of the Nigerian Aladura movement but at the time a prominent Anglican layman, dreamt of a church divided into a larger, dark section and a smaller one ablaze with light. The light was equated with prayer, the darkness with the lack of it in most of his current church. Ultimately the Precious Stone Society was founded, with an emphasis on healing through prayer, and the Anglican connection was broken (Clarke 1986:166-67; Turner 1967, I:9). In periods of ferment, however, in which the founding of new churches is already a part of the prevailing order, there may be little difference between the call to found, the call to exercise special powers and the call to enter, to be discussed below. Such was the dream quoted by Daneel (op.cit; 292-93) of climbing a high mountain and finding baboons there. The baboons were so terrified by the (African) dreamer's white face that they fell over a ledge. On arriving later at the foot of the mountain, he found the baboons lying there dead. Zionist prophets interpreted this dream as indicating that the dreamer would be filled with the Holy Spirit – the white face – and would drive evil spirits – the unfortunate baboons – from many people.

2. Culturally creative dreams

Founders' dreams may well include a cultural element, since uniforms and other symbols of church distinctivness sometimes have a place in them. Variations of practice may also be rooted in dreams, and these may sometimes constitute bids for leadership and may sometimes lead to a new foundation by secession (Fabian 1966: 556). But creative dreams are not necessarily linked to actual or possible foundation or indeed to any particular church. Their context is not therefore necessarily the need for legitimation which is so striking in such instances. Ritual languages have been reported as originating in dreams from both East Africa and Nigeria (Barrett 1968: 177-78), and the "songs of the Holy Spirit" which are such a feature of the Luyia churches of Western Kenya are reputed to originate in dreams, in Tiriki (Sangree 1966: 187, 203) and particularly, on my own information, in Kabras. My direct experience of such churches in Uganda included the dreaming of a new greeting song by a woman accustomed to leading the singing in her church. It was possible in this case, however, that she was merely introducing a song into local circulation rather than creating it. A clearer instance, with an academic character befitting the university graduate concerned, has been reported from ·South Africa. He claimed to have seen in dreams the hymns he subsequently wrote being written up on a blackboard before his eyes (Sundkler 1961: 270)[5].

3. Membership dreams

With his preoccupation with Christians leaving mission churches for Zionist, it is typically the dreams interpreted as calling upon a person to change allegiance on which Sundkler focuses his discussion (1976:263). In dreams told in these circumstances, and in those confirming allegiance to a new church, it is scarcely surprising that the apparently monotonous procession of high mountains, rivers, baptism, green pastures, white clothes, attention to colours and singing should have been found (1961:265-74)[6]. Daneel (1974:143-53) also focuses on membership dreams but provides richer documentation, as well as a more extended discussion. As might be expected, though many of the same images do occur, the more extended treatment reveals the great variety of contexts in which such dreams may be set and the many combinations and permutations which may be drawn from them. The use that is made of them can also emerge. They are seldom narrated during public church meetings but are told to church officials who are "in close contact with the new member during the first phase of initiation". They are, that is to say, part of the means whereby a newcomer is established in a church. They are, though, in this instance clearly not essential: Daneel's evidence as to the prevalence of such dreams has been noted above.

The idea of learning to dream differently and properly as a Christian "spiritualist" has been noticed in West Africa (Turner 1967, II:122-23). The idea of the dream as an initiatory experience has, however, sometimes been more fully developed. A dream narrative which can receive recognition as a direct experience of the divine or as communication with it may be required of entrants. Such a system was first reported by Fabian for the Jamaa movement in Zaire. This movement is distinct from the foregoing examples in having Catholic rather than Protestant roots. Here the required dreams belong to a class sharply distinguished from ordinary dreams; they are *mawazo*, "the thoughts guarded by the Jamaa people". To dream properly is to "get *mawazo*", to prove that one shares in guarding the treasure of the Jamaa. Initiatory dreams are of a distinct kind; they include "Lord Jesus and the Virgin Mary", but these "do not even appear personally but are symbolized by statues (or sometimes by the priest). Nor do they make any important revelations" (Fabian 1971:183-89, 258-67). What is required of entrants is, that is to say, dreams which can be construed as symbolic encounters. The relationship to distinctively Catholic experience is very plain.

A similar system, without the Catholic roots but in a church drawing converts from Catholicism, is reported by Curley in this volume from congregations of the True Church of God (also Curley 1983:27-31). Conversion dreams provide, indeed, the focus for his discussion and, whereas Fabian has difficulty in obtaining the necessary case material to ground his somewhat abstracted account, Curley is able to offer a detailed, documented analysis. Only four out of the thirty five, or possibly sixty five, adult members of the congregation he mainly studied had not experienced conversion dreams. Those who had were generally keen to recite their own, and sometimes others' as well. In particular, the way in which required dreams were achieved becomes clear. No miraculous absorption of a stereotype by the individual psyche was required. It was rather a matter of being coached in church membership, including the expectation of a significant dream, and then trying out those which might qualify. They might do so by including matters related to the particular church, to religion more generally, and above all to miraculous escapes or recoveries of some kind. The possible images or events were in no way predetermined. Reminiscent of Daneel's account, dreams would be tried out first on those coaching the new member. Once a likely dream had been identified, word of it would spread informally, before receiving the public legitimation of recitation at a Sunday service. As in the Jamaa case it was the validating experience to which significance was attached, rather than any message or meaning which might be extracted from it.

4. Contribution dreams

Curley suggests that the particular congregations he studies had a greater interest in dreams than others even of the same church. In his at least, in addition to the conversion dreams, members might in the course of services recount their recent dreams. Elsewhere Daneel has noted and discussed the possibilities for such recounting (1974:154-62): they range from the dreams of leaders, established or aspiring, and typically retailed in the course of preaching, to the dreams of members with or without particular standing in the church which are told as a standard contribution to the progession of services. Daneel provides extensive exemplification of the former, at various organizational levels, concentrating on Mutendi's Zion Christian Church and on Maranke's Apostolic Church. A special version of the latter kind is provided by the Praying Battalions of the Christ Apostolic Church in Nigeria. They come together to pray and sleep in order to have dreams to recount and to be interpeted in a specialized service (Peel 1968:168). I have published accounts of a more straightforward instance, in which dreams are brought into the church to be freely recounted as part of the standard service (Charsley 1973; 1987). Curley's account adds a clear intermediate position. There the dreams of ordinary members are co-opted by the leadership; leaders, knowing already of a dream, would call for its telling in the course of a service and even prompt its teller (1983: 32).

The pattern of contributions across the spectrum from top leaders to ordinary members is clearly variable. Contributions associated with leadership in one way or another are relatively common; it is unlikely that leaders will be found not to be contributing when others are, but others do not necessarily follow the example of contributing leaders. Daneel suggests this in the balance of his analysis and in noting that, in his field, "some of the Zionist and Apostolic preachers made a point of encouraging Church members not only to confess their sins during the opening phase of a church service but also to recount their recent dreams which they regard as important" (1974:161; emphasis added). Even where routine narration is present it may be mainly at the behest of leadership, as is suggested by Daneel's approach, or in pursuit of status at least, as in Curley's account. For the "Indepenent African Church" I have tried to stress the more variable and flexible nature of dream-telling activity.

The difference here can be connected with the contrasted settings of the West and East African cases. Whereas the True Church of God is exclusive and totalitarian in aspiration, signalled by the presence of conversion dreams, and has a strongly institutionalized leadership exercising controls over members, the "IAC", competing for members within a generally Christian population sharing a single religious culture, lacks exclusivity and is better likened to a voluntary association than a total institution (c.f. Kiernan 1985:304). Leadership is weakly institutionalized and always precarious in its hold on members. Accordingly no conversion dreams are found, dream-telling has a regular place in meetings with no control exercised as to participants, and there is relatively little leadership involvement in or use made of dreams told. It is characterized in consequence by a particularly variegated set of narratives, arising, as I have recently exemplified, out of the lives of their tellers. Issues of membership, status and leadership remain salient in these dreams because they are salient in the tellers' lives. It is not in these circumstances easy, however, to draw distinctions between types of dream, or between religious and secular spheres, or indeed to say why many dreams are told at all or to what effect. In such an open situation they are nevertheless an important contribution to the texture of membership of a particular church at a particular time and of the everyday lives of the people concerned.

5. Dreams in the acquisition of special powers

Call dreams may be not to leadership or to membership as such but to the exercise of powers of prophecy and/or healing. Such dreams echo the membership dreams discussed above in that they may take the form of initial calls, often resisted and associated with sickness, or they may be connected with recovery and the experiences which confirm and authorize the use of the new powers. They harp back most strongly to the initiatory dreams of doctors, diviners and mediums already well established in parts of pre-Christian Africa (Berglund 1976:136; Hunter 1961:321; Lee 1969). Like them they may occasionally be associated with cult membership, and new Zionist or Apostolic churches would scarcely be formed without the possession of special powers by their leaders. Kiernan stresses the combination of prophet and preacher at all levels as "an essential partnership in the work of Zion" (1976). Such powers may, however, transcend any particular organization, and this is indeed the typical situation apparent in West's (1975) survey of churches, prophets and healing in Soweto. Prophets there had become practitioners of alternative medicine, not only within the context of church activities but as doctors to be consulted privately. They had amicable if somewhat one-sided relationships with official medicine (c.f. Kiernan 1976:363). In this sophisticated urban world, dreams, though they may rarely appear in any of their other contexts, remain a standard part of the qualification of the healer.

Dream exegesis

There is less to be said about the interpreting of dreams in African churches than about their telling. It appears at present that neither any detailed teasing out of supposed meaning nor the development of more than fragmentary ideas about principles for interpretation are at all common, but rather little systematic research or analysis has so far been directed to the matter. Sundkler addressed it briefly, but entirely in connection with the key symbols of supposedly stereotyped dreams, those marked by distinct church-related meanings. More systematic attention appears to be given to the matter in the Nigerian Church of the Lord (Aladura), but Turner's account (1967, II:124-25) derives mainly from church publications and scarcely comments upon practice. Officially, the keeping of dream journals was encouraged and Christian interpretation had to compete with handbooks circulating in the society at large. Sundkler has the interesting conception, which deserves to be followed up, of meanings in process of creation. Zionists in South Africa had succeeded in monopolizing as referring to themselves and their own religious practices the symbolic reference of water, rivers, pools and shining white clothes: "... from a general sociological point of view, I suggest, an additional item of interest is that in the case of Zionist dreams the historical or time element can be controlled. One can within the limit of so many months or years show how the stereotype has evolved" (Sundkler 1961:271-72; see also 1976:265-66). Sadly he goes no further towards performing such an analysis, but Daneel does take up this matter of standard church-related symbols and their interpretation. He concentrates particular attention on whiteness, revealing in the process the way in which, in the ever more complex and diversified world of southern African religious independency, monopolies have not been sustainable. In his field in Zimbabwe (Rhodesia), it was the Apostolic Church which was "inclined to interpret white garments (in dreams) as a divine sanction of their official attire". For Zionists and others, who also dreamt of Church people in white whatever their own colour of dress might be, "the whiteness connotes the angelic fashion, the closeness to God or simply an ethically correct disposition" (Daneel 1974:163; c.f. Aquina 1969:123).

Interesting as this discussion is, it represents meanings generally available in church circles and likely often to be embedded in primary interpetation, rather than techniques for deciphering the initially mysterious in particular dreams. Daneel distinguishes between such meanings and the "codes" developed by a few "imaginative individuals" for attaching meaning to miscellaneous objects and events (c.f. Freud 1913:81-2). He offers as examples dreaming of much fish, of many locusts, catching an eel, puddling mud and entering water (1974:166). Such items differ from the stereotypes in not having any clearly religious marking. They are not, as yet at least, part of church-related patterns of meaningfulness such as might get into the primary interpretation of dreams appearing in a church context, though Daneel notes that there are rational connections of various kinds to be drawn. Fabian writes of the leaders of the Jamaa "formulating specific 'theories' about the nature and interpretation of dreams and … reserving the application of these theories to themselves" (1971:187), but neither here nor in his original article entitled "Theories of dreams in the Jamaa movement" (1966) does he discuss the process of interpreting particular dreams. West records sessions of dream analysis as having taken place in the course of converting a diviner into a Christian prophet and mentions training in the interpretation of dreams as part of the preparation of prophets in general (1975:184, 186). Both these latter authors therefore imply the recognition of special principles and special skills but neither offers the results of any enquiry into them.

My own study allows me to attempt to delineate processes of interpretation in a context in which apparently stereotyped elements scarcely featured. In the "IAC", dream-telling had its regular place in religious meetings. The secretary running the meeting would call for dreams and visions to be told and it was expected that there would be interpretation. At first sight however, the interpreting seemed to be meagre, altogether overwhelmed by the recitations themselves. Indeed a view of it as little developed was shared by the actors. The capacity to interpret was regarded not as a learned skill but as a "gift" (kihaanwa; Luragoli) in an inexplicit sense shared with speakers of English, though here specifically grounded in the Biblical discussion of "gifts of the spirit" in 1 Corinthians. It was a gift thought to vary in degree and perhaps to need cultivating. Few in this immigrant community of busy farmers resident in Uganda – no-one belonging to the "IAC" at the time – were though to have any marked measure of it. An old man who had had a considerble reputation as a dream interpreter in Kenya before migrating was thought since to have been too hard at work farming to have maintained his gifts.

Closer inspection reveals that there was nevertheless a process of some subtlety operating. This can be seen in the set of dreams and their interpretation as recorded on one particular occasion which I have recently published (1987). Here selection, unsignalled and presumably often unnoticed, was the basis of the process. Even within the simplest of narratives, particular parts would be selected for attention and others discarded. In one very brief narrative money awaiting collection in the local postal town was attended to, the bearing of a message about it, which also appeared in the dream, ignored. In another it was the "sickness" of a fellow congregation member, rather than either the fetching of pastors to pray for her, the dustiness of her house, or the medicine a neighbour had offered her but held back on seeing the pastors. An unusually fantastic and moderately complex narrative involved a hippopotamus in the dreamer's house, unuccessful attempts to spear it, blood like water dropping on the dreamer, assistance from a fellow member of the church, the animal speaking and declaring its intention of dying in the house and so on. The interpretation was simply that there was an enemy in his house but he, the dreamer, had overcome it.

What was going on here was clearly not any kind of quasi-scientific enterprise attempting to account for the incidents of dreams as thoroughly as possible. It was, rather, a matter of selecting out what should be treated as significant. It was as if there were a tacit acknowledgement of random noise in the system from which the message-bearing signals had first to be extricated. Such selection was not mere chance: I discuss in the same article the ways in which local and momentary factors affected it, and particularly the state of play in the relationships of those involved. It could also, it must be supposed, be affected by theories or codes of meaningfulness subscribed to by interpeters, but this was rarely apparent in practice.

To such basic selection a second stage is added. One of three possibilities of interpretation, or perhaps a combination of them, is chosen. In the first, the interpreter may assert that the items selected are simply and literally true. They may already by true, simply the revelation of a hitherto unknown state of affairs, like the money awaiting collection in the town; they may be treated as prediction, as in another dream were the doings of "missionaries" expected to arrive shortly from Kenya; or they might offer a directive. Explicit messages as to what particular people should do were almost certain to be handled in this last way.

The most usual alternative to asserting literal truth in one of these forms was to shift meanings beyond the literal by picking up values, metaphors and linguistic ambiguities available in the culture. This is to extend the process which already occurs in primary interpretation. Failure to eat normally with fellow members in one narrative was here interpreted in terms of church membership and underlying moral problems by the manipulation of the concept "heart" (omwoyo: a Luragoli term which can sometimes also be translated "spirit", see below). An analagous though not identical ramification of significance (Wagner 1949:160) is available in English too. An initial identification of the dream as including not eating wholeheartedly with church members was transformed into the dreamer not having her heart in "the meeting", this latter readily standing for the life of the church more generally. She was thinking of earthly things – the dream had included going to fight in Rhodesia, it being the period of UDI in 1966 – and her heart was spiritually weak. Death and lameness in other dreams, physical conditions if taken literally as they could be, also allowed transformations of meaning by taking them as metaphors for the spiritual. Having body beads, cigarettes or drinking might again be taken literally – one woman exploited this possibility in rebutting an accusation against her by talking of the body beads she had been keeping for someone else – but they also stood for values, the paganism which the true Christian should reject. In terms such as these, interpretation could, if desired, formulate messages. Successful interpretations arrived at in this way are likely to strike an external observer as being imposed on the original narrative, but to the actors they seem, if successful, no more than a drawing out of implications which were already within it.

It is only with the third possibility for interpreting that culturally and situationally determined common sense is transcended and special knowledge about dreams is invoked. Such special knowledge does not here amount to very much. There is the idea that dreams may not mean what they seem to – though they may – and there are occasional assertions of symbolic equivalences of the kind that Daneel, cited above, attributed to imaginative individuals. The locally senior pastor in the course of interpreting on one occasion predicted a death in unusually precise terms. This produced surprise in the meeting and a semi-humourous challenge from the senior woman present. He therefore justified his interpretation by asserting that a motor vehicle into which someone was refusing to enter always meant their death. Actual deaths reported in dreams might, if they were not interpreted metaphorically as in one recorded case, be understood literally but as referring to someone else whose identity would be revealed only retrospectively (cf. Wagner 1949:211, 214). A dream that one was drowning might refer to being upset by gossip about oneself, to which one should really be paying no attention. The symbolic principle might also be operated on an *ad hoc* basis, as with the identification of the hippo in the house with an enemy[7]. It was sometimes possible to elicit such examples, but usually there would be a rapid retreat to the idea that interpreting was a gift, not therefore a matter of any learnable code.

Interpreting was therefore primarily a matter of relating dream narrative to circumstances in ways which would seem natural and obvious to those present. It had also to be controlled and constructive. The problem for a leader engaged in interpreting was in doing both simultaneously, but when successful it avoided startling or needing any sense of special powers or even special knowledge to justify it.

Explanation

The connections between leadership and dream-telling in African churches are very clear. It is not surprising therefore that in seeking to explain findings students have often turned to leadership and its problems. In so far as leaders' positions at all levels are based on the possession of special powers of prophecy or healing, dreams have frequently had a place in the acquisition of such powers and therefore in their legitimation. For the founders of churches, dreams legitimate their organisation's existence and their own pre-eminent place in it. Similarly, for all whose present eminence rests on a rejection of former colleagues and superiors in separating from a former church, the dream as an apparently higher intervention can provide justification. The opposite situation is also interestingly discussed by Daneel (1974:161), with followers asserting allegiance to leaders and claiming special standing in relation to them by narrating dreams about them. The dreams of followers may also, he suggests, be useful to a leader in giving him access to preoccupations and problems for which solutions and therapy can then be attempted.

Such a summing of possibilites makes dreams sound an ever-ready resource at the disposal of any leader. This is of course misleading. It fails to acknowledge that neither accounts of dreams themselves nor the significance given to them are unproblematic. As far as the dreams are concerned it is the claim that they are communications from divinity that gives them their power. As was apparent in the first section above, in no society or context are all dreams regarded as of the same nature; we have come across the extreme position which asserts that particular dreams come from Satan – in my own field this idea occasionally emerged in connection with fantastic dreams of the hippopotamous-in-the-house kind. More generally, it is allowed in practice that dreams are often, in whole or in part, without meaning or significance. There is always therefore a potential issue over the identification of a particular dream as significant and of proper origin (Daneel 1974:167). In the Church of the Lord (Aladura) there is recognition of the sin of "lying against the Holy Spirit", the deliberate uttering of false dreams, visions and prophecies (Turner 1967, II:133). In addition, as has been seen over the identification of white-clothed figures and over the senior "IAC" pastor's prediction of death, interpretations may sometimes be challenged. Dreams can therefore be no more than a part of the armoury of leadership, themselves requiring validation from the accepted pre-eminence of the leader which they then in turn help to validate.

Where leaders telling dreams might find themselves in competition with others, something of a retreat from dreams may occur. Kiernan (1985) has described a firm distinction which has developed between dreams, thought to occur in sleep, which are in principle available to all, and waking visions which are a "prerogative of prophecy" (but c.f. Daneel 1974:141). By this is meant not that it is only established prophets who can have them but that having them is, according to perspective, either a bid for prophet status or an indicator of prophetic powers. Visions, Kiernan claims, tend to be explicit in their meaning but, as befits direct experiences of the divine perhaps, lack grounding in the familiar world; dreams tend to be the opposite, grounded but obscure as to meaning. They therefore require interpretation, another "prerogative of prophecy": "No private interpretation of a dream, particularly if it concerns the welfare of the group or has a bearing on the dreamer's status as a Zionist, can enjoy any currency without the firm backing of prophetic revelation" (Kiernan 1985:310). This pulling back from dreaming to visions and interpretation provides a subtle and therefore probably more effective strategy for maintaining dominance, and it is observable in at least embryo form elsewhere (e.g. Fabian 1971:187-88). In the Nigerian Aladura churches studied by Peel in the mid 1960s, with the exception of the Praying Battalions mentioned above, the emphasis is on visions and messages received in the controlled context of the service, rather than on dreams at all.

Consideration of the strategies of leadership has certainly provided the main problematic to which dreaming in African churches has been related. A lurking functional perspective should also be noted, however, though the acute instability of independent religious organizations in much of the continent does not encourage the assumptions of stability on which functional analysis rests. Nevertheless Daneel invokes this kind of idea with reference particularly to a residual category of dreams told within Spirit-type churches. What he classifies neither as call, control, loyalty, nor healing dreams deal, he claims, with domestic and in-group tensions. Such dreams "serve the important purpose of bringing submerged frustrations to the surface". As such they are "no less valuable as a group-integrating factor" than the other kinds of dream (1974:162). It needs only to be noted that this is an example of the weakest kind of functional explanation, in which the entity allegedly being maintained remains ambiguous: is it here the psychological health of individual members, their domestic units, the church group itself, or possibly all three? There is a typically functionalist sense here that whatever is going on must be useful in some way. In the absence of research directed to establishing the effects of dream-telling, little in the way of explanation seems, however, to be offered by such ideas. My own field experience leads me to doubt whether dream-telling solves more problems than it creates, but its possible therapeutic value perhaps deserves further investigation.

Directly historical explanations of dream-telling in African churches are also available. Sundkler speaks confidently of "the dream level of life" and is prepared to accept at face value explanations of behaviour in terms of instructions received from God in a dream. In earlier days some Zulus joined his Lutheran Church because, he says, of such instructions, though "It is obviously impossible to show now the approximate percentage of conversions prompted by dreams". It is, for him, at the dream level that "people experience their deepest conflicts and somehow try to come to terms with them" (1976:265-66). A persisting preoccupation with dreams has therefore been a part of "a Search for a New Identity", for a new Zulu wholeness to replace the old which missionary Christianity had shattered but for which it had not of itself known how to achieve a replacement (1976: 310). This is a powerful vision but, as I have argued above, it exaggerates the generality of the phenomenon even for Zulus, and it fails to come to terms with the need for a contextualized understanding of the evidence for dreaming. Dream life divorced from contexts of dream-telling must as a concept remain problematic for the purpose of any empirical study.[8]

Finally, can it be argued that Christian use of dreams varies according to the place of dreams in the pre-Christian culture concerned? Traditional concern with dreams would need to be measured on three dimensions. In the first place it might be suggested that the general level of interest within the traditional culture, difficult as it is to envisage measuring it, should correlate with the salience of dreams in church life. Secondly, it might be suggested that, amongst those displaying a certain level of interest, there would be a difference between cultures in which dreams had a generally negative significance, being primarily linked with witchcraft or with malicious or demanding and dangerous spirits – the Nyakyusa are a case that comes to mind here (Wilson 1951:96; 1957:46, 63-64, 213-14) – and those in which positive significances predominated. In the former, one might expect to find Christianity devaluing dreams as an aspect of "pagan" culture from which to escape with relief, whereas in the latter traditional uses of dreams would be ambiguously regarded and, in time and at least by some, Christianized. The Zulus would have to exemplify both a high level of interest and the generally positive valuation, leading to a salience of dreams in church life. But thirdly, the Tiriki, a Luyia people of western Kenya, draw attention to the further need to distinguish patterns of distribution, perhaps for concern with dreams but certainly for their valuation. The Tiriki, as reported by Sangree (1966:42-43, 234), had dream-prophets (*bangoli*), specialists by whom dreaming was harnessed as a positive resource, whereas for ordinary people dreams remained undesirable and to be avoided. It cannot be assumed, therefore, that all cultures are equally susceptible to a simple collective classification as positively or negatively oriented towards dreams.

Such ideas are inviting. Links of this kind do appear to be traceable at a more minute level in the Luyia area. Both Tiriki and their Luyia neighbours, the Logoli, provide bases which have nurtured dream-using churches. Both are recorded as having had dream-prophets and a traditional concern with dreams (Wagner 1949:212-14), but the patterns of dream use, as reported by Sangree (1966:187) particularly for the African Israel Church Nineveh in Tiriki in the 1950s and by myself for the "IAC" with its predominantly Logoli origin, diverge.

As has been seen above, in the "IAC" case an easy and democratic attitude to dreams and their telling was displayed, with little worry about their status as godly or satanic and little attempt on the part of leadership to control them. Sangree's experience in Tiriki was distinctly different, with leaders emphasizing the need to test dreams against biblical precedent and to exercise control over both the telling and the interpretation. This, Sangree asserts, amounts to a direct Christianizing of the traditional pattern. In Tiriki the gift of dream prophecy was not inherited or confined in any particular lineages or clans, but elders stressed the peculiar level of control that they in Tiriki, as compared with other Luyia, had always maintained over its exercise. By the 1950s there were no longer any "pagan" dream prophets, but plenty of Christian. The Logoli case, as reported earlier by Wagner, was different. Their dream prophecy had been confined to a single family, and the last dream prophet had died in 1918. There was not, however, the popular negative orientation to dreams noted for Tiriki above. Whereas Tiriki dreams might be characterized as rendezvous with the ghosts of relatives and friends who had been dead for some time, and might portend, if one ate with them, one's own death (Sangree 1966:42-43), Logoli dreams were the travels and encounters of the *omwoyo*, the spirit, life principle or consciousness of one individual, with those of others. It was an altogether different fraction of the self which was thought to encounter ghosts of the dead. Such encounters were not remembered and therefore did not constitute dreams (Wagner 1949:160). Whether or not such ideas are still prevalent, they provide a remarkable grounding in traditional culture for the divergence in the Christian practices relating to dreams which has been reported.

There is nevertheless a crucial difficulty in making such a connection. It is that there is a lack of coincidence between the church as a unit and anything that could be recognized as an indigenous culture or society. On the one hand there is commonly a multiplicity of churches amongst people who share a common pre-Christian culture and often to a considerable extent the contemporary culture too, and such churches invariably differ considerably in the uses made of dreams within them. On the other hand churches migrate, taking structures and practices with them. The fact that both the "IAC" and the True Church of God (Curley, this volume) were observed as immigrant congregations has been noted. More subtly, there is a flow of churches, of individuals and of influences of all kinds across boundaries of the kind represented by such names as "Tiriki" and "Logoli". Ideas about dreams, interest in them and ways of handling them may therefore either be imported or develop locally, and they may be taken up by people of varying origins. The particular circumstances of particular churches or even congregations will affect the choices made. For some it may be as important to reject as to accept, to eschew "pagan" practices or indeed the practices of other churches, and practices involving dreams may well be amongst those subject to this kind of selection.

The most that can be said at this stage of research into a complex topic is therefore that there are dynamic relationships between specifically Christian dream practices and their non-Christian contexts which, encouraged by such examples as the above and more generally by such a review of the presently patchy evidence as has been attempted here, merit further exploration.

NOTES

1. From outside Africa, Bourguignon (1954:264-66) provides a striking example of the way dreams may sometimes be peeled like onions. The dreamer, here in Haiti, called Annette, first recounted a dream as a simple message from Erzili, a female deity. The anthopologist felt there must have been more to it and tried for further explanation of what Annette had "actually perceived". The ground then began to shift.

> In the course of Annette's comments we note that she told us at first she had dreamed of Erzili, later, Erzili in the appearance of a man, indeed a specific man of Annette's acquaintance wearing white. This is later translated into an appearance of Ogun as sent by Erzili, with some comments on the inappropriateness of his clothing [– as Ogun he should have been dressed in yellow, not white]. Thus, Annette sees a man of her acquaintance in her dream and tells it, indeed appears to perceive it, as a dream involving the deity Erzili.

How then did she identify Erzili? "… one knows the identity of a dream visitor by what he says, by the message which is the main purpose of the dream". Though Bourguignon is not approaching this case in the radical spirit I am advocating, it is clear that the various performances here are filled with culture by processes of primary interpretation. As with an onion, it is not obvious that "peeling" a dream produces any reality at the centre which is different in nature to the layers removed.

2. The extent to which the "headings" are his own classifications or those of his informants is unclear. See *Dream exegesis* below.

3. Dreams in a church context has been reported from southern, eastern and west Africa, but the authors who have given the topic detailed attention in any respect are few. From South Africa we have Sundkler writing about mainly rural Zulu Zionist churches (1961; 1976) and Kiernan about urban ones (1985). Pauw (1975) pays a good deal of attention to dreams in his study of Xhosa Christians in both country and town. Outside South Africa, Daneel (1971; 1974) attends similarly to dreams in his study of independent churches amongst the Southern Shona of Zimbabwe, and the place of dreams in the Jamaa movement in Katanga, Zaire, has been studied by Fabian (1966; 1971). From East Africa, dreams feature in Sangree's (1966) monograph on Tiriki in western Kenya, and I have focussed on them in writing about the pseudonymous "Independent African Church" or "IAC". This was also of western Kenyan origin but observed chiefly amongst Luyia immigrants in Uganda (Charsley 1973; 1987). For Curley, from West Africa, it is the True Church of God which provides the context. By an odd coincidence this is also an immigrant church, here of Nigerian origin but amongst Igbo immigrants in Cameroun (1983 and this volume). Turner reports the role of dreams in the history of an African Independent Church (1967), the Nigerian Church of the Lord (Aladura), and ideas about dreaming which had been developed by some of its leaders. Peel's (1968) study of two other Aladura churches within Nigeria provides interesting parallels and contrasts in its attention mainly to visions rather than dreams in contemporary practice.

With the partial exception of southern Africa, the list is manifestly slight and miscellaneous, though there is, as will be seen, a certain amount of supplementary evidence to be called upon. It has also to be noted that dreams have rarely been a major research interest even for those authors who have focused articles on the topic. Kiernan's research focus was on healing and my own on immigrant settlement and ethnicity. Some authors have been concerned mainly with single whole churches, their founders and leaders, others with communities in which congregations of an array of different churches were to be found. Such differences are important: they may lead to distinct biases in the kinds of data recorded and hence in the characterizations of local situations which come to be compared with one another.

Similar considerations apply to accounts of dreams in non-Christian African contexts. The present collection makes a relatively massive contribution here, though there are classic texts which pay important attention to dreams and to which reference will necessarily be made. Evans-Pritchard's (1937) study of *Witchcraft, Oracles and Magic among the Azande* of the Southern Sudan is one, Wilson's studies of the Pondo of South Africa (Hunter 1936/1961) and of the Nyakyusa of southern Tanzania (1951; 1957), and Field's ethnopsychiatric study in Asante, Ghana (1960), are others. Wilson's work on the Nyakyusa provides a neat illustration of the ease with which misleading impressions can be established by varying foci of interest. From her earlier study, *Good Company*, it might well be inferred that Nyakyusa dreams were essentially concerned with witchcraft, whereas her later work suggests equally strongly a preoccupation with ancestral dreams. Ranging further afield, Malinowski (1929/1932), Firth (1934), Wallace (1958), and in a different vein Freud (1913) still provide essential contextual reading.

4.   Aquina's (1967) and Jules-Rosette's (1979) writings about the Apostolic Church of John Maranke may be compared with Daneel's examples (1974:155, 159-60).

5.   Callaway (1868-70:187) reports a pre-literate precedent from the same part of the world.

6.   But see Peel (1968:206-7) for a Nigerian instance in an apparently different idiom.

7.   Such an identification made more sense to people for whom elephants and other wild animals were occasional marauders from the neighbouring Merchison Falls National Park than it may to those of us for whom they are, on film or otherwise safely separated from ourselves, merely objects of sympathetic curiosity.

8.   Callaway (1868-70:188-89) appends to a fine text by Umpengula Mbanda on the plight of a convert who had lost his faith, amongst "apparitions and strange life-like dreams", an account of one of the dreams previously recorded:

> He dreamt that he was crossing a river with Umpengula in a boat. When they were in the middle of the river, without any apparent cause, the bottom of the boat opened and let him through, and, after struggling for a time in the water, he found himself on a sand bank in the midst of the stream, and saw Mpengula on the other side, he having reached without difficulty the place of their destination. ... He found himself surrounded by huge dogs, which appeared ready to devour him, and many black people, among whom he observed his own mother, who expressed her wonder at finding him among them.

Callaway's comment on this suggests an interesting model of "dream life" in a culture in which, as clearly here, dreams are told and seriously discussed: "This is just one of those prophetic dreams which is suggested to a man by his own thought and wishes, and which help on its own fulfilment by placing before his mind during sleep a distinct tableau of the future such as whilst awake he would be afraid to form for himself".

REFERENCES

AQUINA, M., 1967, The People of the Spirit: an Independent Church in Rhodesia,

Africa 37: 203-219.

1969, Zionists in Rhodesia, *Africa* 39: 113-136.

BARRETT, D.B., 1968, *Schism and Renewal in Africa*. Nairobi: Oxford University Press.

BERGLUND, A.I., 1976, *Zulu Thought-Patterns and Symbolism*. London: Hurst.

BOURGUIGNON, E., 1954, Dreams and dream interpetation in Haiti. *American Anthropologist* 56: 262-268.

1972, Dreams and altered states of consciousness in anthropological research. In F. L. K. Hsu (ed.), *Psychological Anthropology*, 2nd ed, Cambridge, Mass: Schenkam.

CALLAWAY, H., 1868-70, *The Religious System of the Amazulu*. Springvale, Natal: Blair.

CHARSLEY, S.R., 1973, Dreams in an Independent African Church. *Africa* 43: 244-257.

1987, Dreams and purposes: an analysis of dream narratives in an Independent African Church. *Africa* 57(3): 281-296.

CLARKE, P.B., 1986, *West Africa and Christianity*. London: Arnold.

CURLEY, R., 1983, Dreams of power; social process in a West African religious movement. *Africa* 53: 20-38.

DANEEL, M.L., 1971, *Old and New in Southern Shona Independent Churches I*.

1974, *Old and New in Southern Shona Independent Churches II*. The Hague, Mouton.

DILLON-MALONE, C.M., 1978, *The Korsten Basketmakers*. (Zambian Papers 10-11). Manchester: Manchester University Press.

EVANS-PRITCHARD, E.E., 1937, *Witchcraft, Oracles and Magic among the Azande*. Oxford: Clarendon Press.

FABIAN, J., 1966, Theories of dreams in the Jamaa movement. *Anthropos* 61: 544-560.

1971, *Jamaa, A Charismatic Movement in Katanga*. Evanston: Northwestern University Press.

FIELD, M.J., 1960, *Search for Security: an ethno-psychiatric study of rural Ghana*. London: Faber.

FIRTH, R., 1934, The meaning of dreams in Tikopia, In E. E. Evans-Pritchard *et al* (eds.), *Essays Presented to C.G. Seligman*. London: Kegan Paul.

FREUD, S., 1913, *The Interpretation of Dreams*. London: Allen and Unwin.

GREGOR, T., 1981, "Far, far away my shadow wandered ...": dream symbolism and dream theories of the Mehinaku Indians of Brazil. *American Ethnologist* 8: 709-720.

HUNTER, M., 1961, *Reaction to Conquest*. London (1st. ed. 1936): Oxford University Press.

JANZEN, J.M., 1985, The consequences of literacy in African religion: the Kongo case. In W. Van Binsbergen and M. Schoffeleers (eds.), *Theoretical Explorations in African Religion*: London: KPI.

JULES-ROSETTE, B., 1979, Women as ceremonial leaders in an African Church: the Apostles of John Maranke. In *The New Religions of Africa*. Norwood, N.J.: Ablex Publishing.

KIERNAN, J.P., 1974, Where Zionists draw the line: a study of religious exclusiveness in an African township. *African Studies* 33: 79-90.

1976, Prophet and preacher: an essential partnership in the work of Zion. *Man* (NS) 3: 356-366.

1985, The social stuff of revelation: pattern and purpose in Zionist dreams and visions. *Africa* 55: 304-318.

LANTERNARI, V., 1976, Dreams as charismatic signifiants: their bearing on the rise of new religious movements. In A. Bharati (ed.), *The Realm of the Extra- Human:*

ideas and actions, The Hague: Mouton.

LEE, S.G., 1958, Social influences in Zulu dreaming. *Journal of Social Psychology* 47: 265-283.

1969, Spirit possession among the Zulu. In J. Beattie & J. Middleton (eds.), *Spirit Mediumship and Society in Africa*. London: Routledge.

LINCOLN, J., 1935, *The Dream in Primitive Cultures*. London: Cresset Press.

MALCOLM, N., 1959, *Dreaming*. London: Routledge.

MALINOWSKI, B., 1932, *The Sexual Life of Savages*, 3rd ed.. London: Routledge (lst. ed. 1929).

MBITI, J.S., 1976, God, dreams, and African militancy. In J. Pobee (ed.), *Religion in a Pluralistic Society*. Leiden: E. J. Brill.

PAUW, B.A., 1975, *Christianity and the Xhosa Tradition*. Cape Town: Oxford University Press.

PEEL, J.D.Y., 1968, *Aladura: a religious movement among the Yoruba*. London: Oxford University Press.

SANGREE, W.H., 1966, *Age, Prayer and Politics in Tiriki, Kenya*. London: Oxford University Press.

SHORTER, A., 1978, Dreams in Africa. *Afer* 20, 281-87.

SUNDKLER, B., 1960, *The Christian Ministry in Africa*. London: SCM.

1961, *Bantu Prophets in South Africa*, 2nd. ed.. London: Oxford University Press.

1976, *Zulu Zion and Some Swazi Zionists*. London: Oxford University Press.

TURNER, H.W., 1967, *History of an Independent African Church*, 2 vols. Oxford: Clarendon Press.

TYLOR, E.B., 1913, *Primitive Culture*, 5th ed.. London: John Murray, (1st. ed. 1871).

WAGNER, G., 1949, *The Bantu of North Kavirondo*, Vol 1. London: Oxford University Press.

WALLACE, A.F.C., 1958, Dreams and the wishes of the soul: a type of psycho-analytic theory among the seventeenth century Iroquois. *American Anthropologist* 60: 234-248.

WEBB, W.B. and CARTWRIGHT, R.D., 1978, Sleep and dreams. *Annual Review of Psychology* 29: 223-252.

WEST, M., 1975, Bishops and prophets in a Black city. In *African Independent Churches in Soweto*. Cape Town: Philip.

WILSON, M., 1951, *Good Company: a study of Nyakyusa age-villages*. London: Oxford University Press.

1957, *Rituals of Kinship among the Nyakyusa*. London: Oxford University Press.

AFTERWORD

ROY WILLIS
University of Edinburgh

Dreaming is at once a universal and a peculiarly private experience, a mode of perception lacking an identifiable percept, a vehicle of information communicable only in the already transmuted form of memory, a sign of a sign that itself refers, one must presume, to yet another sign written in the arcane language of the unconscious. It is understandable that dreams and dreaming, according to a common-sense view prevalent in our culture, a view that originates in the positivist and mechanist dogma of an earlier scientific era, are inherently devoid of meaning.

This is not the view of the various African peoples discussed in this volume, nor was it the opinion of our ancestors in mediaeval Europe or classical antiquity. More recently, the significance of the dream for our understanding of human nature was rediscovered by the founder of modern psychoanalysis, Sigmund Freud, for whom the interpretation of dreams was "the royal road to a knowledge of the unconscious activities of the mind" (Freud 1965: 647). In pointing to the governing factors that mould the form taken by dreams, the trope-like devices of "displacement" and "condensation", "identification" and "symbolism", Freud established that this seemingly most whimsical and arbitrary domain of human thought was shaped by universal cognitive processes. When the structural linguists Roman Jakobson and Morris Halle noted the apparent affinity of Freud's pairs of "governing factors" (Freud 1965: 343, 345) with the linguistic polarity of metaphor and metonym, the formerly absolute distinction between the dreaming and waking worlds became a relative one (Jakobson and Halle 1956: 95). An important further step in the same direction was taken recently by Adam Kuper who, in a contribution alluded to by several scholars in this volume, has argued that the manifest content of dreams is structured by the same system of binary oppositions and mediating concepts that Lévi-Strauss has shown to underly the language of myth (Kuper 1979; Kuper and Stone 1982; Kuper 1983).

Dreaming, Religion and Society in Africa usefully builds on the series of discoveries inaugurated in 1900 with Freud's epochal masterpieces, and it does so in two ways. Firstly, as the editors observe, it fills a longstanding lacuna in the ethnography of Black Africa, where the cultural role of dreaming has generally received little attention (Evans-Pritchard's discussion of Zande dreams [1937] and Fernandez [1982] on dreaming in the Fang *Bwiti* cult being notable exceptions). The reasons for this comparative neglect are presumably to be found in the fact that Black Africa was for many years the *locus classicus* of functionalist studies. Secondly, while the various essays in this volume well examplify the interesting differences between one African context and another in cultural attitudes to dreams and dreaming, the essays are informed by congruent theoretical approaches which, it might be argued, favour universalist conclusions. Where an older anthroplogy, with its relativist bias, projected a picture of a normatively unchanging social system that moulded individual thought and action, this newer approach sees the social person as actively participating with his/her fellows in a continuing process of cultural creation. Independent support for this vision of human beings as "meaning makers" has recently come from the discipline of infant psychology. There is solid and growing experimental evidence suggesting that the human newborn is innately, and hence universally, predisposed to construct cultural meaning in interaction with others (cf. Bower 1977). Taking account of the structural commonalities that, since Freud, have been shown to relate the waking and oneiric modes of consciousness, we may see the possibility of a conceptual framework constructed of elements of biology, pyschology, and socio-cultural anthroplogy, a framework that will treat the dreaming and waking worlds as complementary manifestations of a unitary, inter-subjective process.

Meanwhile, the essays contained in this volume collectively suggest that the ideational resource provided by the dream-state is, within the customary or institutional modalities peculiar to specific societies, in one way or another made available for the purposes of cultural creativity. As Reynolds remarks of Zezuru healers, "using power and information derived from spiritual sources in dreams, the healer diagnoses, treats, predicts, interprets and analyses". The possibility of such useful "feedback" between dreaming and waking forms of consciousness is officially ruled out by the reigning Cartesian cosmology in Western culture, which invalidates oneiric information as a source of knowledge about the "real", "objective" world. Thus, the two-way connection we have been led to assume between the two domains of cognition is, in our "scientific" culture, normatively obscured or suppressed. Here we are obliged to take account of the ideas of Freud who, against the grain of popular and scholarly opinion, argued that dreams contained significant information. However, it is also true that Freud excluded the possibility of dream images communicating *social* information with the flat statement that "dreams are completely egotistical" (1965: 358). In saying this, the Master apparently forgot the well documented case of the pioneering German chemist Friedrich Kekule, who in 1865 experienced a dream of a rotating serpent biting its own tail, an image that revealed to Kekule the secret of the molecular structure of benzene as a six-carbon ring and inaugurated modern organic chemistry. Kekule's dream, and the similarly heuristic dream reported half a century later by the brilliant French mathematician Henri Poincaré appear to have been of a kind regularly experienced by the Tukolor weavers of West Africa, as described by Dilley in this volume. For these craftsmen, dreams are held to be a constant source of ideas and innovation in their work. Yet unlike the socially-legitimated dreams of the Tukolor weavers, the dreams of Kekule and Poincaré lack such legitimation and are regarded by science as officially inexplicable events falling within the shadowy domain of parapsychology. It would seem that Freud's blanket characterization of the dream as "egotistical" could be a valid description of the normal dream experience in a cultural region pervaded, as Louis Dumont has insisted, by the dominating concept of the "Autonomous Individual" (Dumont 1966). After all, Emile Durkheim had earlier recognised our modern sense of individuality as a product of the form of *conscience collective* peculiar to advanced industrial society.

Dreaming, Religion and Society in Africa is a timely contribution to the investigation and understanding of dreams and dreaming not only in Africa but also in human experience generally. Of course, the oneiric faculty is not unique to *Homo sapiens* but appears to be possessed by all the higher primates and probably by all mammals. However, because of the peculiar development in our species of an innate drive to construct systems of cultural meaning (Trevarthen and Logotheti, 1989), human dreaming is inevitably animated by images filtered through the screen of cultural experience. It seems likely that the dreaming consciousness in its turn works on this material to construct culturally significant "messages" which find their way into the waking world and subtly influence social thought and behaviour in a fashion similar to that of skilful subliminal advertisements. As the examples in this volume show, the process of translating dream experience into mundane thought and action is in Africa typically mediated through socially recognized "experts" such as Zezuru healers, Temne or Ingessana diviners and Tukolor weavers.

In all these different cultural universes, as generally elsewhere in the non-Western and pre-modern European worlds, the social significance of oneiric knowledge is openly acknowledged and exploited. Only in our modern Western culture is the dreamworld degraded and trivialized. As E.B. Tylor remarked of the high value given to dreams by the North American Indians, "that the white men should look upon a dream as a matter of no consequence is a thing they cannot understand" (Tylor 1865: 8). In our time the once semi-autonomous dreamworld has been, as it were, colonized by the imperialism of the waking consciousness. The solar world of the Ego has sought to dominate the lunar domain of an Unconscious that in Freudian psychology is pictured as a jungle inhabited by fearsome beasts, a region to be controlled at all costs. It is conceivable that the resultant psychic imbalance in our civilization is connected with the well known dominance of the left cerebral hemisphere, the seat of linguistic and logical thought, over the "mystical" and artistic right hemisphere, what Victor Turner called "the left-hemispheric imperialism written into Western culture" (Turner 1985: 285). Interestingly, there is evidence that hemispheric dominance is reversed in the dream-state (cf. Cohen 1979: 46-7). The essays in the present volume attest to the continuing existence, in Black Africa, of alternative and relatively libertarian traditions of psychic management.

REFERENCES

BOWER, T.G.R., 1977, *A Primer of Infant Development.* San Francisco: W.H. Freeman.
COHEN, D.B., 1979, *Sleep and Dreaming.* Oxford: Pergamon.
DUMONT, L., 1966, *Homo Hierarchicus.* London: Paladin.
EVANS-PRITCHARD, E.E., 1937, *Witchcraft, Oracles and Magic among the Azande.* Oxford: Clarendon Press.
FERNANDEZ, J.W., 1982, *Bwiti: an ethnography of the religious imagination in Africa.* Princeton: Princeton University Press.
FREUD, S., 1965, *The Interpretation of Dreams.* New York: Basic Books.
JAKOBSON, R. and HALLE, M., 1956, *The Fundamentals of Language.* The Hague: Mouton.
KUPER, A., 1979, The structure of dreams. *Man*, 14, 4: 645-662.
  1983, The structure of dream sequence. *Culture, Medicine and Psychiatry*, 7: 153-175.
KUPER, A. and STONE, A., 1982, The dream of Irma's injection: a structural account. *American Journal of Psychiatry*, 139: 1225-1234.
TREVARTHEN, C. and LOGOTHETI, K., 1989, Child in society and society in children. In S. Howell and R. Willis (eds.), *The Anthropology of Peaceful Societies.* London: Routledge and Kegan Paul.
TURNER, V.W., 1985, Body, brain and culture. In L.L.B. Turner (ed.), *On the Edge of the Bush.* Tucson: University of Arizona Press.
TYLOR, E.B., 1865, *Researches into the Early History of Mankind.* London: John Murray.

INDEX

STUDIES ON RELIGION IN AFRICA

SUPPLEMENTS TO THE JOURNAL OF RELIGION IN AFRICA

1. MOBLEY, H.W. *The Ghanaian's Image of the Missionary*. An Analysis of the Published Critiques of Christian Missionaries by Ghanaians, 1897-1965. 1970. ISBN 90 04 01185 4
2. POBEE, J.S. (ed.). *Religion in a Pluralistic Society*. Essays Presented to Professor C.G. Baëta in Celebration of his Retirement from the Service of the University of Ghana, September 1971, by Friends and Colleagues Scattered over the Globe. 1976. ISBN 90 04 04556 2
3. TASIE, G.O.M. *Christian Missionary Enterprise in the Niger Delta, 1864-1918*. 1978. ISBN 90 04 05243 7
4. REECK, D. *Deep Mende*. Religious Interactions in a Changing African Rural Society. 1976. ISBN 90 04 04769 7
5. BUTSELAAR, J. VAN. *Africains, missionnaires et colonialistes*. Les origines de l'Église Presbytérienne du Mozambique (Mission Suisse), 1880-1896. 1984. ISBN 90 04 07481 3
6. OMENKA, N.I. *The School in the Service of Evangelization*. The Catholic Educational Impact in Eastern Nigeria 1886-1950. 1989. ISBN 90 04 08632 3
7. JĘDREJ, M.C. & SHAW, R. (eds.). *Dreaming, Religion and Society in Africa*. 1992. ISBN 90 04 08936 5